PYRAMID PROPHECIES

By Max Toth

Destiny Books
Rochester, Vermont

Dedicated to my daughters,
Ginger and Peggy

Destiny Books
One Park Street
Rochester, Vermont 05767
www.InnerTraditions.com

First Quality Paperback Edition 1988
Copyright © 1979 by Max Toth
Copyright © 1988 by Max Toth

Copyright Acknowledgments:
"Metaphysical Foundations of the Great Pyramid," Chapter 1
Copyright © 1979 by Bernice B. Cousins

Illustrations Chapter 2, Figures 4, 5, 6, 7
Copyright © 1976 by Rocky McCollum

Library of Congress Cataloging-in-Publication Data
Toth, Max.
     Pyramid prophecies / by Max Toth.—1st quality pbk. ed.
       p.   cm.
     Includes bibliographical references and index.
     ISBN 0-89281-203-6
     1. Pyramids–Miscellanea. 2. Pyramids–Egypt–Miscellanea.
    3. Prophecies (Occultism)   I. Title.
    BF1999.T644 1985
    001.9—dc19

Printed and bound in the United States

10 9 8 7 6 5 4

Destiny Books is a division of Inner Traditions International

CONTENTS

ACKNOWLEDGMENTS

No acknowledgment can be sufficient enough for the tremendous assistance, information, and support I have received for the material in this book. No one individual or single source can be given precedence over any others, because each contribution is invaluable in its own right. The order of acknowledgment is presented for editorial simplicity rather than merit.

It has been my pleasure to be able to include the contributions of: Bernice B. Cousins, in Chapter 1, for her work entitled "Metaphysical Foundations of the Great Pyramid"; Mr. Rocky McCollum for permission to quote from his book *The Giza Necropolis Decoded,* in Chapter 2, along with allowing me to present his theories regarding the Giza complex; Mr. Kenneth Lloyd Larsen, for permission to quote from his two books *Great Pyramid Designs, UFO's and Planet Earth* and *The Topstone,* in Chapter 2; Manly P. Hall, for permission to quote from his world-renowned Encyclopedic Outline of Masonic, Hermetic, Qabbalistic, and Rosicrucian Symbolical Philosophy entitled *The Secret Teachings of All Ages;* Mr. Robert Nelson, for contributing his theory of damming the River Nile as a possible solution to the question of how the pyramid was constructed, in Chapter 4; the late Adam Rutherford and his Institute of Pyramidology, for permission to quote the definition of pyramidology in Chapter 8; Mr. Robert J. Ellwanger, formerly chairman of the Religious Studies Department at St. Joseph's High School, Brooklyn, New York, for his comments, some of which I have incorporated into Chapter 9; Rev. William Stemper of the Church of the Epiphany in New York City, and Margaret Vincent, instructor at St. Joseph's High School, Brooklyn, New York, for their constructive criticism and support concerning the religious topics of Chapter 9; Dr. Ray Brown, for permission to quote from several of his lectures about his finding the Pyramid Crystal, in Chapter 10; Peggie Donnigi, for her inestimable contributions throughout the book and her invaluable secretarial assistance in the preparation of the manuscript; Mary Freda, for research assistance and manuscript preparation; and Carole Kane, for final proofing, indexing and her fantastic editorial assistance.

I am also deeply indebted and grateful for the voluminous material contributed by innumerable books, publications, organizations, and especially the many interested individuals who have contributed directly and indirectly to this book.

FOREWORD

The 1970s is experiencing a resurgence of interest in pyramids—more specifically, the Egyptian pyramids. Once again the accomplishments of ancient civilizations have coursed through their cycle of influence to our present day.

The cycle of influence was accentuated when Howard Carter discovered the burial chambers of King Tutankhamen in 1922. Within a few years, the riches of the boy Pharaoh's tomb had influenced every civilization of the world to one degree or another. Myths, legends, and mystiques began to resurface; new stories germinated, from seeds planted by the minds of the romanticists and the opportunists; life-styles showed the influence this fabulous discovery had made upon the dress of the well-to-do in Europe and America. Fact and fable blended into one seemingly coherent chapter about the life and times of ancient Egypt. And now, fifty-seven years later, the treasure of Tutankhamen is again inspiring the minds and imaginations of people, as it makes its way through the museums of principal cities in the United States.

Few people realize that Tutankhamen reigned in the

Eighteenth Dynasty (see Dynasty List, pages 104–15), which actually was near the end of the great Egyptian era. Fantasies conjured from this period are generally applied to the entire ancient Egyptian civilization so flamboyantly that hardly anyone bothers to consider the true heritage of this particular King. In fact, many people think that Tutankhamen was buried in a pyramid—which of course is not true.

According to classical Egyptologists, the ancient Egyptian civilization seemingly dates back to approximately 4500 B.C. There is much controversy concerning the chronological classification of dynasties and their respective dates, which is discussed in Chapter 5.

The First Dynasty of United Egypt occurs around 3100 B.C., and is also considered to be the birth of the pyramid age. The Fourth Dynasty marks the height of this age, which declines by the end of the Sixth Dynasty. Then a renaissance occurs in the Twelfth Dynasty, with renewed interest in pyramid construction, lasting until the first Persian invasion about 500 B.C.

The Mayans, Peruvians, Chinese, and other ancient peoples had also built pyramid-oriented civilizations around the world. Why? What was their purpose in choosing this particular shape as the dominant form of construction in their age? Was there one major civilization that taught the others—so widely dispersed—the technical skills necessary to accomplish such herculean feats? Or was world influence based upon the migration of the pyramid-building Egyptians?

Whichever is the answer, the ancients—earlier than all known civilizations—had reached the zenith in their knowledge and ability to prophesy, along with the ability to erect huge edifices, and the knowledge of mathematics, astronomy, medicine, etc. All that the ancients learned culminated into the principal faculty of prophesying events that recur, in the cyclical order of nature wending its way throughout the history of every civilization.

The word "prophecy" or "prophet" comes from the Greek word meaning "interpreter" or "spokesman in the name of a deity." We are accustomed to knowing the prophet as the one who speaks the will of God, interpreting the events in the framework of a religious order. From this Greek word "sermon" developed, and is considered to be equivalent to the word "prophecy."

But the word "prophecy" is applied differently in the scientific sense. The growth of science passes through three phases of maturation. The first is that of observation, where events are collected and stored. The second phase is classification or generalization, where the collected events are categorized according to laws regulating their rule and order. Finally, the third phase is that of prophecy, when these laws are applied in such a manner as to accurately predict events that will occur or recur.

It's not surprising that contemporary science has not progressed out of the shadow of our ancient heritage. Scientific endeavor is still in phase two, adding and refining the classification of the collected events. For instance, even with sophisticated computers and elaborate satellites circling our globe, meteorologists only do slightly better than chance in predicting the weather at any given time.

Astronomy is the only science that has completely reached the last phase, and even for this our scientists can take credit only for refining the phase, rather than for achieving it. To this day we are still only on equal grounds with the ancients in this field of science—for as far back as 1722 B.C. the Chinese and Chaldean astronomers were able to predict or prophesy eclipses with unerring accuracy.

It is well documented that our basic foundation of knowledge in every branch of science and the arts stems from the ancient school of the mystics, masters, or wise men. Much that has been considered the superstition of past civilizations is now proving to be the core of an ancient secret coded science; many a modern discovery betrays its origin and basis in this secret science. This rudimentary correlation has kept mankind obsessed in attempting to decode the fragments of ancient civilizations now extant to learn another minuscule piece about life—which we reluctantly confess the ancients knew more about then than we do now.

The Great Pyramid of Giza, along with other pyramids throughout the world, offers the most reasonable fragment of the ancient mysteries, coded in such a unique way that our decoding efforts may not as yet have hit upon the key.

But what is it for which we are searching? It is the ability to prophesy the cycles of nature which the ancients had so expertly achieved! As the ancients knew, the ultimate knowledge of life—prophecy—would elevate any science, religion, or art form to the highest degree.

Enough evidence exists to suggest that the ancient masters of knowledge had reached the third phase in not one, but possibly all branches of science. The achievement of the masters still shines in our era as brightly as ever. Their effortless endeavor in prophesying nurtured the succeeding civilizations such as the Egyptians, Persians, Greeks, Romans, Mayans, Peruvians, Orientals, and Tibetans,· to name a few. Each and every successive civilization possessed strong foundations in all their sciences, religion, and art; they all paid tribute to their predecessor civilization; and they all acknowledged the pyramid structure as their great mystery.

The prophecies of the ancient masters are locked into the pyramid form, much like a combination lock where the correct sequence of numbers must be selected before the lock opens. This has been the task of mankind since the mysterious disappearance of the masters—laboriously seeking the near-infinite combination of sequences to unlock the code of the pyramid.

Conceivably, given that the prophecies prove to be relevant, once they are finally unlocked, the knowledge that the pyramid reveals can never be made completely known to the public, because the masses will not be able to understand or cope with the tremendous power of the knowledge. Such is the basic tenet of the secret societies throughout the world. These societies claim they possess certain teachings of the ancients, and there is no reason to believe otherwise; indeed, to prove it would mean exposing the ancient wisdom to an immature humanity, bound to misuse it. Thus exposed, tremendous conflicts would arise with the current concept concerning the balance of nature and life, leading quite possibly to disastrous results.

Explore with me that mysterious structure found the world over. The pyramid. The word is a definition! The definition symbolizing the ascent of life from its lowest form to that of majestic man governing every aspect of nature, and writing prophecy in the most abstract symbols. Accompany me through the halls and corridors of time, as a long line of tradition establishes the teachings of the masters for posterity.

Suddenly fallen silent, the legacy of knowledge will once again speak through the cosmic monument, revealing the characters of universal script, through the *Pyramid Prophecies!*

"There is an unbelief which grows out of ignorance, as well as a scepticism which is born of intelligence. The people nearest to the past are not always those who are best informed concerning the past."

Ignatius Donnelly
(1831–1901)

From *Atlantis: The Antediluvian World* (1882)

{1}

INTRODUCTION

The pyramids of Egypt evoke an image of immense structures soaring upward from a vast ocean of sand—three massive triangular-faced monuments and a huge, half-human, half-animal statue—arbitrarily grouped together, parched by a searing sun, and eroded by relentless winds. Tangible enigmas, ancient remnants of a time beyond memory, beyond history, beyond understanding.

Along with the lesser-known pyramids around the world, these colossal architectural edifices have, over the centuries, provided archeologists, historians, and mystics with material for thousands of volumes, numberless theories, endless debates, and inner meditations.

The Great Pyramid of Giza heads the list of the Seven Wonders of the World, and is considered the last remaining survivor. Scholars attribute the first listing of the Seven Wonders of the World to a Greek writer, Antipatros, about 100 B.C. His list is the one most familiar to us:

1. The Great Pyramid of Giza
2. The Hanging Gardens of Babylon

3. The Statue of Zeus by Pheidias at Olympia
4. The Temple of Artemis at Ephesus
5. The Tomb of King Mausolos of Karia at Halikarnassos
6. The Colossus of Rhodes
7. The Pharos, or Lighthouse, of Alexandria

Then later writers substituted or added to this list the Temple of Jupiter in Rome, the Walls of Babylon, the Tower of Babel, the Walls of Jericho, the others. And had they known, for example, about the tremendous Buddhists stupas of Ceylon, the huge dam in Arabia, and the Great Wall of China, the list would of course have been more extensive.

The Great Pyramid of Giza is also referred to as simply the Great Pyramid, or the Pyramid of Cheops—"Cheops" being the Greek form of "Khufu," the name of the Pharaoh who was the son of Seneferu and successor to his throne.

The Great Pyramid has become the apogee of world pyramid building with respect to size and quality. Scores of attempts have been made to illustrate its size by comparing it with other famous structures.

It is thought to have originally been 481.4 feet high; the centuries have eroded it to its present height of 450 feet. It covers 13.1 acres, and each side measures approximately 756 feet in length. Its four triangular faces incline at an angle of approximately 51 degrees, 52 minutes to the ground, and the entire structure was initially oriented in line with true north and south.

There is a great deal of mystery surrounding pyramids—from the enigma of building the colossal Egyptian, Mayan, and Peruvian pyramids to the perplexing and inexplicable powers seemingly intrinsic to the pyramidal shape.

One mystery of the pyramids is that of the origin of the name itself. Obviously, the English word is derived from the Greek *pyramis* (plural, *pyramides*). Less obvious is the derivation of the Greek word itself. It does not seem to be derived from *mr* (pronounced "mer"),

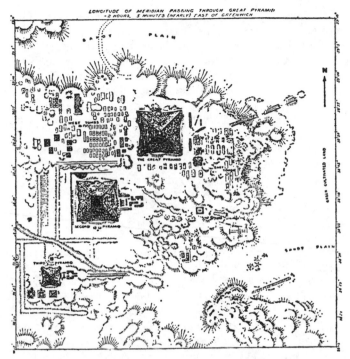

1. Aerial view of the Giza Pyramids

which is the Egyptian word for the four-sided, triangular-faced, square-based structure. To add to the confusion, this Egyptian word itself has no descriptive significance, according to I. E. S. Edwards in *The Pyramids of Egypt*.

A possible ancestor of *pyramis* is a word found in the *Rhind Mathematical Papyrus*. This word, *per-em-us*, is described in the Egyptian mathematical treatise as indicating the vertical height of a pyramid. Literally translated it means "what goes (straight) up . . ." (from "something," signified by the final syllable "us"; unfortunately, the meaning of this syllable is not known, and therefore the word is only partially clear).

3

To accept the explanation that *pyramis* is actually derived from *per-em-us* would be to imply that the Greeks either misunderstood the meaning of the Egyptian term or, by the linguistic process known as synecdoche, named the entire pyramidal structure after the Egyptian word for a part of it. Egyptologists, finding this explanation unacceptable, have accepted the term *pyramis* as a purely Greek word with no known connection with Egyptian terminology.

It has been suggested that the Greeks facetiously chose this word because in their language it means "wheaten cake," and when seen from a distance, the pyramids did indeed seem to them to resemble large cakes. Another example of the Greek custom of humorously applying a descriptive word from their own language to an object having no exact parallel in their own architecture is *obeliskos,* which now means "obelisk," but which also means "a little spit, or skewer."

An entirely different derivation is suggested by Gerald Massey in *Ancient Egypt: The Light of the World.* Massey traces the word back to the Greek *pur* (pronounced "pyr"), meaning "fire," and the Egyptian *met,* meaning "ten" or "a measure." Thus, he asserts, the word stands for the ten original measures or arcs traced by the god of fire—the sun—through the zodiacal circuit. Since the Great Pyramid of Giza, among others, seems to have been constructed according to sidereal measurements, this theory is plausible. The word would then literally mean "a ten-form measure of fire," a symbolic figure for manifest life.

Obviously there is much controversy over the derivation of the word "pyramid." However, there is even greater controversy concerning the purpose of the pyramids themselves, as evidenced by the many theories vying for substantiation in this regard.

A good friend of mine, Bernice B. Cousins, has specifically written an overview of the metaphysical concepts embodied in the Great Pyramid, based on Western occult and esoteric traditions. This was compiled from lectures

and articles previously presented by her on the subjects
of the occult sciences, astrology, reincarnation and karma,
and the symbology of occult and esoteric philosophy in
creative activities.

By way of continuing this introductory chapter, I
now present Ms. Cousins' overview:

Metaphysical Foundations of
The Great Pyramid

BY BERNICE B. COUSINS

To the Western mind, the fertile valley of the Nile
has always been a source of mystery, intrigue, and fantasy. Throughout the history of Western civilization, the
Sphinx has guarded the secrets of the Great Pyramid, and
Egypt of old has played an important role as teacher,
inspirer, and entertainer.

As early as the fifth century, B.C., Sophocles, the
Greek playwright-philosopher, presented the drama of
Oedipus the King who, in answering the "Riddle of the
Sphinx," gained the throne of the King he had slain
(Oedipus' father) and married the widow Queen (actually
his mother).

In the early 1600s A.D., Shakespeare tapped the Nile
as a setting for his famous tragedy *Antony and Cleopa-
tra.* In 1871, the majesty of Egypt was again captured
on stage as the background for the music of Verdi in his
classic opera *Aida.* Verdi wrote his innovative music for a
story sketch written by a French Egyptologist who had
been Curator of Monuments in Egypt.

Countless numbers of us have spent the better part
of our young years nurtured on the fantasy generated by
this mysterious land as scriptwriters and directors filled
the screen with miles of film footage of Karis the Mummy
chasing around the ruins of his homeland seeking the ma-

gic life-giving tanna leaves that would enable him to rescue his beloved Princess Atananka and gain immortal life for them both.

In more recent years, in the surrealist presentation *The Abominable Dr. Phibes,* Vincent Price (in the role of Dr. Phibes), with his assistant Vulnavia, played havoc among the ruins of the Kings as he sought to revive his beloved, Victoria, in the River of Life, which flowed through the ancient tombs each millennium.

Not content with simply inspiring our creative activities, the structure of the Pyramid has enlightened and intrigued scholars and other "interested individuals" as well. Any bibliography of the exploration of the Great Pyramid is extensive, and provides an impressive international listing of avant-garde thinkers.

Probably the largest single expedition to tackle the monument was the French scientific expedition assembled by Napoleon in A.D. 1798, during what was to become a thrust to conquer Egypt for the Empire. Mathematicians, architects, engineers, surveyors, artists, and savants accompanied Napoleon in this multidimensional exploration.

Volumes have since been written about this structure of massive stones so finely engineered and perfectly aligned, and the surrounding Giza complex. Each author and explorer has offered a theory as to the how and the why of the structure.

Yet today, after countless years and dozens of books, the questions remain, theories and conjectures are still offered, and the challenge of this mystery continues to beckon to us from the depths of our remote ancestry.

A survey of existing literature will provide several theories about the Great Pyramid. The explanations or theories can be roughly classified into a few general categories.

There are those who believe that the actual structure of the Great Pyramid is a coded history of the human race on earth, and that this code reveals not only past history, but also the future direction. Proponents of this

6

theory find support for their beliefs in the numerous measurements which have been logged—every angle, every block, course by course, each crack, crevice, and sand grain has been taken into consideration.

There are those who believe that the Great Pyramid was a structure to house the remains of the Pharaoh, and as such held the treasures and riches which the royal household had accumulated. In this vein the most acclaimed theory is that this structure was the burial tomb of one Pharaoh Cheops (or Khufu), circa 3350 B.C. The current accepted name for the large pyramid in the Giza complex, the Cheops or Khufu Pyramid, stems from the discovery of several inscriptions found on the ceiling slabs above the "King's Chamber."

The hieroglyphs of the cartouche are taken to represent Khufu (Cheops), therefore ascribing this as his tomb. While no remains were ever found in the "burial chamber," it has been suggested that the structure was designed by priest-doctor-engineer Imhotep, to house the body of the deceased Khufu/Cheops.

Little is known about the actual method of construction of the Great Pyramid, although traditional thinking on the subject still prevails. It is difficult to shake the postulation that the Great Pyramid was built by teams of slave laborers over a period of twenty or more years. There is debate as to whether these laborers were skilled or unskilled, but the logistics involved in the methodology suggested are mind-boggling at best.

It is speculated that it would have taken approximately three months for a team of eight men to bring ten stones from the quarry to the construction site. It is difficult to conceive of the hundreds of thousands of man-hours spent in dragging massive stone blocks weighing in the neighborhood of 2½ tons each up ramps, down causeways, using a system of levers, rollers, pulleys, and plain "sweat of the brow." When one considers that in our soft, contemporary period the average life span ranges from sixty-five to seventy years, the turnover on the construction crew must have been rapid indeed. Cheops may

7

have been a very precocious child when he commissioned the design of the structure, and hopefully he was far-sighted enough to arrange for alternative accommodations in the event that he should take his leave before his final resting place was completed.

Within the past few years, this theory of the method of construction has been challenged by many individuals who have dared to ask impertinent questions and suggest alternatives. However, the association of the structure with burial hangs on, as does the fixation of the Western mind with Egypt and death. This is an interesting phenomenon, and it is only when one looks outside of the confines of traditional Egyptology and academia that insights and understanding of the connection between the two become apparent.

Another widely held theory is that the Pyramid was constructed as an observatory. For that matter, most of the pyramid structures throughout the world are grouped into this classification, as well as the Babylonian Ziggurat. The royal astronomer and company could climb the steep, stepped incline to rest on a rather small, flat surface, where they could gaze at the heavens, make calculations, and do whatever it is that royal astronomers did.

Of course, this would account for the absence of a capstone. If the Pyramid had been capped, as has been suggested, they would have no place from which to observe.

The alignment of the passages to one or another star is also used to support the "observatory" theory. Much has been written about the alignment of the Pyramid to Polaris the pole star, Alcyone in the constellation of the Pleiades, as well as Alpha Draconis and Alpha Centauri. In this theory we deal with apparent phenomena, but neglect motivation. Again, as with the "burial" theme, a meaningful relationship will be found outside the accepted traditional thought processes.

Still other theories hold that the Pyramid was a geographical or astronomical marker, or better still, that it was really an artificially created hill used as a giant road

8

marker so that caravans and travelers would not lose their way as they crossed the desert en route to the sea or distant cities. All of these speculations are not without merit, in that they each contain some kernel of truth. However, each of the theories must be understood in relationship to the background of the theorist.

By and large, the early explorers were from European backgrounds, and as such sought evidence that supported their already well-formed ideas.

Those individuals influenced strongly by theology applied this to the Pyramid and came up with material evidence to support their ideologies. Those with strong scientific backgrounds applied what they found as material evidence to support their ideologies. In so doing, they provided a perfect point-counterpoint, leaving current researchers to sort out the differences.

What is there about this land of the Nile, Thebes, Karnak, Memphis, Dendera, Luxor, Abu Simbal, the Valley of the Kings, and, in particular, the Sphinx and the Great Pyramid, that enables us to become involved in a detective story that spans a period of more than four thousand years? Perhaps we should reflect with Mme. Blavatsky when she quotes Thackeray in the *Secret Doctrine:*

"That which is part of our souls is eternal."

Are we in fact a part of the Pyramid? Is the Pyramid a part of us?

The writers of the esoteric schools seem to think so. In fact, the giants of Western metaphysical science have been quite prolific on the subject of the Great Pyramid and the society that evolved around it. It is from a comparative study of the works of such individuals as Blavatsky, Bailey, Steiner, Churchward, Michell, and Cayce of the esoteric field; Ptolemy, Budge, Velikovsky, and Donnelly from the physical sciences, and the various Hebrew, Christian, Aramaic, and Mormon testaments, that we are able to piece together some interesting relationships that are expressed in part by the various theories mentioned.

The overall growth and development of the universe, our planet, and humanity follow the same general pattern

9

of growth and development as does the individual. Each Great Age and its accompanying civilizations has an overall theosophical concept that it must crystallize or bring to fruition. Rudolph Steiner addresses the "mission" of the various Great Ages and major civilizations in his book *Egyptian Myths and Mysteries.*

According to Steiner and other esoteric writers, the Lemurian and Atlantean ages preceded the Egyptian. The Greco-Roman age followed. The post-Atlantean cultures can be viewed as a gradual coagulation, moving from the lightness of spirit to the denseness of matter. The process reached a peak in the Greco-Roman age. We are currently in a transition period from the Greco-Roman to the "New Age," which is sometimes referred to as the "Aquarian Age." This is a period in which the combined experiences of the post-Atlantean to Greco-Roman ages are lifted by the expanded consciousness of humanity. Matter and Spirit are becoming unified.

The "mission" of the Egyptian age was to clarify, solidify, and delineate the *physical* aspect of human development. To this end emphasis was laid on the development of astronomy, mathematics, engineering, medicine, and the arts.

Emphasis was placed on the solid three-dimensional structure, bringing ideas into a physical form, and the development of the physical body. Egyptian theology and philosophy concerned themselves with techniques for developing the perfect spiritual, mental, and physical being in harmonious balance. Steiner points out that the emphasis on death and the afterlife served to call attention to the reality of the physical body rather than the spirit. Essentially, the spirit, which was immortal, needed the identification with its own physical body, even after it had left the form.

The recurrent cycle of life was known during the early stages of the mission. The spirit incarnated on the earth plane, the physical body grew, developed, and eventually ceased to function. The spirit made its transition from physical form and returned to the land of the "gods." This cycle was repeated again and again. The "mission" of the Egyptian Era permeated the entire cultural development from the earliest periods on through to the decline in the later dynasties, and its imprint can still be seen in the remains of this culture. Somewhere along the line the balance point was lost, and with the passage of time the understanding of the "mission" diminished. Practices and rituals became corrupted and without meaning.

This is a common phenomenon in societies, due in great measure to the fact that an individual's exposure to the truth underlying an action usually diminishes with direct relationship to that individual's status. The general public is rarely entrusted with a knowledge of the meaning behind the rituals they are permitted to participate in. We can find many instances today where the implementation of the law is more important than the intent of the law.

The testament of the mission of the Egyptian Age was written in what is now known as the *Egyptian Book of the Dead*. Edgar Cayce, the famous American psychic, presented extensive commentaries on the Lemurian, Atlantean, and Egyptian ages. These commentaries appear in the psychic readings that Cayce gave while in a self-induced hypnotic trance.

Many of the readings pertaining to the Egyptian Age appear in the publications *The Great Pyramid and Its Builders; The Egyptian Heritage;* and *Earth Changes.* Cayce addressed the significance of the *Book of the Dead* in reading No. 5748-2. He comments, "The *original* formulation of the *Book of the Dead* was undertaken at a great convention in the Nile Valley in a primeval period. . . ." Scholars generally place parts of the text in the predynastic periods (prior to 4100 B.C.), but it is difficult to specifically date the entire work because of the many additions and changes made to it. Reading No. 5748-2, which appears in *The Egyptian Heritage,* states, "The first laws which originally constituted the *Book of the Dead* were concerned with 'The Division of the Mind,

11

The Division of the Solar Systems, and the Division of Man' in various spheres through the earth's plane and through the earth's solar system." This is a provocative statement!

The Egyptians believed in the individual being as a complex entity with many aspects. The first was Khat, the physical body as a whole. The second was Ab, the heart, source of life, a fulcrum of balance and the conscious. The third principle was Ka, a "double" that was a nonphysical "etheric" duplicate that would leave the body while it was entombed. The Ka was capable of entering any statue of the deceased and also of enjoying life with the gods.

The fourth principle was Ba, the "heart-soul." Ba could assume both physical and nonphysical form. Ba was considered immortal, and it could join with or leave the physical body at will. The fifth principle, Khaibit, was associated with Ba. Khaibit, the "shadow" had freedom of movement independent of the physical body, and, like Ba, had a will of its own.

The sixth principle was Sekhen, the vital force or life force. Sekhen was believed to live in heaven with Khu. The seventh principle was Khu. Khu was the spirit-soul, the immortal part of man. Khu went to heaven as soon as the body died. The eighth principle was Sahu. Sahu was termed the "lasting incorruptible spirit body," which incorporated cosmic qualities of the individual within it. The ninth and final principle was Ren. Ren was the name of the individual. The name existed in heaven. The individual existed only as long as his name was preserved. This concept of Ren is embodied in the Gospel of St. John, 1:1: "In the beginning was the Word, and the Word was with God; and the Word was God."

The nine aspects or principles of individuality were bound together, and the well-being of each affected all of the others. Our present concepts of individual personality are somewhat more simplified. The physical body, the mind, and the spirit/soul are separated by us. Esoteric teachings also add the etheric double and the astral body. Perhaps in time we will rediscover these principles.

Esoteric writers appear to agree that the primary reason behind the design and construction of the Great Pyramid was not as a tomb for a Pharaoh but rather as a solid, three-dimensional statement of the concepts detailed in the *Book of the Dead,* and that the structure should serve as a place in which those individuals responsible for keeping these concepts alive and pure—initiates—would experience their training, testing, and passage to adeptship. As a structure embodying the "first laws" we can readily understand why over the years the investigators writing about the Great Pyramid have come up with divergent conclusions.

The astronomical or astrological concepts embodied in the Great Pyramid figure significantly in the matter of dating the construction. The primary accepted date for the construction is placed in the Fourth Dynasty under the direction of the Pharaoh Khufu/Cheops, circa 3350 B.C. This assignment stems from the discovery of a set of quarry marks that bear the hieroglyphic cartouches that have been accepted as indicators of the name of Cheops/ Khufu, King of Upper and Lower Egypt.

2. Khufu's cartouche

The picture writing of the Egyptians can be interpreted in several ways. The symbol can represent the phonetic rendition of a name, or it can represent the idea encompassed by the glyph sound.

13

The accepted meaning of the sedge and the bee is that of the United Kingdoms of Upper and Lower Egypt. The Kingdoms are the physical-political entities that were known as the upper and lower regions of the Nile.

However, the symbols can also represent the upper and lower kingdoms of life—Spirit and Matter. It is thought that the Pyramid is actually situated at the precise juncture of the physical regions of Upper and Lower Egypt. The symbol for Khu can be read as the initial consonant of Khufu's name, but it can also be read as Khu, the spirit-soul principle. The remaining glyphs in the cartouche can also be interpreted in this fashion.

The quarry marks therefore need not be the marks of one individual known as Khufu/Cheops, but rather as an indication of the structure itself, or the area within the structure that represented the Khu principle of Spirit-Soul being born in the earth plane and re-entering the spirit world. The cartouche markings were found on the ceiling slabs above the "King's Chamber." In esoteric writings, the "King's Chamber" has been referred to as both the tomb and the womb.

Fixing dates in antiquity is a rather difficult and ever-changing matter. Astronomical information often assists in setting the time, provided such evidence is discovered for or at the place in question. Such was the case of Eridu, a Babylonian city that was reported to be the seat of commerce with southern Arabia and India. Eridu is now located inland, hardly the place for a busy seaport town.

A great astronomical work, *The Observation of Bel,* brought insight into the changing positions of the vernal equinox. When the Accadian calendar was arranged, the sun was in the constellation of Taurus at the vernal equinox, not in Aries or Pisces, as it is now. This information enabled an accurate placement of the city, owing to a passage of approximately six thousand years, during which the silt deposits of the Persian Gulf had accumulated and "moved" the city inland.

According to H. P. Blavatsky, "Herodotus had been

14

informed by Egyptian priests" that there had been dramatic changes in our earth over the passage of time. The poles, "terrestrial and ecliptic, had formerly coincided." Mme. Blavatsky maintains that this information was verified by Mackey in *The Mythological Astronomy of the Ancients Demonstrated.*

In the chapter "Mistakes of the Egyptologists" in the *Secret Doctrine,* Volume II, Mme. Blavatsky comments on the Dendera Zodiac, and Mackey is quoted further: "The poles are represented in the Zodiacs [this is in reference to two existing zodiacs, Dendera and another unnamed], in both positions and in that which shows the Poles [polar axes] at right angles? [Dendera Zodiac], there are marks which prove that it was not the *last* time they were in that position, but the *first* after the Zodiacs had been traced—Capricorn is represented at the North Pole and Cancer is divided near its middle at the South Pole; which is confirmation that they had their winter when the Sun was in Cancer."*

This is not the only mention of the shifting poles in esoteric writings! Edgar Cayce emphasizes this phenomenon and places the submergence of Atlantis and the subsequent colonization of the Nile Delta following such a shift and its accompanying upheavals.

H. P. Blavatsky also introduces a comment by J. Gardner Wilkenson: "All facts led to the conclusion that the Egyptians had already made great progress as a civilization before the age of Menes, and perhaps *before they immigrated* to the Valley of the Nile."

Menes was the first King of the United Kingdoms of

---

*In the Northern Hemisphere, the winter solstice occurs when the sun is in the zodiacal sign of Capricorn. This usually occurs on or about the twenty-first day of December. At this time it is summer solstice in the Southern Hemisphere. For the inhabitants of the Dendera vicinity to have winter solstice with the sun in Cancer, Dendera, and therefore Egypt, would have had to be below the equator or in the Southern Hemisphere. Giza is located on the same parallel as Houston, Texas, New Orleans, Louisiana, and St. Augustine, Florida.

Upper and Lower Egypt and ruler of the First Dynasty. He is placed some 750 years prior to the Fourth Dynasty at circa 4100 B.C.

The Dendera Zodiac indicates a passage of three sidereal cycles. By solar-lunar precession, a sidereal year is approximately 25,694.8 years ± 281.2 years' variation (C. Jayne; *Encyclopedia of Astrology,* Devore). Other calculations of sidereal cycles are: H. P. Blavatsky, 25,868 years; Plato, 25,920 years; Giza measurements, 25,827.5 years.

Following H. P. Blavatsky's comments: "Assuming that the long narrow downward passage was directed towards the pole star of the Pyramid builders, Alpha Draconis, the then pole star, was in the required position at 3350 B.C. (Fourth Dynasty), as well as 2170 B.C. (Proctor, Wake). The relative position of Alpha Draconis and Alcyone was an extraordinary one, and would not occur for another sidereal year." Since the Dendera Zodiac shows a passage of three sidereal cycles, it is possible to move backward three sidereal years to "obtain the occurrence of the relationship of Alpha Draconis and Alcyone some 78,000 years ago."

Once the mind is freed of the time limits imposed on it by the preconceived notions of evolutionary development in a forward direction, it is possible to accept this significantly earlier time period. We tend to remain in a fixed perspective with regard to seeing our current level of development and the world as it now appears, and to accept the subsequent arbitrary dating of time prior to the Greco/Roman Era.

Why would the Pyramid builders deliberately or accidentally choose this precise alignment of certain stars in the heavens as focal points for the structure? In referencing the esoteric writings—which cover not only the Western, but Eastern traditions as well—we are able to find some meaning for this alignment.

Alice Bailey gives Alcyone in the Pleiades as the center point of our Sun's orbit. In occult/esoteric litera-

16

ture, the Pleiades/Atlantides are connected with the destinies of nations, as is the pole star. While the celestial Pleiades bear little physical resemblance to the Seven Sisters, we have reason to believe that the cosmic nature of this constellation is in fact the essence of the myth connected with these ladies.

The Pleiades/Atlantides were the daughters of Atlas and Atlantis, and were named Maia, Electra, Taygeta, Asterope, Merope, Celaeno, and Alcyone. The sisters were credited with marrying gods and becoming mothers of famous heroes, the founders of many nations and cities.

The Pleiades are the representation of the feminine, magnetic Form nature of the Universe. The association of Western culture with materialism (matter) is not a coincidence, but a definite outgrowth of the "mission" of the Egyptian Age. In contrast, the Asian culture, with its emphasis on the nonphysical, Spirit, assigns its founders, progenitors, and saints to the Rishis.

Gods in male form, the seven Rishis are associated with the northern constellation of the Great Bear, Ursa Major. It is estimated that it has been 70,000 years since the pole of the earth pointed to the farther end of Ursa Minor's tail—Polaris.

In *Esoteric Astrology,* Bailey cites the great triangulation of energy in our solar system as the interrelationship among the seven stars of the Great Bear, the seven stars of the Pleiades—sometimes referred to as the Seven Sisters, or wives of the Rishis, or the Great Bear—and finally the sun Sirius (Dog Star). The energy triangulation manifests as Will/Power, Love/Wisdom, and Active Intelligence—the three qualities that are the marks of humanity.

The alignment of the Great Pyramid to both Alcyone and the Pole Star in the Celestial Sphere is significant, as it becomes the focal point on earth of the Electric-Male principle Spirit and the Magnetic-Female principle Form. These principles are the foundation of the decimal system—the 1 and the 0. The Pyramid was built on the measure of decimal notation, as was the astronomical and geometrical portions of the "secret sacradotal language" (H. P. Blavatsky, *Secret Doctrine*).

The geographical location was precisely chosen, not only as it was the junction of the upper and lower kingdoms of the physical world, or the center of the mass of the continents, but also because of the nature of the geomagnetic force lines that grid the earth.

According to Michell (*View over Atlantis; City of Revelation*) humanity tends to build centers of great spiritual significance where these geomagnetic lines intersect.

From the writings of the esoteric philosophers, we find that in the structure of the Great Pyramid we have a complete physical manifestation of the nature of humanity on earth, and its very special relationship to the universe. The essence of the Great Pyramid can be found in a quote from Bailey's *Esoteric Astrology* on the nature of the message of the Pleiades:

Stanza IV: "Their light is different from other lights. It wakes the response—I am the densest point of all the concrete world (Capricorn AAB). I am a tomb. I also am the womb [Cancer]. I am the rock which sinks itself into the deep of matter. I am the mountain top on which the Son is born, on which the Sun is seen and that which catches the first rays of light—Man takes a nature which is his today. Son of a Mother, born from the tomb and showing after birth, the Light . . ."

The Great Pyramid illustrates the impact of energy on energy units.

References and Suggested Additional Reading

Bailey, Alice A.—Lucis Publishing Company. New York
   A Treatise on the Seven Rays—Vol. III, *Esoteric Astrology*
   A Treatise on the Cosmic Fire
   A Treatise on White Magic
Benavides, Rudolfo—Editores Mexicanos Unidos, S.A., 1974
   Dramatic Prophecies of the Great Pyramid

Blavatsky, H. P.—Theosophical University Press, Pasadena, Calif.
The Secret Doctrine, Vols. I and II

Budge, Sir Walter—University Press, New Hyde Park, New York
Egyptian Magic

Burgoyne, T. H.—Originally published 1889; reprinted, 1969
Light of Egypt, Vols. I and II

Carlson, Vada F.—A.R.E. Press, 1970
The Great Migration

Cayce, E. E. (Ed.), Cayce, H. L.—Paperback Library
Edgar Cayce on Atlantis

Cayce, Edgar Material—A.R.E. Press, Virginia Beach, Virginia
Earth Changes Past—Present—Future

Churchwald, James—Paperback Library, five-part series on Mu (Lemuria)
The Lost Continent of Mu
The Children of Mu
The Sacred Symbols of Mu
The Cosmic Forces of Mu
The Second Book of the Cosmic Forces of Mu

Davidson, D. and Aldersmith, H.—William Margate Ltd., 1926
The Great Pyramid—Its Divine Message

Donnelly, Ignatius—Gramercy Publishing Company, 1949
Atlantis—The Antediluvian World

Gardiner, Sir Alan—Oxford University Press
Egyptian Grammar

Hall, Manly Palmer—Philosophical Research Society
The Secret Teachings of All Ages

Hatt, Carolyn—A.R.E. Press, 1972
The Maya

Heline, Corinne—New Age Press, LaCanada, Calif.
Occult Anatomy and the Bible

Lamsa, George M.—A. J. Holman Co., 1957 ed., from ancient Eastern manuscripts
Holy Bible from the Peshitta

Lehner, Mark—A.R.E. Press, 1974—Based on the Edgar Cayce Readings
The Egyptian Heritage

Lehnert and Landrock—Cairo, Egypt
  Cairo Tourist Map
Lockyer, Norman J.—M.I.T. Press, 1894–1964
  The Dawn of Astronomy
Michell, John—Ballantine Books, New York
  The View over Atlantis
  City of Revelation
Norris, A. G. S.—Weiser
  Transcendental Astrology
Robinson, Lytle, W.—A.R.E. Press, 1958
  The Great Pyramid and Its Builders
Seiss, Joseph A.—Multimedia Publishing Corp., Blauvelt, N. Y., 1973
  The Great Pyramid—A Miracle in Stone, 1877
Steiner, Rudolph—Anthrosophical Press
  Egyptian Myths and Mysteries, 1971
  Occult Science
Urantia Foundation
  Urantia Book
Velikovsky, Immanuel
  World in Collision, Dell, 1950
  Earth in Upheaval, Dell, 1955
  Ages in Chaos, Abacus, 1952
  Velikovsky Reconsidered by the editors of *Pensee*, Warner Books
Waddell, W. G. and Robbins, F. E.—Loeb Classic Library Edition, 1964
  Manetho—Ptolemy/Tetrabiblos
Wake, Staniland C.—Wizard Bookshelf, Minneapolis, 1975
  The Origin and Significance of the Great Pyramid, 1882
Watkins, Alfred—Ballantine Books, New York
  The Old Straight Track
Holy Bible, Old and New Testaments, Confraternity of Christian Doctrine, and R/D versions, King James version
The Book of Mormon, "An account written by the hand of Mormon upon plates taken from the plates of Nephi," translated by Joseph Smith, Jr., Church of Jesus Christ of Latter-day Saints, Salt Lake City, Utah.

As Bernice explains, the ideologies of the scientists and theologists provide a perfect point-counterpoint. They not only leave current researchers to sort out the difference, but we, too, are left with the task. We, who are not satisfied with the simple explanation of our earthly existence: to be born, to die, and to experience a mundane proportion of pain and pleasure in between.

Are we indeed metaphysically inferior to the ancients through regressive evolution, or have we merely been conditioned to become blind with all our senses to the cyclical order of nature wending its way through our lives?

Let us examine the current point-counterpoint aspects in as great a depth as possible, and sift from them the key to the code that we can use to make our life more meaningful, not just for the present, but also for the futures to come.

{2}

PYRAMID INFLUENCE —
IT'S ALL AROUND US

Long before British scholars began investigating the Great Pyramid of Cheops with their measuring implements and mental gauges, the enigma of the Pyramid had already captured the imagination of countless numbers of students and masters of metaphysics. A tremendous amount of qabbalistic and occult symbolism has been attached to and derived from Cheops' Pyramid. Such age-old societies as the Rosicrucians, the Masons, and the Rose Croix have embodied the Pyramid within their mysticism and secret rituals.

Everything dealing with ancient schools of thought and/or philosophies alludes to the possibility that there once was a great order of mystics who—along with the knowledge of man's nature relative to the time rate of his progress on earth—possessed an immense knowledge of astronomy, mathematics, and construction for thousands of years. This order of mystic wise men built their facts not only into the structure designed as the Pyramid of Cheops, but also into the key temples of each great civilization. This is evidenced by the fact that not only are many pyramidal structures found around the world, but also buildings of other civilizations—which did not have the pyramid structure—contain evidence of stone masonry.

The significance of the knowledge of masonry that existed thousands of years ago—among races of people who apparently had knowledge only of farming and cattle raising—is overwhelmingly complex. It is no wonder that scholars of various mystic orders claim that ancient masters brought their knowledge to all civilizations on earth.

Stonemasonry is a craft that both scientists and laymen take for granted, rather than respecting it for the science it had been centuries ago. Today we marvel at the way pyramids and other megalithic structures were constructed by laying squared stones in courses, to achieve the desired height and shape of the building.

Many structures of ancient civilizations are in existence today. We have scant knowledge of these civilizations, who have built as marvelously as the pyramid civilizations. As an example of this construction, one building in South America had stones formed by irregular cuts to fit exactly in place with other irregularly cut stones. These great, many-faceted stones, many of them ten to twenty times larger than the stones of the Great Pyramid, were lifted into place wedging each other together.

The Great Wall at Sacsahuaman, near the city of Cuzco, in Peru, South America, is believed to have been built by the Tiahuanacoans. It is sixty feet high and is nearly a half mile long. One of the largest stones in the wall is reported to be ten feet wide, seventeen feet high, nine feet thick, and well over one hundred tons in weight. Another stone in the wall is so exquisitely chiseled that it has become world famous as the "Stone of Twelve Angels."

No mortar was used and the interlocking of the stones was so perfect that no earthquake could have any effect upon these structures.

The Holy Order of Mystics, carrying on the knowledge of stonemasonry, revealed the significance in the buildings of the Tiajuran and Tiahuanacan temples. Although building differently from any other race on earth, the people of these civilizations were not simply farmers and cattle raisers, but also highly educated scientists with knowledge of astronomy, mathematics, engineering, and other sciences.

The technical ability of the South American civilizations employing the craft of multifaceting stones also included pyramid construction with normally squared stones.

Evidence of the influence of the same Order or Brotherhood of Mysticism is left by the many massive structures found throughout the world. It is obvious that the ancients conveyed one simple fact through their construction—that is, their knowledge is still superior to our present-day technology. Because their ability still surpasses ours immeasurably, we stand in awe at their amazing mental prowess and ascribe to these masters the Order of Mysticism. It is because of this that wise men consistently recognize that the real knowledge of the masters was not written in perishable manuscript form, but rather in the symbolism of construction of enduring rock itself.

The symbolism of the pyramid structure had so embraced the minds of scholars throughout the ages that by the time the Continental Congress of the United States of America resolved to prepare the Great Seal of the United States, the pyramid had already been destined to be incorporated into the design of the seal. All three committees appointed in succession by Congress between 1776 and 1782 included members holding various positions in Freemasonry. Each committee's suggestion for seal design showed Freemasonry influence—in symbolism such as the eye of providence, a triangle, a Pharaoh, Moses, clouds, stars, constellations, olive branch, and phoenix.

The seal accepted by Congress on June 20, 1782, contains on its obverse an American eagle (the symbol of the phoenix) with spread wings, holding an olive branch in its right talon and a bundle of thirteen arrows in the left, with a scroll in its beak inscribed with the motto *E pluribus unum,* and thirteen tail feathers. Over the head of the eagle is a crest, containing a constellation formed by thirteen stars into a Mogen David symbol breaking through a cloud. On the breast of the eagle there is a shield of thirteen stripes, and the entire design contains an azure background.

3. Both sides of the Great Seal of the United States of America

The reverse of the seal is dominated by an unfinished pyramid. The eye of providence is in a triangle depicted as a floating capstone with glorious emanation. *Annuit coeptis* appears over the floating capstone. The pyramid contains thirteen courses, and on the base course is inscribed the Roman numerical letters MDCCLXXVI (1776). Finally, below the pyramid is a scroll containing the motto *Novus ordo seclorum.*

Paul Foster Case, in his *Great Seal of the United States: Its History, Symbolism and Message for the New Age,* claims that a majority of the Continental Congress of 1776 consisted of members of the Masonic lodge, but records were not so carefully kept then, and research by Masonic scholars has turned up evidence that only seven signers of the Declaration of Independence are known to have been Freemasons.

For example, when Benjamin Franklin assisted in the drafting of the Declaration of Independence, he was past grand master of the Pennsylvania Freemasons. George Washington and twelve of his generals were Mason members. When he took office as the first President of the United States, a past grand master of New York swore him in on a Bible brought from a Masonic lodge.

The Freemasons founding this nation drew their inspiration from many ancient schools and philosophies, such as the Hebrew and Christian Scriptures, the doctrines of Pythagoras, the Alexandrian school, Plato, the Qabbalists, and the Rosicrucians. Qabbalistic influence appears to be greatest in Freemasonry and reveals itself very dramatically in the Great Seal of the United States.

The number 13 is prominent throughout the history of the United States. Thirteen letters are contained in each of the following phrases: "July the Fourth" and "American Eagle." The digits "76," as used to designate the year of the Declaration of Independence, add to thirteen $(7 + 6 = 13)$. The peculiarly Masonic phrase "In God We Trust" equals thirteen by modern numerology, in which a numerical value is assigned to each letter, the sum derived, then broken down to a two-digit number. Obviously, the designers of the Great Seal of the United States definitely emphasize the number 13. It appears their primary intention was to commemorate the thirteen states forming the new nation.

Our first Navy consisted of thirteen ships. Although there were only eleven states in the Confederacy, the Confederate flag used in the Civil War contained thirteen stars.

The deliberate repetition of the number 13 in the composition of the Great Seal of the United States seems to develop into tedium when one considers that the motto *E pluribus unum* and also *Annuit coeptis* each contain thirteen letters. In addition to that, there are thirteen leaves and thirteen berries on the olive branch held in the talon of the eagle.

Modern Qabbalists add two interesting facts to this list of "thirteen" symbolism. The first concerns World War I, when the first expedition to France sailed with thirteen ships on June 13, 1917, taking thirteen days to cross. In addition, President Woodrow Wilson's name contains thirteen letters.

The second fact revolves around the horoscope of the

Declaration of Independence, which shows the sun in thirteen degrees of the sign Cancer and makes thirteen degrees ascendant of the sign Scorpio, which sign is also represented by the number 13 in the ancient Rosicrucian and Masonic tarot keys.

It is generally accepted as fact that sacred and esoteric writings made use of a number-letter code in order to preserve a record of arcane knowledge, at the same time concealing the real significance of the writing from all except those possessing the key to the code. It is believed, for example, that the Book of Moses is so written.

The constellation of thirteen stars above the eagle on the obverse of the Great Seal of the United States is said to convey a code message in symbolism, to which the number 13 is the most important key. Each of the thirteen stars contains five points or pentagrams, arranged so that their grouping in toto forms a large, six-pointed star or hexagram. Interestingly, a hexagram can be composed of either two intersecting equilateral triangles or twelve smaller equilateral triangles. Taking any one of the two large equilateral triangles formed by the constellation of thirteen stars, there are exactly ten stars within that triangular figure known as the tetraktys, upon which Pythagoras is said to have sworn his pupils to secrecy.

The symbolism of the six-pointed star dates back to ancient times, when it was used as the standard of Israel, otherwise known as the Shield of David, or "Mogen David." From the beginning of time the hexagram has been the symbol of forces of the macrocosm at work in the heavenly spaces, which supposedly were active aeons before man made his appearance on earth.

With the repetition of the number 13 in the Great Seal of the United States being so obvious, one cannot help but concentrate on this significant fact as a possible key to the destiny of the United States, which in turn will affect the destiny of the rest of the world. Paul Foster Case believes that the number 13 represents an epoch of a thirteen-year cycle, corresponding to the thirteen courses of the pyramid on the obverse of the seal. However, starting at 1776 and adding 13 × 13 = 169 only adds up to 1945.

While the year 1945 was an important one for our nation, it is obvious that the destiny of the United States has far surpassed that date, and one can speculate how many more epochs must pass before there is a definite change in the destiny of the United States.

Ms. Peggie Donnigi, a psychic in New York City, muses over the possible destiny of the United States had it lost in World War II, which was during the thirteenth epoch of thirteen years: "We would have been divided among the winning nations, becoming their possession and thereby losing our own identity." However, she feels that the political administration of our government at that time was well aware of the impending significance of the thirteenth cycle, and that all chances had to be taken in order to beat the odds of a correct prediction for the nation.

Consulting with Ms. Donnigi, she predicts that the destiny of the United States will receive a severely devastating crisis either during or at the end of the seventeenth epoch. Starting from 1776, it puts this crisis between the years 1984 and 1997. She arrives at seventeen epochs by considering the fact that the number 17 appears quite prominently in two points: the date 1776 has a "17" in it, and the number 13 symbolism appears in or relates to the Great Seal of the United States seventeen times.

In questioning Ms. Donnigi further about exactly what the crisis will entail, she said, "We will bring about the destruction of our nation—and possibly the entire planet—if we do not use our technological knowledge rightly and continue our course of ecological suicide by the abuse of chemical knowledge." With the eagle representing the symbol of the phoenix, Ms. Donnigi senses that a new nation will arise out of the ashes of the chemicals of the spoilers, to bring forth a new nation more prudent in the application of its alchemistic knowledge.

The achievements of the architects and builders of

the pyramids throughout the world have greatly inspired the philosophic thoughts of the metaphysicians. Not only have these achievements become an emblem of eternity itself, but they are indeed a sermon in stone.

From the very beginning, initiates of antiquity dogmatically accepted the pyramid as the perfect symbol of the secret doctrine. It is said that the Great Pyramid is related to the fabled Olympus and that its subterranean passages correspond to the tortuous pathways of Hades. It is also thought that the pyramid shape is a symbolical representation of the Holy Mountain, or High Place of God, which is believed to stand in the middle of the earth.

Students of the secret doctrine believe the sides of the Great Pyramid, facing the four cardinal points, signify extremities of dark and light (west and east) and the extremes of cold and heat (north and south). The base of the pyramid further represents to the student the four material elements of nature from which the body of man is formed: air, water, fire, soil. The face of the pyramid, being a triangle, signifies the triune within every object in nature. The twelve signs of the zodiac appear also to be represented by the total number of lines and faces of the pyramid.

The spiritual centers of man are represented by the three main chambers of the pyramid as the heart, the brain, and the reproductive organs. The triangular form of the pyramid is reminiscent of the posture of the body during yoga, meditation, and other ancient exercises.

The Mysteries taught to the initiates claim that the divine energies of the gods descend upon the top of the pyramid, and that their divine wisdom is radiantly disseminated throughout the world by flowing down the diverging sides of the pyramid.

According to the secret doctrine, the pyramid is the first and true temple of the Mysteries—a structure erected to house those sacred truths that are the definite foundation of all arts and sciences. It is the perfect emblem of both the microcosm and the macrocosm.

The greatest pyramid mystery, causing great and serious concern, is the missing capstone. The lack of completeness is peculiar to the major pyramid structures throughout the world.

In his book *The Giza Necropolis Decoded,* author and researcher Rocky McCollum outlines the location of the capstone, a secret chamber, and several artifacts which, in his opinion, would give evidence of the existence of Atlantis and Mu.

The message that Mr. McCollum has decoded from the Giza necropolis is based upon the slopes of the pyramids and the Ancient Rule of Three.

He has found that taking the tangent of the slope angle of Cheops' Pyramid results in a value of 1.27230. Multiplying this value by a constant yields the Radian Number Pi $= 3.1415926$. Therefore, McCollum labels Cheops' Pyramid to be a Pi-slope pyramid.

Applying the same mathematical reasoning to the slope angle of Chephren's pyramid, the result is a tangent of 1.33511. Again, multiplying this by a constant yields the Natural Number $E = 2.7182818$. Similarly, he labels Chephren's pyramid as being an Epsilon-slope pyramid.

According to McCollum's chart, of the sixteen Egyptian pyramids he investigated, he has determined that six are Pi-slope pyramids and five are Epsilon-slope pyramids—a very nearly even distribution. However, five of the remaining sixteen pyramids have slope angles yielding either a larger or smaller tangent value, which does not compute to either of the Pi or Epsilon values.

McCollum states, "To determine Pi a large circle can be drawn and the number can be measured almost directly. But not so with Epsilon. The number Epsilon must be calculated from theoretical considerations only. Some methods are rather complex and a few of them are of comparatively recent vintage (to us, anyhow)."

Where, then, did the Egyptians acquire this knowledge? McCollum questions, and he goes on further to say that simply knowing the existence of Epsilon and its value to within 5 per cent of accuracy is "a real feat" when it is considered that men had this concept five thousand years ago and applied it in the construction of some of the pyramids. It appears that the pyramid builders may have been more certain of the value of Pi than of the value Epsilon.

According to McCollum, based on his mathematical computations, he has no doubt that the pyramid builders needed the values of Pi and Epsilon. His contention is that the builders of the pyramids were closely related to Buddhism and Hinduism. This he infers from an ancient Egyptian masonry symbol and the symbol of Vishnu, the Preserver. The script within the triangle appears to be one and the same with the symbol of Vishnu, even with several minor variations.

5. The symbol of Vishnu, the Preserver

His inference gains even more significance when the symbols are held up to a mirror and the reflected images of Pi and Epsilon are revealed. Using the interesting theory of Pi and Epsilon being cryptically coded into the two "mystic" symbols, McCollum is certain that Cheops' Pyramid (P1) was built first, representing Pi; and then Chephren's Pyramid (P2) was built to represent the value of Epsilon, in that order, yielding the beginnings of a formula containing Pi and Epsilon. According to him, the numerical symbols held in esteem were best perpetuated by having them built into the slope of the pyramid, because even if semidestroyed, the slope of the pyramid's side could still be determined quite accurately; whereas de-

Chart I
The Sixteen Major Pyramids of Egypt*

Pyramid Number	Name	Height in Meters	Base in Meters	(Slope) Angle	Tangent	Symbol
P-1	Khufu	137	230	51°50'	1.27230	π
P-2	Khafre	143.5	215.5	53°10'	1.33511	ε
P-3	Menkhure	66.5	108.5	51°00'	1.23490	π
P-4	Meydum	92	144	51°53'	1.27458	π
P-5	Snefru (Bent Pyramid)	101.5	188.6	54°31'	1.40281 bot.	?
				43°21'	0.94400 top	
P-6	Dahshur (northern)	99	220	43°40'	0.95451	?
P-7	Weserkaf	44.5	70.4	51°41'	1.26546	π
P-8	Sahure	48	75	50°36'	1.21742	π
P-9	Neferirkare	70	106	53°00'	1.32704	ε
P-10	Neuserre	52	80	51°50'	1.27230	π
P-11	Pepi	52	76	53°00'	1.32704	ε

P-12	Amenemhet (I)	58	84	54°00'	1.37368	ε
P-13	Senusert (I)	61	105	49°00'	1.15037	?
P-14	Hawara	58	100	48°45'	1.14028	?
P-15	Amenemhet (III)	80	100	57°20'	1.55966	?
P-16	Khendjer	37.4	55	55°00'	1.42815	ε

*According to Rocky McCollum in *The Giza Necropolis Decoded.*

4.

struction of a portion of the pyramid would leave doubts as to its original height or overall size.

McCollum goes on to question that, if the pyramid builders knew the value for Pi and Epsilon, would they not also incorporate the number 1, the arithmetical symbol 0, and i—representing the imaginary number of the square root of −1? (see Figure 7.)

He could not find a pyramid in Egypt with either a slope angle of 45° or one from which his computations would indicate the number 1. McCollum logically looked for the answer in the third pyramid of the Giza group and found that Mycerinus' pyramid (P3) met his requirements admirably.

According to him, ". . . it is large enough to be significant and yet smaller than its neighbors so as not to compete with them as guardians of the symbolic numbers." Therefore, it had to be built to a minimum requirement, and at the same time be considered as a major or contributing structure of the Giza complex.

By dividing the distance of the base of P3 into the base of P2, the result is 1.987. Thus McCollum postulates that P3 represents the number 1, because there is a 2-to-1 ratio between pyramids P3 and P2.

The Epsilon equation was discovered by Leonhard Euler, an eighteenth-century Swiss mathematician and physicist. It contains the Radian Number Pi (π), the Natural Number Epsilon (ε), the Imaginary Number i $= \sqrt{-1}$, the Unitary Number 1, and the arithmetical symbol 0. $E^{i\pi} + 1 = 0$.

According to McCollum, in order to prove that the builders of the pyramids knew of the Epsilon equation, he had yet to find the imaginary number, i, and 0 depicted in or around the Giza complex. To him it was obvious that a pyramid could not be built having a tangent of 0, because it would mean a slope angle of 0, and the only geometric form satisfying this condition is a straight line.

It was not until McCollum saw a two-dimensional straight line expressed in a three-dimensional flat surface

34

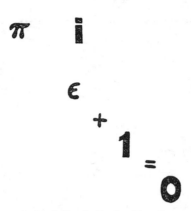

6. McCollum's Epsilon Equation

(the plateau at Giza) that indeed he felt "0" to be represented in the pyramid complex. He intuitively decided that this had to be the area intended by the pyramid builders to indicate the arithmetical symbol 0.

According to McCollum's theory, an Epsilon equation had to be generated from the Giza complex. He claims that the Egyptians wrote mathematical equations obliquely. When viewed from the air, the Giza complex along a northeast-to-southwest axis yields the Epsilon equation. At this point, the equation physically takes shape as depicted by the complex and, amazingly, in proper accord with the rule for exponents in algebraic equations—the imaginary number i is clearly represented by the Sphinx itself.

In McCollum's own words, "Examine the Sphinx; he will serve admirably as (i) and is even located in the proper place. . . . And what indeed is more imaginary than a character having the body of a lion and the head of a man!"

McCollum very ingeniously locates the 0 site in an intriguing way; by fitting the Golden Spiral as formed by the Fibonacci number series through the apexes of the

35

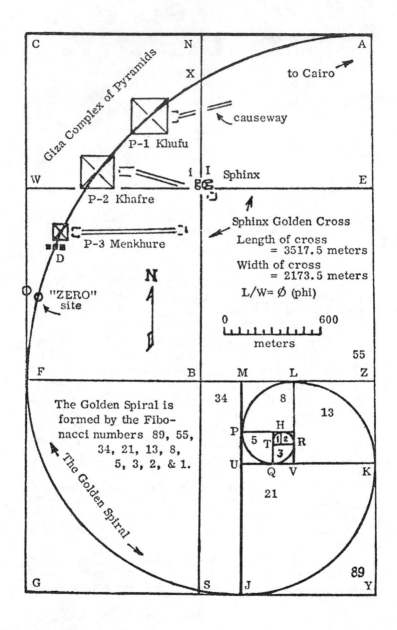

C   N   A

Giza Complex of Pyramids

X

to Cairo →

causeway

P-1 Khufu

W   i I Sphinx   E

P-2 Khafre

Sphinx Golden Cross

Length of cross
    = 3517.5 meters

Width of cross
    = 2173.5 meters

$L/W = \emptyset$ (phi)

P-3 Menkhure

D

N

"ZERO" site

0   600

meters

55

F   B   M   L   Z

The Golden Spiral is
formed by the Fibo-
nacci numbers 89, 55,
34, 21, 13, 8,
5, 3, 2, & 1.

34   8

13

P   5 T   H   R

U   Q V   K

The Golden Spiral →

21

89

G   S J   Y

The Seven Royal Numbers

1. π = 3.1415926 (Radian Number)
2. ϵ = 2.7182818 (Natural Number)
3. ϕ = 1.6180339 (Golden Number)
4. Γ = 0.5772156 (Gamma Number)
5. i = $\sqrt{-1}$ (Imaginary Number)
6. 1 = Unity (Unitary Number)
7. 0 = Zero (Nothingness Number)

The Master Equations of Giza

1. The Gamma Function

$$\Gamma(\alpha) = \int_0^\infty \chi^{\alpha-1} \cdot \epsilon^{-\chi} \, d\chi$$

2. The Golden Gamma Equation

$$\Gamma(\phi) = \int_0^\infty \Omega^{[(\alpha \pm \pi i)^{-1}]} \epsilon^{-\Omega} \, d\phi$$

3. The Integral Maximal

$$\int_{MAX} = \sum_0^\infty + C$$

4. The Epsilon Equation

$$\epsilon^{i\pi} + 1 = 0$$

5. The Differential Maximal

$$\Delta_{MAX} = \frac{\infty}{0}$$

(note: The Gamma Function and the
Epsilon Equation were discovered by
Leonhard Euler. Swiss 1707-83.)

The Golden Gamma Equation contains
all seven of the Royal Numbers plus
(∞) infinity. It was discovered by
Rocky McCollum in February 1977.

7. The Golden Spiral and the Master Equations of Giza,
according to McCollum.

three pyramids, he contends that the "0 site" also has to be within the limits of the Golden Spiral to totally conform to the obliquely depicted Epsilon equation.

It is where this 0 is symbolized on the plains of Giza that McCollum predicts an existence of an underground chamber carved in bedrock, fitted with a stone lid, and covered with sand. He goes on to predict that this chamber is thirty to forty feet below the surface, pyramidal in shape, and truncated at the top. The stone lid is of a solid piece, square and wedge-shaped. The lid will measure four cubits on its side (a function of Cheops' pyramid) and two cubits thick (a function of Chephren's pyramid).

The volume of the coverstone will be 161.4 cubic feet, composed of either hard limestone or granite, and weighing between 12 and 15 tons. The chamber will be 20 meters deep, having a square base of 32 meters per side. There will be a solid pyramid in the center of the chamber, 20 cubits tall and 32 cubits on each side. He predicts the solid pyramid as being truncated, forming a platform 2 cubits square. The surface of this platform would be a mirror of gold.

Among the marvelous objects that will be found inside the chamber, besides the "missing capstone," McCollum postulates the existence of clay tablets stored around the perimeter of the chamber. These tablets will turn out to be records of the history of the Atlanteans and that of the children of Mu, from the land of Lemuria. There will also be records of the earliest Egyptian history from the Fourth Dynasty back in time.

From the floor of the chamber there will be thirteen steps leading to the capstone, each step containing important engravings conveying useful information to mankind. The very bottom step, or base, called the Philosopher's Stone, will reveal many equations and functions in physics and metaphysics, including the integral and differential maximal equations and the Epsilon equation, along with a method of computing the number of atomic elements.

On the west side of the capstone there will be a

doorway leading to an inner chamber, housing the rarest objects of art, gems, jewelry, and prize tablets.

This remarkable mathematical "expedition" to theoretically locate the missing capstone and the hidden chamber has so convinced Rocky McCollum that his assumption is correct, that he formed the Pyramid of Aquarius to acquire the funds necessary to travel to Egypt and excavate at the site located by his calculations.

Kenneth Lloyd Larson, writing in both of his privately printed books—*Great Pyramid Designs, UFOs and Planet Earth* and *The Topstone*—shows how the Great Pyramid, the Nile Delta, Bethlehem, and Mount Sinai serve as a mathematical, historical, and engineering complex on the earth's surface. This basic design has been enlarged by him so that it conforms to another mathematical design over western America, with the date representing certain biblical records and events.

The master plan of the Giza complex's aerial site was superimposed by Larson onto a map of the western portion of the United States containing Salt Lake City. He sees so much similarity in the topography between Cairo and Salt Lake City that he questions the many locations of the topstone proposed by theorists. He doubts that the topstone is located within Egypt in the ground near the Great Pyramid site.

According to Larson's theory, the missing topstone is actually located on the site representing Levelland on the U.S.A. map!

This theory has its merits, and may quite possibly be true in light of the fact that, according to the Church of Jesus Christ of Latter-day Saints (the Mormons), there is said to be a record of ancient civilizations on the American continent prior to the year A.D. 421. It is believed by the Mormons that these early cultures were related to the Jewish people of Jerusalem. In respect to this possibility, it seems quite plausible that these early cultures brought along with them the topstone in question during their migration to the American continent. Once settled, these ancient peoples may have hidden the topstone in the geographical area suggested by Larson.

Larson's theory involving the Mormon belief of migrated people inhabiting Utah receives firm support from the readings of Edgar Cayce, a celebrated seer with most impressive records of psychic perception. In one reading he confirms that either Utah or Nevada were populated by "the first peoples," although his time reference may be too far removed from the Mormons' calculation of A.D. 421.

> . . . in the land now known as Utah or Nevada, when the first peoples were separated into groups as families . . . The entity developed much and gave much to the people who were to succeed in that land, and in the ruins as are found in the mounds and caves in the northwestern portion of New Mexico may be seen some of the drawings the entity then made, some ten million years ago. [Reading 2665-2, July 17, 1925].

As is currently suspected, the land areas of the world have undergone several changes along with the bodies of water, and were quite different from the present. In another reading, Edgar Cayce states, ". . . for the change has come often, since this age of man's earthly indwelling. Many lands have disappeared, many have appeared and disappeared again and again during these periods. At that time, only the lands now known as the Sahara . . . and the plane of [present] Utah, Arizona, Mexico in the northwestern hemisphere [also appeared]." (Reading 5748-1, May 28, 1925).

The correlation of the Sahara region to the western portion of the United States as stated by Edgar Cayce fits quite well with the Mormon doctrines of the early migration of people from Africa to the Northwestern Hemisphere. This transatlantic migration may have indeed been possible, because Cayce said that the waters in ancient times entered the Atlantic Ocean from the Nile region rather than flowing northward.

The drawings in Larson's books make clear how and why the planet earth was measured, weighed, and designed by the Creator, just as represented in the Bible (Isaiah 40:12; 40:22; 19:19; Job 38:4–7; Psalms 95:5; Genesis 1:1). Larson further believes that the Great Pyramid represents a scale model, or "blueprint," of the planet earth, set forth in mathematical and chronological terms and patterns.

One of the authors who offers a metaphysical explanation for the incompleteness of the pyramid is Manly P. Hall, who writes in *The Secret Teachings of All Ages:*

> The size of the capstone of the Great Pyramid cannot be accurately determined, for, while most investigators have assumed that it was once in place, no vestige of it now remains. There is a curious tendency among the builders of great religious edifices to leave their creations unfinished, thereby signifying that God alone is complete. The capstone—if it existed—was itself a miniature pyramid, the apex of which again would be capped by a smaller block of similar shape, and so on ad infinitum. The capstone therefore is the epitome of the entire structure. Thus, the Pyramid may be likened to the universe, and the capstone to man. Following the chain of analogy, the mind is the capstone of man, the spirit the capstone of the mind, and God—the epitome of the whole—the capstone of the spirit. As a rough and unfinished block, man is taken from the quarry and by the secret culture of the Mysteries gradually transformed into a trued and perfect pyramidal capstone. The temple is complete only when the initiate himself becomes the living apex through which the divine power is focused into the diverging structure below.

Hall further sheds light on the mystical use of the pyramid. According to his book, the illumined of antiquity passed through the mystic chambers and passageways of the Great Pyramid. It was the house of the "second birth" or the "womb of the mysteries." Men entered its portals and exited as gods.

An unknown being called "the Illustrious One" or "the Initiator," wearing gold and blue vestments, carrying in his hand the sevenfold key to eternity, is said to reside somewhere in the recesses of the Pyramid. This unknown being is also known as "the Holy One," "Master of Masters," and "the lion-faced hierophant" who never left this house of wisdom. No man ever saw him except those who have passed through the gates of preparation and purification to be born again.

The Mysteries were unfolded to the neophyte by this master of the secret house. The power of the guardian spirit was revealed to the new initiate. The process of separating divine spirit from material body was revealed, along with the divine name. The most high secret and unutterable designation of the Supreme Deity is the knowledge through which man and God are made one. With the receiving of this name, the initiate became spiritually enlightened.

With the world generally knowledgeable of the story of the crucifixion and resurrection of Jesus Christ, Manly P. Hall's description in *The Secret Teachings of All Ages* of the ritual enacted in the Great Pyramid takes on fresh significance:

> In the King's chamber was enacted the drama of "the second death." Here the candidate, after being crucified upon the cross of the solstices and the equinoxes, was buried in the great coffer. . . .
> The candidate was laid in the great stone coffin, and for three days his spirit—freed from its mortal coil—wandered at the gateways of eternity. . . . Realizing that his body was a house which he could slip out of and return to without death, he achieved actual immortality. At the end of three days he returned to himself again, and having thus personally . . . experienced the great mystery, he was indeed an initiate— one who beheld and one to whom religion had fulfilled her duty bringing him to the light of God.
> The King's Chamber was . . . a doorway between the material world and the transcendental spheres of Nature. . . . Thus in one sense the Great Pyramid may be likened to a gate through which the ancient priests permitted a few to pass toward the attainment of individual completion.

8. Artistic representation of the ritual in the Great Pyramid

43

Regardless of what other theorists claim as to the reason for the missing capstone and its location, along with other externally hidden, secret chambers, the time will once again come when the secret wisdom of all ages shall be the dominating religious and philosophical force of the world. Rediscovery of the secret room in the Pyramid, as prophesied, is close at hand.

Our modern world may uncover many secrets that the ancient world knew, but one—that is the secret that confers life and truth. As the sands of time have buried civilization after civilization, the pyramid as truth remains the visible covenant between Eternal Wisdom and the world.

The reason these monuments have remained in clear vision of mankind in the face of the near disappearance of others, is to be a constant reminder to people of their subservience to God. They cause us to search for higher truths, and aid us in rising above our limited and materialistic vision, to more spiritual and metaphysical levels. The teachers of the secret doctrine fervently believe that the Pyramid is the gateway to the eternal.

Once man has relearned the secret of entry into the Pyramid, he will again meet the Masters of the Mysteries, who are silently awaiting him. They shall help remove the shroud of dogma and reclothe him in the vestments of truth. The time is coming when the glorious chants of the illumined will resound throughout the ancient passageways and chambers of the Pyramid, as they did in the many pyramid civilizations that once flourished throughout the world.

⟨3⟩

DIFFERENT TIMES, DIFFERENT PLACES

It seems incredible that the Egyptians created a metropolis with such grandiose architecture as the pyramid shape, in a desert area seemingly inhospitable to life and incapable of affording the proper environment for a developing civilization. This remarkable achievement against all apparent and logical odds has been used by Egyptologist Kurt Mendelsohn to confirm his theory that pyramid projects were developed as a sort of "civil service" effort to stop unemployment and increase prosperity in Egypt.

Mendelsohn postulates that the administrations of ancient Egypt, believing in the necessity to create a more "state oriented" populace, forced the religious significance and ritual traditions embodied in pyramid philosophies to take the "back seat" to their socioeconomic plans.

This modern view of an ancient and highly advanced civilization is at best a theory applicable to much later pyramids paralleling the decline of Egypt.

A socioeconomic theory of history and the movements and works of man hardly holds up even in modern times, let alone to a civilization inspired by a religion and philosophy we are just beginning to penetrate and understand.

One must be careful in accepting the socioeconomic theory for pyramid construction, because it can only be selectively applied, and does not account for the building of the original pyramid in Egypt; nor can this theory be applied to other pyramid-building civilizations that in the past had enveloped the entire world.

According to archaeologists, the pyramid civilizations of Mexico and South America, like the Egyptians, began as nomadic tribes from a cultural start of zero. Within their own time period, their magnificently vast and complex stone cities towered above their environment. In the confines of their own land, all pyramid civilizations had developed delicately wrought artifacts, hieroglyphic writing, all the branches of the sciences, philosophies, and theologies, and a very precise calendar regulating their lives.

From a distant past, unknown influences similar to those of the Egyptians mysteriously produced pyramid cultures—not at the best environmentally suited geographical locations, but rather at extremes such as deserts, dense jungles, and high altitudes. This may be contingent upon the fact that these major pyramid complexes were all built within a 30-degree zone above and below the equator in a strip circumscribing the globe.

With due respect to the many theories attempting to explain the existence of pyramid civilizations in this zone, such as migration and continental drift, one important point has to be considered—that is, the nearly identical geometric pyramid form found throughout the civilizations. This means that the pyramid as a shape is unique to the world, rather than to a specific civilization, and that it is a tradition dating to the beginning of an event in time.

The pyramid civilization of South America seems to have emerged virtually full-blown when two new cultures appeared almost simultaneously at approximately A.D. 200, following a Dark Age period. These two civilizations—the Moche on the northern coast of Peru, and the Tiahuanaco, or Wari-Tiahuanaco, in the southern highlands—were descendants of the Chavin civilization, which

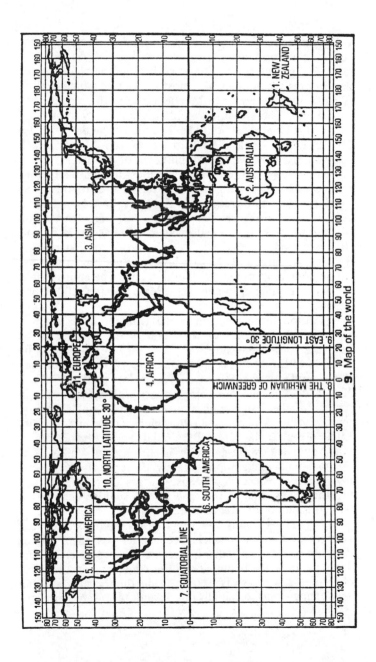

9. Map of the world

1. NEW ZEALAND
2. AUSTRALIA
3. ASIA
4. AFRICA
5. NORTH AMERICA
6. SOUTH AMERICA
7. EQUATORIAL LINE
8. THE MERIDIAN OF GREENWICH
9. EAST LONGITUDE 30°
10. NORTH LATITUDE 30°
11. EUROPE

ostensibly spread throughout Peru and prospered for several thousand years.

The people of the Moche civilization erected massive and impressive temples, the most famous of which are the gigantic twin pyramids at Moche, close to the modern city of Trujillo. These twin pyramids are popularly known today as La Huaca del Sol (The Temple of the Sun) and La Huaca de la Luna (The Temple of the Moon). Each consists of a massive terrace platform of adobe.

The Temple of the Sun is the most immense structure on the coast of Peru, and has a terraced pyramid on its platform. The platform rises in 5 terraces to a height of 60 feet; its base measures 450 feet by 750 feet. On the top of the fifth terrace is a causeway nearly 20 feet wide and 300 feet long, leading to the north end of the pyramid. A 340-foot-square and 75-foot-high stepped pyramid surmounts the platform at the southern end. The entire Huaca del Sol is estimated to contain at least 130,000,000 adobe bricks.

Although the platform of the Temple of the Moon is much smaller at the base than that of the Temple of the Sun (the former measures only 195 feet by 260 feet), the Temple of the Moon is approximately 10 feet higher than the Temple of the Sun. On top of the platform of La Huaca de la Luna are some rooms with fresco walls in typical Moche design, with some colors still remaining.

Another Moche pyramid, which stands just south of Lima, Peru, is the Great Pyramidal Temple of Pachacamac, overshadowing the city in the Lurin Valley. The Pachacamac covers approximately 12 acres of ground and rises nearly 75 feet. So famous was this shrine in Inca and pre-Inca days, that at the time of the Spanish conquest it was considered the Mecca of Peru.

Mystery shrouds the ruins of Tiahuanaco, the last vestiges of a culture which, even at its nascence, rivaled the culture of the Moche. There are some who claim that Tiahuanaco is the birthplace of the Americas, and possibly even of the world's civilization. One theory suggests that Tiahuanaco was originally an island that sank into the

Pacific Ocean and was then uplifted with the Andes Mountain range to its present height. Another hypothesis holds that Tiahuanaco was the seat of a powerful and megalithic empire ruling the entire world.

Tiahuanaco, situated at an altitude of about 2.5 miles, is approximately one dozen miles southeast of Lake Titicaca, the world's highest navigable lake. This place, with its extremely thin atmosphere, cold climate, and nearly treeless surroundings, hardly seems a likely location for the birthplace of a civilization. Yet despite the uninviting surroundings (most people have trouble breathing in this rarefied atmosphere)—or perhaps because of them— many mystics the world over consider Tiahuanaco to be a truly holy site.

The masonry of Tiahuanaco is the best and most monumental in the Andean region. There are four large buildings and a number of smaller ones on the site, altogether occupying approximately 1,475 feet by 3,275 feet —or .17 square mile. The largest here, called Acapana, is a 50-foot-high terraced pyramid that was originally faced with stone. The irregular ground plan of the Acapana measures approximately 690 square feet.

The most publicized structure at Tiahuanaco is the world-famous Gateway of the Sun. This great monolithic gateway, measuring 10 feet high and 12.5 feet wide, was sculpted from a single enormous block of andesite. It is estimated to be between 10 and 15 tons in weight. This is unquestionably one of the archaeological wonders of the Americas.

Another site having mysterious origins is Nazca, situated on the southern coast of Peru. Once a densely occupied area, this site contains a unique spot called La Estaqueria (The Place of Stakes), which is best described as a wooden Stonehenge.

The Moche and Tiahuanaco civilizations are both thought to have reached the height of their magnificence by approximately A.D. 600 and then, like the Chavin civilization before them, seemed to have come to an abrupt halt. There followed another long, culturally stagnant period in Peru, then once again a new culture burst forth, almost full-blown, as if it had been developed elsewhere and been transported in its maturity to Peru. This was the empire of the Inca.

In a period of a little over 300 years, from circa A.D. 1200 to 1534, thirteen Incan emperors extended the domination of their civilization over an estimated 350,000 square miles. This empire stretched nearly 3,000 miles—from what is known today as central Chile, to northern Ecuador. The Incas did not build pyramids. Rather, they apparently rebuilt the existing pyramids in every important Inca town, just as they enlarged the great ceremonial centers in the major cities to accommodate the religious requirements of the Inca empire.

Road engineering was another feat perfected by the Incas. Within the Cuzco area is an example of the Inca system of bridging culverts with a form of the corbeled arch on which the road was actually placed. This corbeling, incidentally, is also found as the primary architectural feature of the walls of the Grand Gallery within the Great Pyramid of Giza.

Another example of Inca road engineering is a coastal road originally 2,525 miles long, stretching between Tumbes, Peru, and Santiago, Chile. Twenty-four feet wide, this road is bordered by adobe walls to keep out sand drifts.

When an Incan Emperor died, elaborate funeral ceremonies were observed throughout the empire. Like the bodies of the Egyptian Pharaohs, the Emperor's body was kept in the palace by an unknown process of mummification. His innards were removed and preserved in special containers; his body was wrapped in the finest of textiles. The mummy was thereafter waited upon as during life. Unlike the Egyptian custom, instead of entombing from sight and virtually leaving the mummy alone, each successive Incan empire catered to and paid homage to the mummies of the previous Emperors.

The Incan commoner was buried much like the Egyptian commoner, in a beehive-shaped tomb above the ground. The body, wrapped in textiles or skins, was placed seated inside with knees to chin. These tombs were made of rude stonemasonry, clay, and mud, and the bodies dried without decomposition.

It is generally assumed that with the Spanish conquest of the Incan empire, any records of pre-Incan civilizations were destroyed. All extant records of the Incan empire, along with the fables and tradition of its genesis, are those compiled by Spanish historians at the time of the conquest. If there were ever any written histories of the Moche, Tiahuanacan, Chavin, and other pre-Incan civilizations, these are now considered lost forever. All that remains are their great pyramids—tantalizing relics of great and glorious civilizations inexplicably cut down in their prime.

As far as can be ascertained, the evolution of the great and ancient Peruvian civilizations was paralleled by the growth of amazingly similar civilizations in the part of Central America known today as Mexico. Although comparatively little is known about the pyramid civilizations in the Western Hemisphere as opposed to those of the Egyptians, two facts are indisputable: All cultures produced extraordinarily massive and complex pyramidal structures, and apparently all the cultures relied heavily on astronomical calculations, not only to regulate their lives, but also to plan and erect all their architectural edifices. At first glance this is not very surprising; but then one realizes that the beliefs of archaeologists and other experts concur in that these cultures were totally insular; it is contended that they had not even the slightest knowledge of each other. This contention is laughable in the face of the existing problems that archaeologists of today have in acquiring knowledge of past civilizations based on "hints" of evidence. Unfortunately, because of this, there are many ancient cultures and civilizations that are obscured in nonexistence because "evidence" has not yet rediscovered them.

Existing evidence places prehistoric Egypt to at least 5000 B.C.; pre-Peruvian history is dated back as far as 9000 B.C.; while Meso- or Middle-American civilizations cannot be traced much farther back than about 2000 B.C. Known as the civilization of the Mayas, the Meso-American culture has challenged the imagination of explorer and scholar alike, due to its elaborate structure and great complexity. Mystics theorize that the Mayans originated from the lost continents of Atlantis and Mu. Less daringly, historians and archaeologists consider the Americas to be the Mayan place of origin and credit these people with carrying to a higher degree a civilization shared by their neighbors.

It is pretty much accepted that the earliest antecedents of the Mayan civilizations are the Olmecs, a people who lived and flourished throughout what is known today as southern Veracruz and Tabasco. Excavations at these and other sites have produced huge stone heads, as well as calendric formulae inscribed on stone stelae.

The art of the Olmecs is notable for the portrayal of beings whose faces are either swollen and infantile or else grotesque visages of tigerlike monsters. This extremely dramatic sculpting style is so distinguishably unique that their carvings cannot be confused with those of other civilizations.

A talented and mysterious people, the Olmecs were known—according to mythology—as the ones who lived in the direction of the rising sun. A symbol appearing profusely throughout glyphic documentation indicates that their wealth consisted of rubber, among other items. This glyph being deciphered as representing the rubber tree has been coined by archaeologists to designate the "Olmecs." The name "Olmec" is actually derived from the word *olli,* which means "rubber."

A dominant figurine of the Olmecs depicts an old man in a sitting position with his head bowed. Supported on his head and shoulders is a bowl, perhaps for burning incense. This god was to be worshiped by successive Middle American civilizations. The Aztecs called him Huehueteotl, "the old god," or Xiuhtecuhtli, "lord of fire." Since Xiuhtecuhtli's worshippers dwelled in a volcanic region, this appellation was peculiarly appropriate. It is also suggested that those who called him Huehueteotl identified him with the antiquity of the mountains in which they lived.

At this point, it is interesting to note a story about the Creator god worshipped at Tiahuanaco, Peru, called Viracocha—who in many respects resembles the Mexican god Quetzalcoatl. Mytho-history states that after traveling throughout the country instructing his people, Viracocha set off across the Pacific, from the shores of Ecuador, walking on the waves!

As the Olmec cultural history is painstakingly reconstructed, their achievements and mannerisms indicate that they had a propensity for body awareness—plucking facial hair, flattening their head, inlaying teeth with jade, and body tattooing; and also for the science of engineering, erecting temple cities centered around the stepped pyramid. There is even the indication that the Olmecs refurbished their buildings many times by basically putting another one directly over the existing one.

The beginning of the disappearance of the Olmec civilization is thought to be marked by the eruption of the volcano Xitli. It appears that after this event, development ceased; the civilization no longer flourished, and in time it disappeared.

The Olmec civilization seems to have been paralleled by that of the Zapotecs, in the highlands of Oxaca, southwest of Olmec country. Their art styles and writing seemingly differ from that of the Olmecs—the Zapotecs' calendric calculations were set forth in distinctive writing and their system fixed dates in terms of fifty-two-year cycles. They too were talented and mysterious people, also having the propensity toward the engineering sciences. The Zapotecs, along with perpetuating the refurbishing and enlarging of buildings, continued the construction of temple cities and pyramids; and they were as advanced in city planning, writing, and sculpture as their contemporaries and predecessors.

Many cultures were responsible for the birth of the

Aztec civilization. Along with the Mayans, the Olmecs, and the Zapotecs, other principal ones were the Mixtecs, the Huastecs, the Totonacs, the Toltecs, and the Chichimecs.

The Mixtecs are known for their story-telling ability. They spoke of the Olmecs, of "giants," and about the pyramid of the plumed serpent, which they considered the greatest in all the Americas. Their greatest contribution to the knowledge of preconquest history are painted picture books illuminating their genealogy and history in manuscript form. The best-known Mixtec painted picture book is referred to as the Codex Nuttall. This Mixtec manuscript is a conceptual, rather than perceptual, mode of visual expression. Concepts and ideas rather than the natural world are given visual form.

The Mixtecs used a hieratic scheme in presenting images. Size differences of figures do not refer to a giant per se, but signify the relative status of the figures. Personages are identified by name, rank, and function, not by physical features.

According to Mexican scholar Alfonso Caso, Mixtec writing employs three categories of images, signs, or symbols, identified as iconographic, ideographic, and phonetic. Iconographics depict recognizable images of people, places, things, and situations, even though they are more symbolically represented. Ideographics—being very closely linked to iconographics—impel the reader to sense the meaning derived from the thought or idea that the symbols are conveying. Pictographic phonetics is the least understood category of writing, referring to sounds or words in the Mixtec language.

Codices scholars are fairly content in believing that the Codex Nuttall has been accurately decoded and translated. Apparently considerable information about each ruler has been scribed into painted picture-book form.

One important convention found within all existing Mixtec manuscripts is the use of a dating system structured after the Meso-American calendar. The Mixtec calendar had a similar structure, perhaps a more local version of

10. Example of Mixtec writing found in the Codex Nuttal

the Meso-American system of time notation. Its "year" consists of two concomitant cycles—260 days within 365 days—along with a "century" of 52 years.

The Mixtec civilization, reputed to have lasted over thousands of years, was one of the greater cultural influences for the Aztecs.

Another civilization known as the Toltecs—perhaps more majestic—had emerged to influence the Aztecs, probably to a far greater degree than the Mixtecs. The Toltecs, apparently having a better management of agriculture, and probably producing constant surpluses, had become an independent cultural civilization by approximately 600 B.C. They were situated roughly thirty-two miles northeast of Mexico City, at a place called Teotihuacan. It was this "place of the gods" of the Toltecs whose imposing cluster of grouped buildings surpassed in magnitude all other cities in Meso-America.

The remains of Teotihuacan cover an area of over eight square miles. The Toltec architects planned and constructed their Teotihuacan metropolis in several successive precincts, extending southward from the Pyramid of the Moon. This was not a true pyramid, but was truncated at the top to accommodate an altar.

The platform supporting the pyramid had skillfully designed terraces. From a rectangular courtyard, a broad staircase leads up the south side of the platform. Flanking the Plaza of the Moon were additional buildings, and several hundred feet to the west and east, two smaller precincts added to the symmetry of the plan. Two impressive rows of buildings of great size lead south from the Moon Plaza.

The Pyramid of the Sun dwarfs all the other buildings in Teotihuacan, and like the Pyramid of the Moon, is truncated at the top. Nearly seven hundred feet square at the base, it rises in four terraces to over two hundred feet. Its builders terraced the base to create the illusion of gigantic mass. The Pyramid of the Sun is thought to be primarily built of adobe bricks and faced in stone with a covering of plaster. Its cunningly calculated planes between terraces are so designed that an observer standing at the base has the illusion of infinite height and space.

Across a river that ends in the south lies a magnificent platform whose walls are faced with carved blocks and whose crowning pyramid temple has disappeared. It is contended that it was built in honor of the rain god, Talaloc, even though it is called the Temple of Quetzalcoatl.

The Toltec city of Teotihuacan obviously was neither an ordinary city nor simply a religious center for temples and houses. It apparently was consciously designed to convey the illusion of massiveness and eminence. The city was constructed with buildings grouped along a north–south axis, laterally interrupted by precincts of edifices oriented along the east–west axis. From whatever angle Teotihuacan was approached, the eye was tastefully led toward a point of interest, guided by the arrangement of the plane and mass. The diminishing effect of distance was thus avoided. Within the precinct, the surrounding walls insulated the observer from the rest of the city, and consequently emphasized the enormity of each precinct temple. Not even the pyramid complexes of Egypt were so carefully and consciously planned to lift the individual's soul by the sheer powers awakened by the place.

One cannot escape the insistent association of ideas

that the greater the temple, the more powerful the god for whom it was built.

Some time after the city of Teotihuacan was built, a mysterious renovation took place. Every building was rebuilt. Façades were covered up and ruins were filled in to create platforms for new pyramids. Not even the gigantic hulks of the Pyramid of the Sun and the Pyramid of the Moon escaped the addition of new stairs and façades.

Strangely, the Temple of Quetzalcoatl underwent the most extreme alteration. Although the reconstruction extended to every building in the entire center, it is not thought that the renovation was the result of a new conquering culture. Instead, the new architecture has all the earmarks, according to the experts, of a religious reformation that destroyed or improved the symbolism of one cult to instill a new.

This majestic city was rebuilt two more times. Among other reasons, the renovation probably fulfilled a traditional requirement of rebuilding and refurbishing at the beginning, or ending, of a fifty-two-year cycle. The third reconstruction was done hastily and with maximum use of the original construction. This final rebuilding introduced new gods to be honored and also heralded the end of the use of Teotihuacan as the sacred capital.

By now, the Toltecs were migratory and developed two other cultural areas—Tula and Xochicalco—at approximately the same time. Tula was once regarded as pure mythology, but is now confirmed by archaeology. Found there is a step pyramid, with the remains of a temple at its summit, containing the symbol of Quetzalcoatl. A debatable question exists about Tula's being the legendary Tollan, which mythology claims was as large and powerful as Teotihuacan.

Xochicalco, or "Place of Flowers," is famous for its Pyramid to the Plumed Serpent, and is thought to have been a ceremonial, even administrative, city for the people who lived in the region.

These two succeeding Toltec cultures were highly

57

cosmopolitan and, although short-lived, established the structure of the tribute empire that the Aztecs later adopted.

The Toltecs were known as master builders. They built their massive pyramids, houses, and palaces of stone and mortar and used a form of the steam bath. They counted their years using 260 days and had a "century" of 52 years. Their supreme god was Quetzalcoatl, a mysterious figure represented by a serpent.

It is assumed that Quetzalcoatl had once lived, because accounts of his autonomous creative force were recorded by the Toltecs and the Mixtecs. In fact, it is assumed he was ruler of the Toltecs for twenty years. Quetzalcoatl was also considered a priest and was conceived years after his father's death by his mother becoming pregnant after she swallowed a piece of jade. The story of Quetzalcoatl ends by his setting sail into the open sea with the prophecy that he would again return on the recurrence of his birth date.

The history and remains of the Toltecs are as tenuous as their sociology and religion. One history, written by Ixtlilxochitl, begins with the creation of the world and the four suns, or eras, through which life has survived.

The first era, the Water Sun, began when the supreme god, Tloque Nahuaque, created the world. Then, after 1,716 years, or 33 52-year cycles, it was destroyed by lightning and floods.

The second era, the Sun of the Earth, saw the world populated by giants called Quinametzin, who almost disappeared when earthquakes obliterated the earth.

The Wind Sun came third, and the Olmecs, human tribes, lived on earth. The Olmecs destroyed the surviving giants, founded Cholula, and migrated as far as Tabasco. A spectacular individual called Quetzalcoatl by some, Huemac by others, appeared in this era, bringing ethics and civilization. When the populace did not appear to benefit from his teachings, Quetzalcoatl returned to the east whence he had come, prophesying, as he went, the destruction of the world by great winds and the conversion of humankind into monkeys. All of this, according to the narrative, came to pass.

The fourth stage, the present one, is called the Sun of Fire, and will end in a general conflagration. Such is the story of the Toltecs as set forth by Ixtlilxochitl.

Because the Toltecs, like the peoples of other civilizations, build upon structures and in turn had their own structures built over by successive cultures, it is difficult to ascertain which pyramids and other edifices belong to which period. It is generally assumed that most of the Mexican pyramids were built by the Teotihuacan-Toltec or possibly by the people of an earlier civilization.

The last and greatest of the Mayan civilizations was that of the Aztecs, which archaeologists believe had its probable source at Cholula, in the state of Puebla, where exists the largest structure in the world in terms of cubic content. They are credited with performing the stupendous task of mammoth constructions.

The Aztec civilization was brought to its greatest height by the Tenochcas, the Mexico City Aztecs, around A.D. 1400. Yet, according to authorities, the Tenochcas did not originate the civilization, nor contribute much to it beyond the introduction of a sacrifice cult.

Like the people of all the great ancient civilizations, the Aztecs had a highly sophisticated knowledge of astronomy. The discovery of the Great Calendar Stone, assumed built by Axayacatl, an Aztec chief, in A.D. 1479, convinced archaeologists that the Aztec knowledge of calendric science was even more refined than that of other civilizations.

Based on an extremely involved mathematical and astronomical system, the Calendar Stone was incomprehensible until discovery of calendric texts led to an understanding of the meaning of the stone and aided in the deciphering of the Aztec hieroglyphics. The Great Calendar Stone, weighing over twenty tons and being thirteen feet in diameter, was hewn from one monolithic chunk of stone. In the center of the face of the stone is the sun god,

Tonatiuh, flanked by four ornamental frames listing the four previous ages of the world. Summed, these represent the date of our present era.

The central element is encircled by the names of the twenty days of the Aztec month. These, in turn, are ringed with a band of glyphs denoting jade or turquoise, sym-

11. The Great Calendar Stone

bolizing the heavens. This band is surrounded by the signs of the stars penetrated by the sun's rays in an emblematic design. Two immense fire serpents, symbolizing year and time, circle the exterior of the stone and meet face-to-face at the base.

The Great Calendar Stone should be an enormous aid to anthropologists and historians in the reconstruction of the chronological history of Meso-America. However, there are numerous opinions as to exactly how the dates on the stone should be correlated with Christian dates.

Several calculations have been designed in an attempt to reconcile the Aztec calendar with the Christian calendar, but each calculation involves an error of some 260 years in the expression of Aztec dating in Christian terms. This discrepancy has naturally led to many divergent interpretations of Meso-American chronology. The disagreement of chronology is as significant as the disagreement between Egyptologists concerning the chronology of dynasties, Pharaohs, and predynastic events.

The chronological dating of Western Hemisphere pyramid civilizations places their pyramid construction over two thousand years after the Pyramid Age of Egypt. This implies that the migratory theory attempting to explain the existence of pyramid civilizations in the Western Hemisphere is less credible. If this were the case, it is very strange that the migrating Egyptians should instruct the South and Meso-Americans in the construction of large pyramids, structures they had ostensibly given up over two thousand years previously!

It would seem more plausible to have pyramid civilizations developing years apart rather than hundreds of centuries distant, based on the theory of migrating Egyptians.

From the opposite viewpoint, if the chronology of Western Hemisphere civilizations is grossly inaccurate, the credibility of the migratory theory is thereby maintained. If the continental-drift theory were more credible than the others, why should it take over two thousand years for the same conceptual idea to develop if it came from a common source, unless, again, chronological dating is in error?

Regardless of which theories can be more acceptable, or how accurate chronological dating is for any civilization, it brings back the insistent possibility that the pyramid shape is unique to the world through the efforts of a highly advanced race perpetuating a tradition of a specific event in time, and more possibly prophesying future events. It also brings to mind again the fact that these various civilizations were not insular, because some element had to interconnect them with the basic concept of the pyramid shape.

Curiously, the peoples of the so-called prehistoric cultures were fire worshippers, while the peoples of pyramidal civilizations were all sun worshippers. Of course, it can be contended that there is a logical correlation between fire and the sun, but it does seem curious that they all should simultaneously and rather abruptly switch from fire worshipping to sun worshipping.

Throughout the mytho-history of each and every civilization, there are tales of "giants" and a race of "sons of the sun," both of whom instructed humankind in all kinds of arts and were responsible for great construction feats. After a certain time period they "disappeared," but with an assurance that they would again return.

The term "giants" may not refer to the physical size, but rather to the mental ability of this race of people, and the "sons of the sun" could have been called that because of the apparent direction from which they had approached —that is, from the east, or the place of the rising sun. This indicates such a strong correlation between these two races that they might in fact be one and the same, with the difference solely attributable to the way the different cultures referred to them.

Metaphysically speaking, there are two planes of humankind: older and more experientially advanced souls, and young, neophyte-type souls. A responsibility is thus assumed by the master plane to assist the neophyte plane in its growth and evolutionary development of passing through the initiate phase. The innate behavioral characteristics of the masters is that of *noblesse oblige*—meaning that their status places them in a position similar to that of the "guardian angel" maintaining the existence of life which, in turn, insures the perpetuity of themselves. In other words, if the masters cease in their obligation, life on earth will end, thereby ending their own existence.

Within this spiritual thought lies the supreme prophecy that the pyramid states. The triangle being the substance of the pyramid is also the key to man's triune existence. The configuration of neophyte at one corner, master at another, and the Creator at the third, clearly expresses all religious doctrinal foundations—that is, a neophyte attaining "priesthood" or mastery level then possesses the ability to be in communion with the Creator.

In addition, the neophyte who quite conceivably receives the divine gift of direct communion with the Creator will then automatically become a master. Man's triune existence not only applies to him spiritually, but physically as well; whereby a secondary triangle exists, placing brother and brother at two of the corners, and the Initiate at the third. As a brother, one is endowed with the sense of *noblesse oblige* and, once aware of it, becomes the Initiate, in turn assisting his brother. But the simple act of brotherly love can automatically elevate him to the rank of Initiate.

Thus, the Initiate position at the corner of the secondary triangle by definition assumes the Neophyte position on the primary triangle. The solidity of man's triune existence is represented by the geometric mass of the pyramid.

Neophyte, Master, and Creator form a strong interacting bond. Architecturally, this is also true of the pyramid; the form insures its integrity. No force can topple it because of the interacting bond between its stones; its destruction can only be brought about by total demolition.

In essence, the physicality of the pyramid represents the transcendent ability of man, and all the apparent enigmas decipherable from the measurements of the pyramid become the universality of nature. Thus, the pyramid introduced to various civilizations is indeed prophesying the event in each man's individual time of his transcendent ability to attain his own *noblesse oblige*.

The physicality of the pyramid is inherently defined by its solidity of construction. Architecturally, construction of the pyramid and its interacting bonds is symbolically significant for its metaphysical as well as its physical strength.

{4}

STARS AND STONES—
THE ARCHITECT'S
MASTERPIECE

Extant records shed only minuscule light on the lives, habits, and customs of the Pharaohs of the Old Kingdom; and virtually nothing is known about the method of construction of pyramids and the subsidiary buildings within each pyramid complex of that period.

Archaeologists have made educated guesses concerning the construction techniques employed by the master pyramid builders. Unfortunately, theories formulated from these educated guesses are accepted as fact now—even though there is no proof whatsoever that any of the massive structures built in the Old Kingdom, or before, were actually erected in the manner that the archaeologists claimed they were.

Egyptologists falsely reason that the Egyptians constructed pyramid complexes on the west bank of the Nile because they wanted to be as close as possible to the setting sun, because the setting of the sun symbolized death. However, if Egyptians were positioning pyramid complexes for purely symbolic significance, it makes just as much sense to have built them on the east bank—symbolizing birth—so that the Pharaoh would be closer to rebirth, and also to the birth or rebirth of the gods. It is more logical to conclude that the original pyramid was built on the west bank for practical purposes, and that the Egyptians simply assumed that the pyramids had to be built on the west bank.

The designers and builders of the Great Pyramid—the Pyramid of Cheops—were the world's best geologists. Because of their technical expertise, they determined that a huge area on the west bank consisted of a solid rock foundation with no faults. Had this not been true, the entire structure would have collapsed, possibly while under construction.

After choosing this construction site, the builders had to clear many acres of sand and stone from the surface covering the solid rock foundation, and current evidence suggests that the foundation itself had to be leveled and smoothed before construction began. The leveled area is so exact that the Great Pyramid is less than .5 inch out of level. Over the length of 756 feet (the length of one of the sides of the pyramid), a .5-inch deviation can be deemed negligible indeed. Considering that .5 inch equals approximately .04 foot, this is an error of only 0.04/756—or 0.00005 per cent. This infinitesimal deviation of accuracy rivals the inaccuracies existing in the most current construction techniques of our day.

Surveying was the foundation of knowledge necessary to begin the building of the Great Pyramid, or even to quarry the stone used in its construction. In order to align the Pyramid to the four cardinal points, the surveyors had to exactly locate one side, and then the remaining three sides would automatically be positioned correctly. Among the various tools and instruments unknown at the time, it appears that the compass heads the list. Yet, with the Egyptologists' distorted vision of the builders' using archaic-type implements such as the set square and plumb bob, not only is the pyramid aligned to within an accuracy of about 1.5 feet, but also the base can be considered a near perfect square.

The pyramid builders' knowledge of astronomy was

far beyond the limits of the science practiced by the civilization of that day, and it is still beyond the ability of our own modern astronomers.

Simultaneously with the preparation of the building sites, quarriers—working at Tura on the east bank of the Nile in the Muqattam hills—were quarrying the limestone blocks necessary for the Pyramid. Farther up the Nile near Aswan, other quarriers were acquiring the necessary granite blocks.

The method of quarrying these tremendous blocks of stone, which weighed between two and seventy tons, cannot be inferred from some simple tools discovered at the quarry site by archaeologists. "Experts" claim that the quarriers dug, chiseled, hacked, wedged, and pounded to split the huge blocks out of tiny tunnels dug deep into rockbeds—and then scraped and polished and finished these monoliths into nearly perfect cubes. Interestingly, none of the copper tools—alleged to have been tempered by highly skilled smiths to impart the strength required to shape stone—has ever been found. It is particularly difficult to accept that a race such as the Egyptians—who could barely contend with the flooding of the Nile, the growing of crops, and the raising of cattle—could take their copper implements, hardly strong enough to cut cardboard, and turn them into instruments durable enough to work stone. Even today we have difficulty maintaining a keen edge on our finest and most expensive cutlery, used for cutting nothing stronger than meat, produce, pulp, or fabric. And even the scientifically advanced alloys of extreme durability and tempered quality offer only limited longevity for such commercial use as oil-well drilling. These extremely costly cutters still require frequent sharpening and expensive maintenance.

Curiously, in the quarries there still exist blocks of stone that were cut but never trimmed or used. They have been identified as coming from a particular "hole" in the quarry wall. These blocks of stone seem to have been removed from their corresponding holes as if they were plugs.

12. Westerly view of the Great Pyramid's north face

With the use of nebulous rationalization, it is conceivable that the Egyptians had the possibility of making the two vertical cuts and the two horizontal cuts of the stone plug; but it is left to one's wildest imagination as to how the cut in the back was accomplished in order to remove the stone plug. The archaeologists and Egyptologists explain this question away rather simply, with the statement that it is not yet understood how the Egyptians actually worked the stone; however, they are certain that once this is explained, it will automatically answer the question of the technical ability for the blind cut.

The stones remaining in the quarry, along with the quarry walls, show signs of being cut with some implement such as a saw blade, and there are also many blind holes that appear to have been made by a drill bit. It is the contention of many engineers evaluating these markings and drilled holes that the masons had exceptional-quality cutting and drilling implements, and that these implements also had to have a tremendous force applied to them in order to work. They speculate that several tons of pressure had to be applied to the drill to cut a hole several inches in diameter and many inches deep. It seems incredible enough that engineering techniques were so advanced in those days that limestone was worked as easily as it appears to have been. But it is almost unfathomable that granite—being many times harder, and therefore even more difficult to work with than limestone—seemed to pose no problem to the masons.

The prevalent theory of the quarrying of various types of stone is the wedge theory, which claims that crawl spaces were tediously hand-chiseled by the masons until they could insert a wedge-shaped piece of wood. The wood was then soaked with water, causing expansion, and this expansion produced a split, shearing the stone from the wall of the quarry. As with all theories, this, too, has its shortcomings and does not adequately explain quarrying methods.

After one wades through all theories postulated by

contemporary experts, it is obvious that no one really knows how the stones were worked.

A theory has been brought to my attention that is as plausible as those already existing. It suggests that a laser beam type of device was employed in the quarries. This is a fascinating twist among the theories, as the laser beam could very easily produce surface marks mimicking those of a saw blade. It is not so farfetched that the laser beam and other electronic devices could have existed during that time, because there is a possibility that an advanced civilization did in fact once exist on earth.

Based on documented evidence such as Von Daniken's work, for example, "beings" depicted as having technical capabilities at least compatible with ours today were intermingling with various backward civilizations. This gives stronger credence to the theory that, although the pyramid shape is in Egypt, it is not necessarily of Egyptian origin.

There is an old Arabian story that was recounted throughout hundreds of generations. It tells of a marvelous piece of paper with sacred inscriptions on it. This was placed on a dressed block of heavy stone ready for transportation and struck by a hammer, causing the block to magically lose its weight so that only a few men were needed to transport it.

Nearly every superstition and fairy tale in the world had some definite truth at the very start by which it was brought into being; and there is every probability that there is here in this one, also, a moment of reality. This probability might be illustrated by considering the following:

Today's electronic technology is making a great effort to satisfy the need for microminiaturization of complicated electronic circuitry. We have such things as pocket-sized calculators and some even smaller components used by various space agencies. When viewed under a microscope, their circuits resemble road maps and even delicately executed yet undecipherable script. I believe that, due to inadequate translation of ancient texts, and the misunderstanding of words in the story passed throughout the generations, the "piece of paper with sacred inscriptions" in the above story was misinterpreted. It could have been an electronic circuit board, wafer thin, which was actually placed on the stone. And the "hammer" may not have been a hammer at all, but rather a battery or an energy cell which, when "touched" to a certain point on the electronic device (as opposed to being "hit"), activated the device, causing it to counteract the effects of gravity. With the piece of stone somewhat "floating" it would then be quite easy for a small group of workers to move it, and perhaps even elevate the stone as necessary.

There are other theories worthy of mention, but not as credible. One suggests that the blocks of stone were not really blocks of stone, nor were they cut from the quarry, but rather there was some formula for liquefying stone, piping the fluid stone to the construction site, and remolding it in place on the Pyramid. Another theory claims that the stones were dematerialized at the quarry and rematerialized in their proper positions on the Pyramid.

A very interesting explanation as to how the cuts were made at the quarry and how the stones were dressed and/or polished relates to the fact that there is a species of bird that builds its nest on the face of a sheer stone cliff wall by ingeniously burrowing into the rock. The bird accomplishes this by gathering several leaves from a certain plant and then rubs the leaves against the rock face. The juices secreted from the leaves soften the stone, so that the bird is able to pick it out. The bird continues the leaf-rubbing and bill-pecking process until the hole is as wide and deep as the bird requires.

When all is said and done, every theory proposed and every theory yet to be formulated is debatable when one realizes that, to this very day, no shred of evidence exists to indicate the kind of tools used for stone cutting and stone working. All these implements seem to have mysteriously disappeared—or perhaps they were purposely removed once they served their purpose. It seems very strange that not even one tool has ever been found, when so many pyramids had been built in Egypt, involving millions and millions of blocks of stone—which in turn would have required a huge quantity of tools to supply the workmen.

A very earnest explanation of the missing tools is correlated to the appearance of Egyptian "graffiti" on the surfaces of the most ancient structures. It seems that their civilizations, like modern ones, had vivacious tourists who wanted to record their pilgrimage to a site which may have been considered holy, by writing their name on the surface, receiving in turn a special blessing insuring spiritual perpetuity. It is quite possible that the voracious nature of the tourists impelled them to take some object as a souvenir of their pilgrimage. And it is also quite possible that what they actually picked up for souvenirs were the stonecutters' tools, rather than taking a piece of the structures themselves. This would have been a sacrilegious act, causing disfavor in the eyes of their god and possibly condemning their future spiritual unfoldment. Therefore, no tools are found in the area today.

On the other hand, it does not seem possible that the team of craftsmen, so diligently and accurately following through every phase of construction to completion of the pyramid, would leave their tools lying around at the end of the job. It is a definite contradiction that a work force which constructed a meticulously designed and detailed pyramid, would be so sloppy as to walk away upon completion of the work and leave all their tools scattered and abandoned. Thus, the tools had to be packed up and taken to the next "job," or to be stored some place for future use. This leaves one firmly convinced that the small number of simple copper tools found at some of the quarry sites cannot be those used as the "working" tools in the quarry, but instead are tools of another craft.

The illusive facts leading to the explanation of how the stones were quarried are numerous, and there is just as much speculation concerning the way in which these stones were transported to the actual construction site. In the

71

opinion of some people, the achievement of transporting the quarry blocks may not be as remarkable as the actual quarrying, but nonetheless, it posed equally challenging and perhaps even more numerous problems to be solved.

Moving a single stone block on a surface of sand is a troublesome task indeed. Obviously, sand will more firmly support an object with a large surface area than a small one. Therefore, a wheeled vehicle could not have been rolled directly on sand without encountering tremendous locomotive difficulties.

This problem is further compounded when one learns that the wheel was probably not yet introduced to the Egyptian civilization at the date the Pyramid was allegedly completed. It is possible that wheeled vehicles were used, because a picture in the Fifth Dynasty tomb of Kaemheset at Saqqara depicts a wheeled scaling ladder. But for some mysterious reason, there is no further evidence to support the wheeled-vehicle theory; no other picture in succeeding dynasties has been found depicting use of the wheel. The concept of the wheel seems to have been literally forgotten.

It is not until the Eighteenth Dynasty that the first reference is made to transporting huge, heavy, and bulky material. But they are using a sledge, not a wheeled vehicle! Paintings on tomb walls from the Eighteenth Dynasty period illustrate men transporting statues and heavy bricks by pulling sledges with ropes along a wood-paved way. It is believed that water or oil was poured under the sledge to reduce friction.

Based on the find of these and similar pictures, Egyptologists were relieved to be able to palatably infer how the blocks of stones used in the Great Pyramid construction were transported. But they so obviously ignore that picture of a wheeled scaling ladder that you have to doubt their credibility. It is inconceivable to accept the sledge theory of transportation as applied to the construction of the Great Pyramid when it is definitely apparent that the wheel was in existence in the Fifth Dynasty! In addition, the mathematical properties of Pi are very dominant in

13. An illustration of the process of transport of sculptures

the Pyramid form, and Pi can only be computed from a circle. This causes one to accept the earlier existence of the wheel. The supposedly great minds of the men involved in the purpose, design, engineering, and construction of the Great Pyramid should have found it a simple task to develop the wheel based on the properties of a circle.

Something dramatic had to have happened to cause the wheel to plunge back into obscurity. This may very well further support the theory that an advanced civilization—temporarily inhabiting the land of Egypt for some as yet unknown purpose—was responsible for the construction techniques and science necessary to create the Pyramid. Having had to make use of the local people for construction, they were forced to expose these people to extremely advanced technology.

A serious philosophical and moral responsibility is placed upon any technically advanced civilization that bears unusual but necessary influence on the normal rate of evolution of a backward civilization. It was probably this concern that caused the advanced civilization not to leave behind any physical tool or device that would grossly interfere with the predestined evolutionary rate of the host civilization. The last vestiges of the Egyptian people as being influenced by an advanced civilization finally fades out like a swan song with the documentation of the wheel in a Fifth Dynasty period picture.

However the case may be, the sledge theory is more popularly accepted, even though this theory raises more questions than it was meant to settle. For one thing, the sandy desert surface had to be leveled and paved over with timber in order to create a smooth surface on which the sledges could be dragged.

It is documented that timber in the area was very scarce. All that was available were palm trees; and the Egyptians, to whom these date-producing trees were essential for food, would not have been likely to cut them down for paving roads.

On the other hand, the lumber for the roadways could have been imported; however, there is no record that tree importation took place until over a thousand years later. If lumber was imported, what kind was it, and from where was it imported?

To compound matters, the timbers used in paving the roadways and for the construction of the sledges would have had to be replaced repeatedly, because they would have splintered from the dynamic pressure and friction of such enormous weight constantly being applied between the two surfaces. Such a replacement procedure would have been exorbitantly time-consuming and costly.

However difficult it was for the shippers to manage the transport of the stone blocks on land, it would seem that they must have faced even greater problems with the task of transporting the stones over water. A massive problem with which the shippers had to cope was the designing of boats, or perhaps barges, that would buoy weights so great that they staggered the imagination.

The blocks of quarried stones are said to have averaged 2.5 tons, while some subsidiary buildings in the pyramid complex required individual stone blocks of over 200 tons in weight. Not only would the barges have to have been extremely large to handle such weights, but also the conditions in this case would dictate a barge having a flat-bottom design in order not to capsize. No remnants of these barges have ever been found, nor does any record of them exist.

It is obvious that the quarriers at one site actually had to ship the stones upstream, while the other quarriers had the simpler task of sending them downstream. However, the experts could not cope with such simple logic. They totally ignored the mode of power the barge had to employ to overcome the force of current flow to proceed upstream (which is accounted for by one theory claiming that hundreds, if not thousands, of people tugged on ropes tied to the barge and laboriously pulled it upstream along the banks of the Nile). Instead, the experts were more concerned with the distance the stones had to travel across land before reaching the shoreline. In their opinion the Egyptians would have had more difficulty transporting tonnage over land than on water. Therefore, the Egyptians would have thought of a way of reducing the distance of land to travel. This, the experts claim, could only have been done during the time the Nile was flooding. The shippers would then be afforded the best possibility of arriving closer to the quarry site and also to the building site. However, this may actually have created an additional problem for the shippers: When the river is overflowing, the tremendous force of current would make it virtually impossible to navigate on the Nile.

Mr. Robert Nelson of New Jersey, a student of metaphysics, has the most rational explanation I have heard. He claims that the Nile River was dammed at some point below the Tura quarry site. Then, when the Nile flooded, a large portion of the geographical area would become evenly inundated with water, to a nominal depth of three or four feet. This damming alleviates all navigational problems for the people concerned; the water can be brought as close to the quarry as needed by controlling the flood level. In addition, there would be no current force to contend with, because the flooded area develops the surface calmness of a small lake. The result of this magnificently simple theory is that only a few people would be required to pull and control the loaded barge between the quarry and the construction site. This may also account for the finding of seashells and other encrusted marine fossils dispersed at various depths around the base of the Great Pyramid.

Mr. Nelson further asserts that as the height of the Pyramid rose during each construction phase, the area was correspondingly flooded to the height necessary to raise the barges level with the course of the Pyramid; the stone would simply be slid off the barge and into place. One can see a similarity between this technique and our present-day lock system.

Mr. Nelson's theory is so elementary that it also eliminates the need for the ramp theory of construction, and the theory necessitating the development of the powerful and complex lever-arm devices to lift the heavy stones very high; and, of course, the sledge theory. With this theory of dam-controlled flooding of the Nile, the engineering feats performed by the Egyptians in loading, transporting, and unloading the stones no longer rivals those performed today with the use of the modern techniques and equipment of our experts.

I am certain that noted Egyptologists will forever tenaciously cling to the ramp and sledge theories, because there is considerable evidence construed as favoring the use of ramps to build pyramids. This contention is based on tomb paintings of the Eighteenth Dynasty that depict a ramp used in the erection of columns in the temple court-yard, and the discovery of the remains of ramps at several dig sites, including Giza. These ramps, found near pyramids, had a slope of about 15 degrees, which is claimed to be a manageable angle along which to pull the stones.

Of course, all theories are certainly debatable; there is no solid evidence to support any one of them. In fact, arguments that offer evidence for any theory must be confined to the dynasty period in which the evidence was uncovered. In other words, illustrations of construction or transportation on walls of Eighteenth Dynasty tombs are not contemporary to, say, the Fourth Dynasty—any more than stainless-steel statues of the present day would be considered contemporary to the twelfth century.

Just because ramps were discovered near pyramids does not prove that ramps were used to build all the pyramids on the site. It is possible that the ramps were used only in the construction of the latter-dynasty pyramids; or that they were actually used in the dismantling of the outer casing stones of older-period pyramids, which stones were then used in new construction.

It is extremely important to realize that many archaeological sites contain relics of several thousands of years; and it seems rather foolish to unequivocally attribute a particular artifact to a certain age or dynasty. It is human nature to speculate as to whether or not a certain find can be related to an earlier time period, but it is certainly folly to become convinced that a formulated theory that really has no facts to support it should be considered above any of the others.

It is interesting to note at this point that, while archaeologists and Egyptologists feel relatively secure and content in ascribing building practices of the Eighteenth Dynasty to those of the first five dynasties, these same authorities have the naïveté to point out that the pyramids of the latter Pharaohs are obviously inferior, in terms of craftsmanship and technical expertise, to the pyramids of the Old Kingdom. Oddly enough, these Egyptologists see

77

absolutely no inconsistency in their attribution of identical building techniques to structures that differ so widely in the quality of their construction.

Mr. Nelson's theory becomes increasingly tantalizing in light of the fact that the natural inundations of the flooding Nile brought the Pyramids of Giza only a quarter mile from the river's bank; and the pyramid at Meidum was about three city blocks from the river's edge. It seems that the pyramids were purposely built on the west bank of the Nile, on high ground, so that the complexes would not be flooded whenever the Nile rose. Yet the complexes had to be close enough so as not to make the dam-controlled flooding of the Nile too difficult.

Still, no matter how tempting it is to embrace Mr. Nelson's theory, one must maintain perception of the total problem within the proper perspective of its scope. This becomes evident when one considers the event of the Aswan High Dam nearing completion in the 1960s. A united effort was made by many engineers, using sophisticated equipment from all over the world, to save as many temples, palaces, and statues as possible before the Aswan damming would inundate these colossal masterpieces forever. But all the modern equipment and expertise of the highly trained and skilled engineers could not lift many of the individual monoliths. The stones actually had to be broken into smaller pieces in order to relocate them. Because the experts needed to cut up the blocks of stone, which the Egyptians obviously had been able to handle intact, a very small percentage of the actual targeted edifices could be saved from the inundating waters of the Aswan High Dam.

There are still a number of other related and unsolvable mysteries that arise in connection with the actual construction of the Great Pyramid. For example, what were the materials used on the outer surfaces of the Old Kingdom pyramids? The development of this controversy focuses on the same hieroglyphic sign appearing on the wall of each burial chamber in every pyramid of the Old Kingdom. The glyph represents a white pyramid having a black base, with brownish-red speckled sides and a capstone in either blue or yellow.

There are Egyptologists who interpret this glyph to indicate that the surface of the finished pyramid was painted, possibly after the application of a plasterlike coating, to give the surface a smooth finish. Other Egyptologists believe that the white of the glyph symbolizes the naturally white Tura limestone. They speculate further that another type of stone with a speckled appearance was used on the sides, and only the capstone and base were painted.

The only extant records on the subject of the Great Pyramid construction are the writings of the Greek historian Herodotus. He visited Egypt in the fifth century B.C., which was at about the time of the twenty-eighth Dynasty, and at least two thousand years after the completion of the Great Pyramid. According to this historian, the pyramid was built in twenty years by four hundred thousand laborers. The laborers were divided into four groups of one hundred thousand men each, and each group worked on the construction of the Pyramid for a period of four months per year.

If this number is accepted as being correct—and currently there is no information source other than Herodotus'—then it must be concluded that Egyptian officials were confronted with the unusual problem of providing food, shelter, sanitation facilities, etc., for one hundred thousand workers. Even if the total figure were to be cut in half, leaving two hundred thousand men, each working for a period of six months, the same problem would still have existed. Yet no evidence exists of any structures or facilities having been used to house such a massive number of laborers.

There is the alternative possibility that the masses did not live at the site, but commuted to it from their homes. The only modes of transportation available in that era were basically those of foot, waterway, or animal back, and three hours could be reasonably estimated for the one-way travel time. This means six hours of total travel time per day. The daily work schedule in that era more than likely was ten or twelve hours long. Therefore, the individual foregoing all other personal activities was left with a maximum of eight hours of sleep time in which to recuperate from what had to have been excruciating, exhausting labor.

Another dispute involving the laborers is the contention by some authorities that the laborers were executed when they completed the Pyramid so that they would not reveal the secret passageways leading to the burial chambers. Mass graves would have been required if this were the case, and as yet none have been found. Of course, there are other possible methods to dispose of bodies, such as the use of gigantic funeral pyres, or allowing the Nile to wash away the bodies into the Delta. However, no evidence exists confirming these methods. Common sense implies that any type of mass execution would have been impractical, since it would have wiped out a major portion of the Egyptian population—not to mention a significant percentage of the total world population. The Pharaohs would have a reduced military force; and, in addition, at least fifteen to twenty years would have to pass before the population regenerated itself to the size where there once again were enough people to build a new pyramid.

Oddly enough, according to the same archaeologists, several pyramids were built within several years of each other, raising an interesting paradox between these two beliefs. Men cannot simultaneously be executed and function as construction workers.

Archaeologists have also eagerly accepted Herodotus' claim—which is totally unsupported—that it took twenty years to build the Great Pyramid; and therefore all pyramidal construction is assigned to a twenty-year time period.

An experiment was performed by the Japanese in 1978, to test several of these theories. Being a highly practical people, they decided to try to erect a 60-foot-high pyramid using the same methods alleged to have been used by the original pyramid architects. They did in 1978 what should have been done decades earlier.

The Nippon Corporation received permission from the Egyptian government to build a mini-pyramid, to be located southeast of Mycerinus' pyramid at the Giza plateau. However, the stone from the Giza complex could not be used; and when completed, the mini-pyramid could only remain for a few days. It would then have to be totally dismantled and the surrounding area restored to its original topography.

With these stipulations agreed to, the Japanese began the arduous task of quarrying and transporting the blocks of stone, and constructing their mini-pyramid, stone by stone. The blocks were taken from the same quarry which had supplied the facing stone for Cheops' pyramid, some nine miles away, on the east bank of the Nile.

Once cut into approximate one-ton blocks, the stones could not be barged across the River Nile. Flotation apparently was not the simple answer, as had been suggested. The blocks finally had to be ferried across by steamboat.

Then, teams of one hundred workers each tried to move these stones over the sand—and they could not move them even an inch! Modern construction equipment had to be resorted to, and once again, when the blocks of stone were finally brought to the building site, the teams could not lift their individual stones more than a foot or so. In the final construction step, a crane and helicopter were used to position the blocks.

The modern world possesses technological abilities unequalled by any known previous civilization, yet even after using the latest techniques and the best of the workers' ability, the mini-pyramid did not have the characteristics of the ancient structure.

The entire project was filmed for documentation by the Nippon Corporation, and then the mini-pyramid was demolished.

This venture by the Japanese, who are considered to be the most resourceful, industrious and enterprising people of the modern world, showed that the methods theorized for the construction of the pyramid by tradition-

Chart II
Major Pyramids of Egypt*

Dynasty	Pharaoh	Base Dimensions	Location
Third	Zoser	411 by 358 ft.	Saqqara
Third	Sekhemkhet	395 sq. ft.	Saqqara
Third	Khaba	276 sq. ft.	Zawiyet el-Aryan
Fourth	Seneferu	473 sq. ft.	Meidum
Fourth	Seneferu (Bent)	620 sq. ft.	Dahshur
Fourth	Seneferu	719 sq. ft.	Dahshur
Fourth	Cheops (Great)	756 sq. ft.	Giza
Fourth	Djedefre	320 sq. ft.	Abu Roash
Fourth	Chephren	708 sq. ft.	Giza
Fourth	Mycerinus	356 sq. ft.	Giza
Fifth	Userkaf	247 sq. ft.	Saqqara
Fifth	Sahure	257 sq. ft.	Abu Sir
Fifth	Neferirkare	360 sq. ft.	Abu Sir
Fifth	Niuserre	274 sq. ft.	Abu Sir
Fifth	Isesi	265 sq. ft.	Saqqara

Fifth	Unas	220 sq. ft.	Saqqara
Sixth	Teti	210 sq. ft.	Saqqara
Sixth	Pepi I	250 sq. ft.	Saqqara
Sixth	Merenre	263 sq. ft.	Saqqara
Sixth	Pepi II	258 sq. ft.	Saqqara
Eighth	Ibi	102 sq. ft.	Saqqara
Eleventh	Neb-hepet-Re Mentuhotep	70 sq. ft.	Deir el-Bahri
Twelfth	Ammenemes I	296 sq. ft.	Lisht
Twelfth	Sesostris I	352 sq. ft.	Lisht
Twelfth	Ammenemes II	263 sq. ft.	Dahshur
Twelfth	Sesostris II	347 sq. ft.	Illahun
Twelfth	Sesostris III	350 sq. ft.	Dahshur
Twelfth	Ammenemes III	342 sq. ft.	Dahshur
Twelfth	Ammenemes III	334 sq. ft.	Hawara
Thirteenth	Khendjer	170 sq. ft.	Saqqara

*According to I. E. S. Edwards in *The Pyramids of Egypt*.

14.

al investigators have been highly inaccurate all this time! And yet—in the light of this undeniable evidence—Egyptologists still refuse to correct their doctrines.

The purpose to which pyramids were finally put seemingly presents less of a problem to Egyptologists than does pyramid construction. In other civilizations around the world there is evidence of the use of pyramids as temples; and more than two dozen of the initial pyramids built in Egypt were found not to contain mummies or any other signs of burial. Yet the Egyptologists are steadfastly convinced that the pyramids were used to inter the bodies of the deceased Pharaohs.

All the pyramids scattered for miles up and down the Nile have had elaborate devices built into them, which the Egyptologists believe were for the protection of the mummy in its burial chamber. Entrances were hidden and a network of passages built to baffle tomb robbers. Also included were false sepulchers, assumed to be designed to lure the thieves in the wrong directions. Burial chambers had trap doors blocked with stones of incredible size and weight; some even had no doors at all, but a hole cut in the roof of the chamber through which the sarcophagus could be lowered. The hole could subsequently be plugged or blocked with a great slab of stone. These slabs of stone were often of leviathan size. For example, the doorless chamber of the Pyramid of Ammenemes III, at Hawara, had a slab of stone weighing more than forty-five tons. It could be reached only by descending a steep, multiple-twisting corridor and then negotiating three trap doors that were barricaded with huge stone blocks. However, all these devices were in vain. Each of the pyramids and all their burial chambers were entered and robbed. Not one escaped this fate.

When Howard Carter, with the financing of Lord Carnarvon, located Tutankhamen's tomb, he found that the seal on the outer door had been broken and then resealed. When that door was opened, another door at the end of a narrow empty corridor—which was the door to the tomb itself—was found by Carter to have been forced

84

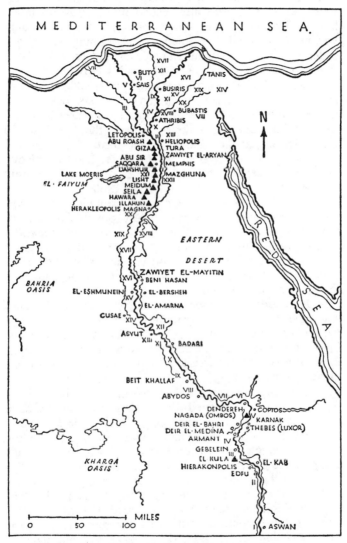

15. Location of pyramids from Aswan to the Delta area

85

open and then resealed. He theorized that grave robbers had been there before him, and that the treasures might have already been taken out of the tomb. When the tomb was finally entered, it seemed that everything was in disorder, and it was thought that thieves had probably been there shortly after the young Pharaoh's burial.

Howard Carter surmised that apparently the grave robbers were surprised by guards or priests, causing the robbers to flee, and therefore very little was taken and very little damage was done. If this were the case, it would seem logical that the disarray would have been corrected to re-establish the burial site as it was originally set. However, this apparently was not done. The doors were simply resealed, which is a curious mystery in itself.

Tutankhamen's tomb is a prime example of an Egyptian's tomb having to contain every possible article for the use of the dead. His tomb is very important to the fields of Egyptology and archaeology in that even though it seems to have been entered and resealed after his burial, it is a virtually intact tomb of a Pharaoh—the only one that has ever been found to date.

It is judged by the archaeologists that in the days when the Pharaohs were entombed, the masses were very, very poor; and the amount of wealth buried with the Pharaoh was sufficient justification to warrant the development of a new profession of a highly specialized nature—namely, tomb robbing.

Probably the coffin makers worked with the robbers. As the makers fashioned the coffins, they could have occasionally included a small door in one end, cleverly masking their alteration. Then it was a simple matter for thieves breaking into certain tombs to open a secret door and pull out jewels along with the mummy.

Then there was the sealer of the tomb, who faithfully sealed the last door in the presence of the family, but purposely left the inner doors unsealed and unprotected, allowing the robbers unobstructed access once they tunneled past the sealed outer door. Also, the guardians of tombs could have let plunderers in, looking the other way in exchange for their share of the treasure. There had to be corrupt officials, and priests themselves, who accepted bribery in return for the protection of the thieves.

Apparently there must have been robbers who felt guilty about desecrating bodies, for there are examples of the thieves trying to rewrap mummies after removing the jewelry and precious stones. It looks as if they then hurriedly put them back together, pasting bandages in place with a slipshod mixture of sand and resin.

The concept of an afterlife manifested itself most emphatically in the proper mummification or preservation of the body. Mummification was an embalming process performed under most secret religious procedures. Contrary to popular belief, the energies of the pyramid shape were unknown to the Egyptians and were not responsible for the dehydration of the body. In fact, no mummy has ever been found in a pyramid in Egypt. Mummies were only discovered in underground quasimausoleums or other burial sites.

The processing of the body and the interment procedure for the mummy is quite detailed in the *Papyrus of Ani,* otherwise known as the *Egyptian Book of the Dead.* There are no extant records of mummification or the embalming process except those found in the writings of Herodotus.

Herodotus was the firsthand observer of the mummification procedure, and he attempted to write down exactly what he saw. The translation of his writings showed that mummification involved the principle of drying out the body—known as the desiccation process. According to the Greek historian, the brain was removed through the nasal cavities, and vital organs like the stomach, liver, lungs, intestines, and kidneys would be wrapped in resin-soaked cloths after being removed, and placed in proper Canopic jars. The jars, with their lids sealed on with wax, would then be set aside to await the day of burial.

The lids of the four primary Canopic jars bear the likenesses of the sons of Horus. One depicts the baboon-headed Hapi; another depicts the jackal-headed Puamute

16. Canopic jar

(f); a third represents the human-headed Inseti; while the fourth represents the falcon-headed Quebusenue (f).

The disemboweled body was desiccated by soaking it in an aqueous solution of a chemical known as natron, which is a sodium carbonate in crystalline form. For centuries, no one questioned the validity of this mummification process; then an English scientist conducted some experiments with chickens. Alfred Lucas felt that dehydration of a body could not be accomplished in an aqueous solution, but rather would have to be done with a dry chemical. His experiments showed that chickens soaked in a solution of natron did not dehydrate, while those embedded into dry natron crystals became mummified. This research convinced Lucas that natron in dry crystalline form was the only process that could have been used to desiccate the body.

As a result of these experiments, students of the ancient Greek language took a closer look at the translation of Herodotus' writings. They found that a key word could either mean "preserving by drying out" or "preserving by placing in a brine or pickling solution." Based on the results of the English scientist's experiments, it was judged that the original interpreter had apparently chosen the wrong definition as the translation of the key Greek word.

In the 1800s, a British archaeologist, James Quibell, was digging in a flat desert area of a known ancient cemetery when he uncovered a square-shaped box. In this box he found the body of a woman, positioned with her knees drawn up to her chin. This was the burial custom of the Early Period of Egypt dating to about 3000 B.C. The woman's body was completely wrapped in a complex series of bandages, which Quibell counted as approximately sixteen intact layers. He estimated that sixteen others had probably been destroyed. Quibell noted that each limb was bandaged separately and that the body was carefully wrapped.

There was a mass of corroded linen between the bandages and the bone, which is indicative that some chemical had been applied to the body as a preservative. But this chemical had not succeeded in accomplishing the chief aims of mummification, which were (1) to preserve the once-living form of the person, and (2) to preserve the body tissue. The female mummy found by Quibell, despite the bandaging and chemical application, could not have been recognized or identified, because no tissue had survived. The only things remaining were the fine bone structure of her skull; her strong, even teeth, indicating that she was a young woman; and her body skeleton, in good shape.

A few years following Quibell's discovery, British Egyptologist Sir William M. Flinders Petrie found an oblong coffin while excavating along the Nile in the desert region of Meidum, which he dated to approximately 2500 B.C. Upon investigation, it was found that the outer wrappings were soaked with resin and were molded carefully into shape, so that every feature of the man's face and body was highlighted in the wrappings. This mummy was so well wrapped that those who had known him in life would probably have immediately recognized his wrapped mummy. This mummy is the oldest one ever found that showed success in outwardly preserving the living form and identity of the person who had died. But it, too, was an unsuccessful mummy; for although the wrappings were lifelike, the mummy inside was not preserved.

When portable X-ray machines became available in the mid-1960s, mummies were X-rayed in order to locate amulets and to determine the condition of the body. This saved the mummies from destruction, as they did not have to be unwrapped in order to learn about their condition or state of preservation.

The X-ray pictures revealed more than the physical condition and location of amulets. One X ray of a mummy revealed a surprising discovery, which to this day is unexplained. This mummy was a wrapped figure of a much larger size than usual. It proved to be not one but four bodies. The largest was the body of a big-boned man, and bandaged with him were two infants and a child. The two infants, possibly twins, were each placed on the thighs of the man; the child, estimated to be a boy of 10 years of age, was laid head down on his side along the man's right leg. It was not uncommon to find the mummy of a newborn infant buried with its mother; presumably both would have died as a result of childbirth. But why would two infants and a child be wrapped up with a man? No one yet has hazarded a guess.

Many mummies are not in existence today because they were used as medicine during a period of four hundred or more years, and a great destruction of them for profit occurred. From the early thirteenth century A.D. well into the seventeenth century, mummies were ground into dust and sold throughout Europe as medicine for the sick. The resin that was used in wrappings to preserve the bodies had turned black and glasslike, resembling a mineral pitch called bitumen. It was this resemblance that was misunderstood and was responsible for the use of mummy dust as a cure for many diseases.

Taking mummy medicine to cure ills was not a practice limited only to the superstitious and ignorant. Sir Francis Bacon, the great English philosopher of Shakespeare's day, consumed and also recommended it "for the staunching of blood." It is not known whether Shakespeare used it, but he does mention this medicine in several of his plays, and it is one of the magic ingredients in the witch's brew in *Macbeth*.

Mummies were also the victims of paper manufacturers. Paper made from cloth, termed "rag" paper, is of high quality and always in demand. If the mummy cloth was not heavily impregnated with resins, it was very useful for this purpose. It was not unusual for a mummy to be wrapped in 150 yards of this cloth, if not much more.

It is also known that the poor people of Egypt unwrapped the mummies, discarded the body, and used the resin-soaked cloth for fuel.·

On a smaller scale, mummies were ground into powder for use by European artists. It was believed by the artists of the Renaissance period that paint would not crack on canvases if mummy powder were added to the pigments.

Alexander, the tenth Duke of Hamilton, who died August 18, 1852, left instructions that his body was to be mummified. About thirty years before his death, with mummification already in his mind, the Duke purchased an ancient sarcophagus and had it shipped to Hamilton Palace, his estate in England. He also had a large mausoleum built on the palace grounds to contain the sarcophagus.

At that time, there was a prominent London doctor,

Thomas J. Pettigrew, a professor of anatomy, who had developed a scientific interest in the techniques of mummification over a period of about twenty years. When the Duke died, this doctor was called in to mummify the body. Pettigrew followed as best he could the ancient art of mummification, which he had gathered from the knowledge he had from his years of study and years of unwrapping mummies. No one knows, of course, how good a job has been done, for Duke Alexander has not been disturbed since.

When the mummy of Amosis I, son of King Seqenenre, was unwrapped, scholars were astounded to find that the brain had not been removed in the usual way. Instead of the brain's being removed through the nostrils, an incision had been made on the left side of the neck, and the Atlas vertebra had been removed. The brain was then apparently drawn out through the foramen magnum, a passage that carries the spinal column out of the skull. The medical experts of that time questioned whether the procedure were possible even with the then modern-surgical knowledge. The proof was before them that it had been successfully done more than thirty centuries earlier by some skilled surgeon or surgeons. However, the mummy of Amosis I was the only one ever found having the brain removed in this manner; and no one is certain to this day why the procedure was done using this rather complex technique.

Thirty mummies of Pharaohs ruling Egypt for a period of about three hundred years, between the Seventeenth Dynasty and the Twentieth Dynasty, were not found in their individual tombs in the rock cliffs of Thebes, but were found in one mass grave-site. Among these mummies were some of Egypt's most famous Pharaohs, such as Amenophis I, Tuthmosis II and III, Seti I, and Ramses I, II, and III. In 1874 French Egyptologist Gaston Maspero aided in the uncovering of the mass re-entombment site of these thirty mummies.

Before unification, burial customs of the upper and lower regions of Egypt were completely different. Lower

Egyptians buried bodies beneath the floor of one of the rooms of the house, while Upper Egyptians buried their dead in cemeteries at the edge of the desert. The Upper Egyptian graves, usually lined with brick, had roofs constructed of wood and were marked with a mound of sand. Egyptologists assert that the Upper Egyptians later adopted the burial custom of Lower Egypt when Egypt was unified, and that there was a simple transition to the massive pyramid tombs.

In retrospect, the question of pyramid construction remains unanswerable, and the facts concerning related feats remain deafeningly mute, while the experts quarrel among themselves—each vying to have his theory accepted for the time being. The metaphysicians industriously profess, in the clear light of their revelations, that the Great Pyramid of Giza is the oldest building in Egypt, a library in stone, a huge safe-deposit box, a shrine, and, of course—through our patient examination—an oracle.

Indeed, the more one attempts to learn any one part of the seemingly infinite amount of secrets locked within the Great Pyramid, the more one is faced with an enigma. It is like standing before the Sphinx itself and attempting to exact an answer to a question that has, indeed, no answer. Through the Great Pyramid one can gaze far down time's misty corridors. It is speaking with amazingly uncanny accuracy, and yet we stand in awe in front of the miracle of ages, insensitive to the sounds of the past and the whispers of the future.

Dressed in its garb of antiquity, the Great Pyramid stands before us with an indestructible truth that it in fact is the past, present, and future; and among its many prophecies, it is clearly making the statement of the universality of man.

The history of the Great Pyramid and its relationship to Egypt is, as we shall see, as great a mystery as the afterlife, and the culture that was raised in its shadow.

⟦5⟧

YESTERDAY AND TODAY
IN THE LAND OF THE NILE

The land of Egypt is considered to be the cradle of a magnificent ancient civilization that ranks highest among the two most ancient cultures of the world.

The idyllic natural setting, complemented by very unusual climatic conditions, afforded a paradiselike atmosphere. The vast desert surrounding the fertile Nile Valley was extremely conducive to the early and rapid development of its peoples' cultural abilities. Some may see the desert as a barrier isolating the Egyptians from the world around them, and vice versa. However, this barrier was not absolute, but acted more like a filter, allowing in only those intrusions that could enrich and develop the traditional Egyptian civilization, a civilization that was the "envy" of the world—and not just for one time, but for all times.

The life-giving force of this area has always been the River Nile. Traversing over 4,000 miles, it is one of the longest rivers in the world, and its northerly flow makes it the most unique in the world. From June to as late as November, the Nile floods to a height of about 25 feet in the Cairo region. Originating from the great lake basin of

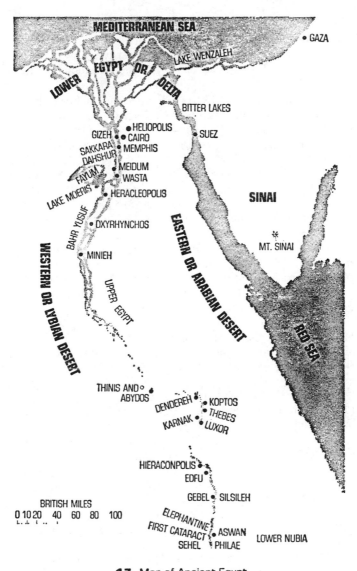

17. Map of Ancient Egypt

95

Equatorial Africa, the Nile carries from the Abyssinian Hills a rich deposit of loam, which it leaves on the land when the water recedes. This ageless renewing of detrital soil has earned the land of Egypt the nickname "The Black Land."

The thin band of rich soil extending on both sides along the Nile from Aswan past Cairo has a comparatively small area. Within a total Egyptian land area of 386,660 square miles, there are no more than 13,000 square miles of habitable land, of which 12,500 square miles are cultivatable. Therefore, the density of the population maintained by this tiny area has traditionally been very large. Records of ancient times set the figure to about 7 million, and the current count is recorded at 40 million.

Along with its fertilizing powers, the Nile has forever been the highway linking distant communities by the most economical, convenient, and least troublesome mode of transportation. Interestingly, for nearly four-fifths of the year, a steady wind blows from the north and simplifies the general problem of upstream transport.

The Nile Valley was not as easily accessible as other lands of the ancient world. Guarded by the deserts on both sides of the valley, the Egyptian culture was protected from the more aggressive races. The Egyptians have always essentially been an unaggressive people. However, there were times in Egyptian history during which its people rallied with an aggressive and militaristic behavior, establishing themselves periodically as conquerors.

According to present archaeological inference from unearthed relics, the typical developmental story is reapplied to the initial habitation of Egypt, where the hunting life of the nomads flows into a settled life of an agricultural community. Through scant evidence, a highly detailed community scene is presented, with herds of animals domesticated to varying degrees, and the growing of wheat and barley.

Present-day Egyptians are apparently descendants of a short and slender race, with heads of the "dolichocephalic type," called the Badarians, also known as the first cultivators. The Badarian structure is said to have some affinity to the black race, and also closely resembles the more ancient races of India and Ceylon.

The earliest remains of the Badarians discovered by archaeologists showed them to be a village society, cultivating wheat and barley, and maintaining dogs among its domesticated animals. The cultivation of flax and the rudiments of a weaving industry, establishing a dress of linen along with animal skin, is attributed to these people.

Badarians produced remarkable pottery during an era that was expected to be quite primitive in the arts. Thus they were called "the first civilized Egyptians." Naturally, knowledge of these early Egyptians has come from the contents of their graves. The Badarian grave was a simple shallow trench into which the body was placed in a fetal position. The bodies, wrapped in goat skins or a mat, were usually placed on a twig-covered platform. Graves contained carved ivory or clay-modeled figurines that are thought to represent a female—either a goddess or a representation of the dead man's wife.

The Badarians exhibited a stage of extraordinary refinement in their life-style. They used ivory pins to fasten their garments. Bracelets, necklaces, and other ornaments were made of shells from the Red Sea; and copper was formed into tubular beads while quartz and other stones were glazed into beads. Carved and decorated ivory combs were in common use, along with eye and face makeup for decoration.

A similar, but backward, Fayum community was also flourishing concurrently with the Badarians in this prehistoric period. Less is known about the Fayum tribe; however, archaeologists see its existence as an indication of general increasing incursions of various peoples into the Nile Valley. The evidence of this incursion allows archaeologists to classify this epoch as the first predynastic period.

It is in this period that traces of the formation of tribes into districts appears. But there is still no indication of any individual leadership, even though the various districts appeared to use an identifying symbol. Craftsmanship is already a finely executed art, as seen in the oar-powered vessels.

Although a startling difference seems apparent between this first predynastic period and the one before it, grave contents only suggest cultural advancement. Figurine models thought to represent water bearers and cattle, along with pottery comparable to the craft of the prehistoric period, have been found in the graves. However, the vase makes its debut among the relics in the graves of this period. These painted vases exhibit good attempts to scenically depict life-styles. Cultural advancements developed steadily as community life progressed into the middle predynastic period, which indicates a conscious change in culture.

The first appearance of a house approximately rectangular, with a wood-framed doorway, found at El Amrah, is credited by archaeologists as belonging to this middle predynastic period.

Districts were now established in a clan system whose emblems are clearly indicated on boats painted on vases of this period. The vases themselves show the craft of the day reaching greater perfection because they were worked in hard stone.

Archaeologists label a very crudely painted grave as the "most remarkable feature" of this era. They claim it heralds the initial stages of the painted tomb. This grave at Hierakonpolis has mud-coated walls covered with a yellow ocher-type paint, serving as a background for scenes of what is thought to be war and pursuit, and possibly ceremonial dances. This work, executed in white, black, and red pigments, illustrates social development reaching the stage of distinction where a leader or chief is evident.

Archaeologically speaking, the late predynastic period appears to have developed in a rather ordinary fashion, and is classified as a transition period preparing for the unification of all the clans into a nation.

The general knowledge and characteristics of developing civilizations in both the prehistoric and predynastic periods is deduced entirely from a scant amount of relics found in graves. Occasionally, graves undeniably assumed as belonging to these periods are excavated, and the contents curiously disrupt the archaeologists' predetermined framework of civilization development. Confusion curiously laces the archaeologists' or Egyptologists' "facts" exuberantly concluded from mere theory. Even though chieftainship or leadership is evidenced as developing in the middle predynastic period, graves preceding this period notably exemplify definite class distinction as a result of developed aristocracy.

A proportionate quantity and quality of objects accompanied the interred body according to its social or economic status. There are graves that indicate notable examples of various aristocratic levels; bodies are raised as much as twenty inches from the floor; planks tied together form a fence around the body; definite roofing is evident; furniture and household articles are included; and the size and depth of the grave finalize the status.

Whether rich or poor, each body was accorded standard ritualistic process. The corpse was fetally positioned, mainly on the left side, lying with the head southerly directed and the body parallel to the Nile. A fascinating and strange oddity found among many children's corpses is that mice bodies were found in the stomachs. The fact that the mice were purposefully ingested is evidenced by their being skinned before being swallowed. This is confirmed from ancient Egyptian pharmaceutical records that regularly prescribe mice as medication for children near death.

For some unknown reason, skeletons are found in a patently undisturbed grave, with bones not in their natural order. It is inferred that these bodies were dismembered after death, perhaps for some religious significance. This inference is supported by the finds in early dynastic tombs in which dismembered bodies were wrapped in linen. The scarcity of graves indicating practice of a dismemberment ritual denotes that it might have been specific to one tribe. In addition, the ritual indicates advanced religious ceremonialism, and plainly distinguishes this practicing tribe from all the others.

Mysteriously, fractures of the forearm are evident in a large proportion of skeletons found in predynastic cemeteries. Adding to the mystery, some cemeteries show that a large portion of the women have their left forearm broken.

By interpreting the meager remains of history, the level of culture attained is surprisingly high. There flourished a considerable degree of advancement in knowledge, however obscured by the long shadows of time. Many secrets abound throughout the predynastic periods, manifesting in equipment and techniques. The native not only had command of these secrets, but he also had it at an incredibly early date in history.

Some of the secrets he commanded included firing and glazing pottery; pigmentation; mining, smelting, and smithing of various metals into tools and weapons; masonry; looming; making and using cosmetics; and pharmacopoeia and its administration. Most importantly, he had to have the knowledge of designing and fabricating the equipment to be used in all of the aforementioned categories. It was these and other secrets that dramatically launched Egypt into the dynastic periods, ranking her highest among the cradles of civilization.

Overall, there is no solution in sight to the enigma of the original source of Egyptian culture. An even greater enigma prevails concerning the history and dating of the first several dynasties, which include the pyramid builders.

The earliest dynastic records clearly indicate the existence of a well-established and fully developed system of hieroglyphic writing. This system of written communication was so far advanced in the First Dynasty that a modified form of it, classified as Early Hieratic, which was scribed in ink, had already evolved and was adopted. Intellectual attainments abounded at the dawn of the early dynastic period, and it is not so surprising that an established calendar was also in existence.

According to some Egyptologists, a calendar of 360 days was adopted by 4241 B.C. It was conveniently arranged, having 12 months of 30 days each, and at the end of which 5 days were added, to compensate for the deficiency that the Egyptians knew existed in their calendar. However, there is nothing extant to indicate how they accounted for the sixth day occurring every 4 years. Debates over the development of the Egyptian calendar continue to rage, offering ingenious theories, and scholars will probably never arrive at the correct solution. However, the incontrovertible point remains: No matter how hard these scholars ignore it, the science of astronomy and its necessary equipment was another one of the secrets, along with writing, of which the native had perfect command.

The inability of scholars to resolve the problems concerning the origin of Egyptian achievements pales in comparison to the attempts of dating and properly fitting various events with Kings currently known to us. Vexing questions concerning Egyptian history and its chronology have Egyptologists widely split. Their opinions as to the chronology of the Pharaohs, the length and time of the reigns, and dynasty duration and dating have resulted in severe disagreement among them.

Basically, the issue rests upon which of the existing documents, or amalgamation of them, should be accepted to answer the burdensome question of chronology. The more universally accepted—but highly questionable—documentation comes from classical writers quoting from the now lost text *History of Egypt*. This missing text is claimed to have been written by Manetho, a high priest living in Lower Egypt during 300 B.C. The *History of Egypt* apparently also contained a list of Kings. The list, along with short quotes from the missing text, were first documented by a Libyan historian named Julius Africanus around A.D. 300.

In the list of Kings, Pharaohs are divided into dynasties or houses. Archaeologists believe this listing an arbitrary grouping, but nonetheless it serves a convenient arrangement.

101

Another documentation consists of two records, labeled the Abydos List and the Sakkara List. The first is a list of kings found upon a wall of the Temple of Abydos by Seti I of the Nineteenth Dynasty. It states all Kings recognized in the archives of Upper Egypt, with each Pharaoh identified with the name he was known by in that locality. The second is a list of Kings of Lower Egypt acknowledged by Memphis historians. It was found in the tomb of Thunuroy, buried at Sakkara in the Nineteenth Dynasty during the reign of Ramses II.

Then there is the Turin Papyrus, simply a listing of Kings judged to be written in the Seventeenth Dynasty. And last, there is what is known as the Palermo Stone, believed to be only a small fragment of a larger stone tablet nine feet long and of unknown origin. The brief annals of the first five dynasties are allegedly documented on both sides of the original tablet. Archaeologists speculate that a second fragment from the same tablet exists, and possibly even two more smaller pieces. These pieces become insignificant when compared to the immenseness of the overall tablet. Thus attempts to reconstruct the entire tablet based on existing pieces have baffled researchers.

Arthur Weigall, in his two-volume work *A History of the Pharaohs,* documents his attempts at reconstructing the annals inscribed on that tablet. He has done an admirable job in deducing the annals of the first five dynasties, but disappointingly, the fruits of his labor have not become popularly accepted.

Mr. Weigall also places the beginning of the Egyptian calendar some seven years after the establishment of Menes, the apparent first King of the First Dynasty—or about 3400 B.C. He further contends that other Egyptologists dating the institution of the calendar at 4241 B.C. have done so on incorrect premises. Mr. Weigall presents very strong and convincing arguments to support his research findings. In fact, all the Egyptologists are able to present their theories very convincingly.

As I am not in a position to judge who among all

the scholars is more nearly correct, an interesting dilemma presents itself, asking what is really the truth of dynastic Egypt. With due respect to as many Egyptologists as is simultaneously possible, I present three charts of dates:

1. The Table of Dates as compiled by Arthur Weigall.
2. The Chronological List of Egyptian Dynasties and Kings tabulated by James Baikie in his two-volume work *A History of Egypt.*
3. Manetho's Chronology as presented by I. E. S. Edwards in *The Pyramids of Egypt.*

Chart III
The Table of Dates Compiled by Arthur Weigall

	B.C.
Establishment of the dynasty of Lower Egypt (Turin)	5507
Establishment of the dynasty of Lower Egypt (Manetho)	5224
Establishment of the dynasty Heracleopolis and Memphis	5197
Establishment of the dynasty Hieraconpolis	5012
Establishment of the dynasty Thinis	3757
Accession of Menes and establishment of First Dynasty	3407
Institution of calendar with October 20–21 as New Year's Day, and June 17–18 (rising of Sirius) as first day of season of Shom	3400
Establishment of Second Dynasty	3144
Rising of Sirius, June 22, coincided with calendar New Year's Day, and hence the beginning of a Sothic cycle may have been recognized	2895
Establishment of Third Dynasty	2887
Establishment of Fourth Dynasty	2789
Establishment of Fifth Dynasty	2715
Establishment of Sixth Dynasty	2587
Beginning of six kingless years at end of Sixth Dynasty	2458
Establishment of Seventh Dynasty	2452

Establishment of Eighth Dynasty	2377
Establishment of Ninth and Eleventh Dynasties	2271
Establishment of Tenth Dynasty	about 2221
End of Tenth Dynasty	about 2197
Establishment of Twelfth Dynasty	2111
Establishment of Thirteenth Dynasty	1897
Arrival of the Hyksos and establishment of Fifteenth Dynasty	1850
Adjustment of calendar from Mesore year to Thoth year by postponement of intercalary days for one month	1767
Death of Khyan and establishment of Seventeenth Dynasty contemporary with Hyksos Sixteenth Dynasty	1728
Establishment of Eighteenth Dynasty	1577
Beginning of Sothic cycle of Menophres, when rising of Sirius (July 6) coincided with first Thoth	1317
	A.D.
Beginning of Sothic cycle, when rising of Sirius (July 17) coincided with first Thoth	139

18.

105

Chart IV
Chronological List of Egyptian Dynasties and Kings, Tabulated by James Baikie in His Two-volume Work A History of Egypt

Shorter Dating
Predynastic Kings of Lower and Upper Egypt

Lower	Upper
Tiu	
Thesh	
Hzekiu	
Neheb	Ka-ap
Uazonz	Ro
Emkhet	

First Dynasty, 3500–3350?
Scorpion
Narmer
Aha-Mena
Zer (Khent?) Atoti

Sir F. Petrie's Dating

Ka-ap, c. 5650 B.C.
Ro, c. 5600 B.C.

First Dynasty, c. 5546–5293
Narmer, 5576–5484
Aha (Mena), 5484–5437
Zer-ta, 5437–5406
Zet-ata, 5406–5383

Za
Den Semti (udimu)
Merpeba
Sermerkhet
Ka-sen

**Second Dynasty,
c. 3350–3190**

Hotepsekhemui
Raneb Kakau
Neneter
Sekhemib
Perabsen
Senedi
Neferkara
Neferkasokar
Kara (?)

**Third Dynasty
c. 3190–3100**

Khasekhemui
Sa-nekht

Merneit (Queen)
Den-setui, 5383–5363
Azab Merpeba, 5363–5337
Semerkhet, 5337–5319
Qa-sen, 5319–5293

**Second Dynasty,
c. 5293–4991**

Hetepsekhemui, c. 5293–5255
Ra-neb Kakau, c. 5255–5216
Neteren, c. 5216–5169
Perabsen Sekhemab, c. 5169–5152
Send, c. 5152–5111
Kara, c. 5111–5094
Neferkara, c. 5094–5069
Khasekhem, Neferkasokar, c. 5069–5021
Khasekhemui, c. 5021–4991

**Third Dynasty
c. 4991–4777**

Sa-nekht, c. 4991–4975

CONTINUED

Shorter Dating

Zeser
Nebkara
Neferkara Huni
Snefru

Fourth Dynasty
c. 3100–2965
Shaaru, c. 3100–3098
Khufu, c. 3098–3075
Radedef, c. 3075–3067
Khafra, c. 3067–3011
Menkaura, c. 3011–2988
Shepseskaf, 2988–2970
Imhotep (?), c. 2970–2965 (?)

Fifth Dynasty
c. 2965–2825
Userkaf, c. 2965–2958
Sahura, c. 2958–2946
Kakau, c. 2946–2936

Sir F. Petrie's Dating

Nebkara, c. 4975–4947
Zeser (Neterkhet), c. 4947–4918

Snefru, c. 4803–4777

Fourth Dynasty
c. 4777–4493
Shaaru, c. 4777–4748
Khufu, c. 4748–4685
Khafra, c. 4685–4619
Menkaura, c. 4619–4556
Radedef, c. 4556–4531
Shepseskaf, c. 4531–4509
Imhotep, c. 4502–4493

Fifth Dynasty
c. 4493–4275
Userkaf, c. 4493–4465
Sahura, c. 4465–4452
Kakau, c. 4452–4432

Shepseskara, c. 2935–2929
Khaneferra, c. 2929–2925
Neuserra, c. 2925–2891
Menkauhor, c. 2891–2883
Dadkara Assa, c. 2883–2855
Unas, c. 2855–2825

Sixth Dynasty
c. 2825–2631
Teta, c. 2825–2795
Pepy I, Merira, c. 2795–2742
Merenra, c. 2742–2738
Pepy II, c. 2738–2644
Merenra II, c. 2644–2643
Nitokris, c. 2643–2631

Seventh and Eighth Dynasties
(nox alta premit)

109

Shepseskara, c. 4432–4425
Khaneferra, c. 4425–4405
Neuserra, c. 4405–4361
Menkauhor, c. 4361–4352
Zedkara Assa, c. 4352–4308
Unas, c. 4308–4275

Sixth Dynasty
c. 4275–4077
Teta, c. 4275–4251
Pepy I, c. 4245–4192
Userkara, c. 4251–4245
Merenra, c. 4192–4185
Merenra II, c. 4090–4089
Pepy II, c. 4185–4090
Nitokris, c. 4089–4077

Seventh and Eighth Dynasties
4077–3907 (nox alta premit)

CONTINUED

Shorter Dating

Ninth and Tenth Dynasties

2500–2300

Khety I, (Ekhtai)
Khety II, Meryabra
Khety III, Uahkara
Khety IV, Merykara

Eleventh Dynasty

c. 2375–2212

Antefaa Uahankh, c. 2375
Antef II, Nakhtnebtepnefer
Mentuhotep Sankhabtaui
Mentuhotep II
Mentuhotep III, Nebhapetra,
   c. 2290–2242

Mentuhotep IV. c. 2242–2212

Sir F. Petrie's Dating

Ninth Dynasty

c. 3907–3807

Khety I, c. 3907–3880
Khety II, c. 3880–3855
Khety III, c. 3855–3830
Khety IV, c. 3830–3807

Eleventh Dynasty

c. 3733–3715

Antefaa, c. 3733–3715
Antefaa II, Uahankh, c. 3715–3665
Antef III, c. 3665–3660
Mentuhotep I, c. 3660–3645
Mentuhotep II, c. 3645–3640

Mentuhotep III, c. 3640–3592
Mentuhotep IV, c. 3592–3588
Mentuhotep V, c. 3588–3574

Twelfth Dynasty
c. 2212–2000

Amenemhat I, c. 2212–2182
Senusert I (coreg.), 2192–2147
Amenemhat II (coreg.), 2150–2115
Senusert II, c. 2115–2099
Senusert III, c. 2099–2061
Amenemhat II, c. 2061–2013
Amenemhat IV, c. 2013–2004
Sebekneferura, c. 2004–2000

Thirteenth and Fourteenth Dynasties
c. 2000–1800 B.C.

Ugaf Khutauira, c. 2000 (?)
Sekhemkara
Sankhabtauira
Sneferabra, Senusert IV
Sebekhotep I
Sebekemsaf I

Twelfth Dynasty
c. 3579–3368

Amenemhat I, c. 3579–3549
Senusert I (coreg.), 3559–3515
Amenemhat II (coreg.), 3517–3482
Senusert II (coreg.), c. 3484–3465
Senusert III, c. 3465–3427
Amenemhat III, c. 3427–3381
Amenemhat IV, c. 3381–3372
Sebekneferura, c. 3372–3368

Thirteenth and Fourteenth Dynasties
3366–2729 (about 70 kings of
whom more or less important
relics have survived)

Ugaf, c. 3366–3358
Sekhemkara, c. 3358–3352
Yufni, c. 3338–3336
Sankhabra, c. 3336–3314
Sebekhotep I, c. 3286–3278
Sebekemsaf I, c. 3260

CONTINUED

Shorter Dating

Sebekemsaf II
Mermeshau
Menuazra
Sebekhotep II
Neferhotep, 1900(?)
Sebekhotep III
Merneferra Ay
Sebekhotep IV
Sebekhotep V
Antef III
Antef IV
Antef V, c. 1750(?)
Khaza

Fifteenth and Sixteenth Dynasties
c. 1800–1580 (Hyksos Kings)

Semken

'Ant-hal
Yekeb-baal

Sir F. Petrie's Dating

Sebekhotep II, c. 3254–3244
Mermeshau, c. 3236–3228
Sebekemsaf II, c. 3225
Sebekhotep III, c. 3212–3200
Sebekemsaf III, c. 3220
Neferhotep, c. 3209–3194
Sebekhotep IV, c. 3166–3160
Merneferra Ay, c. 3144–3120
Khaza(?)

Fifteenth and Sixteenth Dynasties

Semken, c. 2497–2453
Oauserra, Apepa I, 2416–2335
Khyan, 2355, 2305
Oaqenenra, Apepa II

Yekeb-hal . . . Salatis (?)
Maa-ab-ra Pepi (?) . . . Bnon (?)
Aahpehtira Nubti . . . Apakhnas (?)
Apepa I . . . Apophis (?)
Khyan . . . Iannas (?)
Apepa II, Oauserra
Oasehra
Appepa, Oaqenenra

**Seventeenth Dynasty, Theban,
c. 1635–1580**
Seqenenra, Ta-aa, 1635–1615
Seqenenrq, Ta-aa-aa, 1615–1605
Seqenenra, Ta-aa-ken, 1605–1591
Kames, 1591–1581
Senekhtenra, 1581–1580

113

Nebkhepeshra, Apepa III
Maatnebra
Maatabra
Antef V ⎫ Seventeenth Dynasty,
Antef VI ⎬ Theban, begins
Antef VII ⎭ about 1738 B.C.

**Seventeenth Dynasty
Theban**
Seqenenra, Ta-aa, 1660–1635
Seqenenra, Ta-aa-aa, 1635–1610
Seqenenra, Ta-aa-ken, 1610–1597
Kames, 1597–1591
Senekhtenra, 1591–1587

The two streams of dating, which have been converging for some time, now virtually co-alesce, and from this point it is needless to maintain any division between dates, which only dif-fer by a year or two.

CONTINUED

Eighteenth Dynasty
c. 1580–1322
Aahmes I, 1580–1558
Amenhotep I, 1558–1545
Thothmes I, 1545–1514
Thothmes II, 1514–1501
Hatshepsut, 1501–1479
Thothmes III (coreg., 1501–1479),
  1479–1447
Amenhotep II, 1447–1420
Thothmes IV, 1420–1412
Amenhotep III, 1412–1376
Akhenaten (Amenhotep IV), 1376–1358

Semenkhara, 1358–1355
Tutankhamen, 1355–1346
Ay 1346–(?)

Late Minoan I begins

Late Minoan II begins

Tushratta of Mitanni,
Burraburiash of Babylon,
Shubbiluliuma of Hatti

Destruction of Palaces of
Knossos and Phaistos,
c. 1400 B.C.

The second stage of the New Empire opens with the accession of Horemheb, 1346(?), who gathers up the fragments from the collapse under Akhenaten, and prepares the way for the active Pharaohs of the Nineteenth Dynasty.

19.

114

Chart V
Manetho's Dynastic Periods*

3100–2686 B.C.	Early Dynastic Period	First and Second Dynasties
2686–2181 B.C.	Old Kingdom	Third to Sixth Dynasties
2181–2133 B.C.	First Intermediate Period	Seventh to Tenth Dynasties
2133–1786 B.C.	Middle Kingdom	Eleventh and Twelfth Dynasties
1786–1567 B.C.	Second Intermediate Period	Thirteenth to Seventeenth Dynasties
1567–1080 B.C.	New Kingdom	Eighteenth to Twentieth Dynasties
1080– 664 B.C.	Late New Kingdom	Twenty-first to Twenty-fifth Dynasties
664– 525 B.C.	Saite Period	Twenty-sixth Dynasty
525– 332 B.C.	Late Period	Twenty-seventh to Thirty-first Dynasties

*According to I. E. S. Edwards in *The Pyramids of Egypt.*

20.

As can be seen from the three charts of dates, a very significant variation is apparent in the dating of the dynasties. For example, if it is accepted that Cheops' Pyramid was constructed and/or completed in the Fourth Dynasty, the range of dates from 2686 B.C. to 4777 B.C. involves a discrepancy of a little more than two thousand years.

It is no wonder that squabbles among Egyptologists are forcing more and more students to seek acceptable answers from other fields, and rightly so. Present-day theorists have allowed themselves to become so preoccupied with their own theories, and are so busy defending any challenges to them, that they are unable to deal with other hypotheses that might very well be as sound as their own.

With the presently existing contradictory evidence, the blatant disagreements among Egyptologists, and the outright clash among these Egyptologists with archaeologists of other pyramid civilizations, one cannot blame the student for approaching the school of metaphysics in search of universal knowledge.

Contradictory evidence and discrepancies increase among scholars when early dynastic Egypt is viewed with an attempt to organize the fragmentary evidence thought to date from that period.

⫷6⫸

OF PHARAOHS, GODS, AND FARMERS

Major sequences of Egyptian chronological events, and their relationships to one another, are known to be incomplete and perhaps even inaccurate. In spite of the difficulties involved in developing a chronological listing of Kings (it is difficult and/or impossible to date in terms of years much before the beginning of the Christian era), Egyptologists present publicly as accurate a sequence that among themselves they disagree about vehemently. For convenience, and because over "a century of study has demonstrated that it is fundamentally sound . . . ," the known Kings of Egypt are grouped into thirty-one dynasties, which are further segmented into nine main periods. Rather than developing a more exact dating technique, Egyptologists have acquiesced in accepting such a questionable substitute as the chronologies in Manetho's *History of Egypt,* providing a false standard for universal acceptance. (See Chart V in Chapter 5.)

The first dynastic ruler of Egypt has been traditionally accepted to be Menes. The Greek historian Herodotus states that Menes gave Egypt a new capital called Memphis. From extremely scant evidence, it is thought that

Menes came from the Egyptian city of Thinis, and there are doubts as to his actual identity.

Many elements are involved in the traditional conception of Menes. Some historians believe that he was really King Narmar and was responsible for the beginning of all things in unified Egypt. There is a possibility that "Men" was the personal name of Narmar, which evolved into a title of Meni, Mena, or Menes, which seems to signify "the established." Memphis is viewed to be a Greek corruption derived from Men-nefer, "the well established."

As discussed in the previous chapter, it is certain that kingdoms existed before the time of Menes. A dynasty of Kings reigned over Lower Egypt, whose dominions extended from the shores of the Mediterranean to the beginning of the Delta region. About sixty Kings are judged to have reigned in Lower Egypt before the unification. There are no existing records of these Kings other than their being included among several lists of Kings' names written thousands of years later on papyri and stone. It is supposed that these Kings did not necessarily evolve from a single dynasty or the same lineage. Although hieroglyphic writing was just evolving, Lower Egypt is known to already have developed two major cities. It is assumed that these kings reigned at the city of Sae or Sais, which succeeded the city of Buto or Beutho.

The Kingdom of Lower Egypt was known as the North Land, or Papyrus Land, with a hieroglyphic symbol of a tuft of the papyrus plant. The King's title was Baya, Biti, or Bati, standing for bee or hornet. He wore the now-famous red crown, having a high peak at the back and a curved projection from the front. The royal color was red, and the treasury was known as the Red House. The city of Sae had a patron goddess called Neit, and her symbol consisted of a shield and two crossed arrows. The city of Buto had the cobra symbol for their patron goddess called Utho or Uto. She later became patroness for the entire Delta region, whereas the cobra became the pharaonic symbol of royalty.

The Kingdom of Upper Egypt is placed several centuries after the establishment of the Lower Kingdom. The approximately thirty Kings who reigned were called "Insi," "Suten," or "Seten," meaning "the Reed." They wore the familiar tall, white-colored, pointed cap or crown as their symbol of royalty; and interestingly, they called their treasury the White House. Unlike the Lower Kingdom, which was symbolized by a tuft of the papyrus plant, Upper Egypt has no known glyph symbol representing its geographical position. I believe that the River Nile, the pyramid, or the cow—possibly in combination—could

21. The Three Crowns of Egypt
(left) The White Crown of Upper Egypt
(center) The Red Crown of Lower Egypt
(right) The Combined Crown of Unified Egypt

have conceivably served as the hieroglyphic sign for the upper region. The River Nile and the pyramid appear to be the more logical symbols because the river was a very important element in the lives of the people, and pyramids are obviously the dominant structures of the land. However, the cow as a hieroglyphic sign was as important, if not more so, than the other two symbols designating the upper geographical region. The people in Upper Egypt were basically the cattle raisers, and the cow symbol may have preceded the Nile or pyramid symbol, embodying the female aspect of nature in its life-giving and -sustaining qualities. Many ancient texts refer to a "land of

119

milk and honey," and this reference may actually apply to the Unified Kingdoms of Upper and Lower Egypt. The hieroglyph for milk, represented by a pitcher with tufts of the sedge plant coming out of it, could indeed substantiate the belief that Egypt was, in fact, a "land of milk and honey."

For lack of the proper designation of Upper Egypt, it is classically referred to as the Land of the Reed; and its capital was Het-Insi, or Eheninsi, which means "House of Insi."

It should be noted at this point that when the term "King" or "Pharaoh" is used in Egyptian history textbooks, it signifies rulership rather than sex. This is differentiated from the title "Queen" applied to the wife of a King or a Pharaoh. Female rulers are chronicled in the pre-dynastic period, and it is fascinating that a female Pharaoh is documented as having reigned in the middle of the Eighteenth Dynasty.

Manetho claims that two dynasties existed before that of Menes. He called the first "The Dynasty of Gods" and the second "The Dead Demigods." The Bee King of the Delta and the Reed King of Upper Egypt are part of Manetho's Second Dynasty. The two kingdoms thus independently established, along with their successor Kings, formed the foundation for unification under Menes, the traditional founder of the pharaonic line of dynastic Egypt.

Egyptologists view Menes as having united both kingdoms, and establishing the title Insi-Bya—"Reed and Hornet." He also wore either crown on separate occasions, and, at other times, the double crown (see Figure 22), further symbolizing the combining of the two kingdoms. However, a contradiction appears, because instead of believing that Menes and Narmar were one and the same, most scholars theorize that Menes was actually the son of Narmar and not Narmar himself. Historians arrive at this conclusion from the evidence of a decorated great slate palette unearthed at Nekhen, which is deciphered as depicting Narmar wearing not only the white crown but

22. The Palette of Narmar

also the red crown. This palette appears to predate any
recorded evidence of Ménes. Based on the evidence of
this palette, this theory states that Narmar was the hereditary King of Thinis. He was also the heir of Nekhen, a
city that his ancestors founded. Either by marriage or inheritance he was also the Reed King, signifying sovereignty
of all Upper Egypt. Adding to this his conquest of the
Hornet Kingdom of the Delta, his son—assumed to be
Menes—inherited unified Egypt.

By his birthright, Menes was a Hawk King and had
taken the name Ohe, "the fighter"; thus he is listed as
"Ohe Meni" or "Aha Mena." He is known more for his
administrative abilities than as a conqueror; and he was
not accepted as King by the Lower Egyptians because he
was not of their blood line. This is supported by the

evidence that the royal title "Bya" (Hornet) was not applied to him, and that in Lower Egypt he was known simply as "the Hawk."

Menes married a Lower Egyptian princess, Neit-hetep or Neithotep, whose name signifies the peace or satisfaction of the goddess Neit, and therefore he also became the ruler of Lower Egypt. He then assumed a new title, "Lord of the Vulture and the Cobra." The Egyptians referred to dual lordship titles by the general word "Nebti." The Vulture in Menes' Nebti name was the equivalent of the queen's symbol for Hawk. The Vulture is the hieroglyph for "motherhood." Its egg-shaped body and great protecting wings express this function. But even though he was then legally considered the sovereign of a united Upper and Lower Egypt, he was still referred to as either the Hawk or the Dual Lord, but never as Insi-Bya.

Due to the accomplishment of Menes and his successors, the term "Pharaoh" is applied when speaking of the sovereigns after the unification of Egypt. Before the unification of Egypt, the sovereigns are simply called Kings. The word Pharaoh is a Hebraic derivation from the Egyptian word Peroe, which means "the Great House" —or more specifically, "the Great Hereditary Proprietor," *per* being the word often used for inheritable chattel and real estate.

Menes is credited with establishing the ritual of divine worship and the tradition of elegant and sumptuous modes of living. Upon his death he was buried, either at Abydos or at Nakada. It was a common practice for a ruler to have two burial sites—the tomb was for his real body and the cenotaph was for his *ka* or double.

Menes' successors in the First Dynasty are acknowledged as the developers of the *mastaba,* which is a superstructure of sun-dried mud brick placed over the burial pit. Because tombs were regarded as the place where the dead dwelled, every mastaba was a close copy of a house or palace. A mastaba, dated to the reign of Menes in the First Dynasty, covers a shallow rectangular pit divided into five compartments. Archaeologists speculate that the middle compartment contained the body, while the adjoining compartments probably housed the most intimate possessions. The mastaba itself was divided into a rectangular, twenty-seven-celled interior containing nine rows of three cells each. The outer walls of the superstructure slope inward from the base to the truncated top. Corridors to interconnect rooms were not provided because they were considered unnecessary. The ancient Egyptians believed that the spirit of the deceased could pass unhindered through any material barrier. Mastabas of this type were almost certainly copies of the deceased person's domiciles, indicating the progressive life-styles of the First Dynasty.

Accomplishments credited to the First Dynasty include the unification of Egypt, the establishment of a new royal line, governmental formation, and organization of priests and temples. The chaos in the Second Dynasty clearly reflects what the First Dynasty had actually accomplished: heightening the existing antagonism between the two kingdoms as a result of forced unification. This dynasty was beset with tremendous civil wars compounded with natural disasters, all of which became the growing pains of Egypt's greatness.

The annals of the Second Dynasty are extremely obscure and afford minimal information on this period. As a result, it is viewed as a transition period, and some Egyptologists consider this and the Third Dynasty as one. This dynasty experienced an epoch of bitter struggles between political and royal factions of both Kingdoms, along with great clashes among the various religious philosophies. Throughout the entire Second Dynasty there were constant reversals of administrative policies and royal doctrines as each new Pharaoh attained office. There were two dominant religious sects—the solar or sun worshipers, and the Nile worshipers, and there was a perpetual power shift between them. The god of the Nile was called Osiris, and the sun god was Ra. Adherents of these two major gods of Egyptian life and thought, because of

23. The Sun God, Ra   **24.** The God of the Nile, Osiris

the attempted unification, were forced into bitter rivalry, each vying to become the principal religion of unified Egypt.

The many references to stories and the origin of Osiris are frustratingly incomplete and elusive. He probably was a King, as commonly regarded, who perpetuated an old tradition of royal martyrdom whereby a King sacrifices himself, or is sacrificed, for the good of his kingdom.

Sparse Egyptian religious history records Osiris as the great fertility god, who was eventually transformed into the Nile god, and who finally came to be regarded as the god of resurrection and immortality.

According to Egyptian legend, Osiris is the first-born of the five children of the goddess Nut and the god Seb, and he eventually became King of the Egyptians. His brother Set, the third-born child, was very jealous of

25. Osiris' mother, the Goddess Nut

26. Osiris' father, the God Seb

Osiris' office and accomplishments, and decided to kill him. Through trickery, Set got Osiris into a chest, which was tossed into the Nile. The casket with the drowned body of Osiris was washed to the sea. Osiris' sister and wife, Isis, the fourth-born child, searched for and found Osiris' body, and brought it back to Egypt. She hid the body, but eventually slackened her guard over it, at which time Set, while hunting, stumbled onto it.

Knowing of Isis' magical skill in revivifying corpses, Set stole the body. In order to prevent her from resurrecting Osiris, he dismembered the body into fourteen or sixteen parts and hid them throughout Egypt. Isis then searched for and recovered all the parts. She was able to reconstruct Osiris' entire body, but she was unsuccessful in fully reviving the corpse. Her partially successful efforts were rewarded in that she was able to conceive his child,

27. Osiris' brother, the God Set

Horus. At the end of the ritual, then, Osiris' body historically became the first mummy.

When Horus was born he inherited all of his father's earthly regal powers. Osiris, now the dead King, ruled the realm of the dead as the lord of afterlife. Hence, all Egyptians desired to become Osiris when they died.

Although Osiris became the national god of life after death, he did not attain the level of a universal god, because he was able to satisfy the needs of the Egyptian people only in their afterlife. On the other hand, Ra, the sun god, more than adequately satisfied the Egyptians' temporal and spiritual needs, because he was considered the god of the living.

Both Ra, the sun god, and Osiris, the god and judge of the dead, have definite positions and duties assigned to them; and it is also exceedingly clear that ceremonies performed in connection with them were extremely ancient by the Fifth Dynasty.

Legends and religious history of the Egyptians intimate that sun worshipping was the original religion. The

28. Osiris' sister and wife, the Goddess Isis

first sun-worshipping city is considered to be An or In. The Bible refers to it as On, whose glyph symbol is a pillar; the Greeks renamed it Heliopolis, the "City of the Sun."

The inhabitants of On worshipped the sun god, Ra, who is thought to be derived from an Asian deity. The symbol of Ra or Re was a small pyramid or pyramidion—perhaps conical—called either Ben or Benben, which stood on a pedestal in an open court. This seems to have been the sun worshippers' most sacred object, and probably symbolized a primeval mound that emerged from primordial waters at the creation of the universe. In later dynasties this pedestaled pyramid, or Benben, became the familiar obelisk—now considered to be the oldest monument to God. From the theology of sun worshipping there developed a powerful priesthood that is credited with evolving

127

29. Osiris' son, the God Horus

nine deities and is later known as the great Ennead of Heliopolis.

Along with the Second Dynasty's constant administrative and economic upheavals, it is evident that this dynasty did not follow a hereditary succession of Kings; rather, monarchs ascended the throne supported by the particular faction in power at the time. Of the nine monarchs during this dynastic epoch, four were sun worshippers claiming to have been given ascension to the throne by the sun god, Ra, while the other five claimed to have acquired their position through royal inheritance.

It is interesting to note that, as in the Mixtec tradition, in which giants were believed to have existed, Manetho records that in the Second Dynasty, a "giant" Pharaoh, Neferkasokar, whom he called Sesochris, reigned. This Pharaoh was between seven and eight feet tall and had a fifty-two-inch chest measurement. However, there is no evidence of this Pharaoh other than Manetho's mention of him.

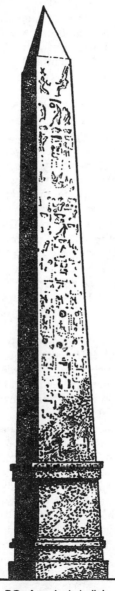

30. A typical obelisk

The second monarch of this dynasty, Kekeu, is also listed under the name Nebra, and this is the first time in Egyptian chronicles that the sun god's name, Ra, is incorporated into a Pharaoh's name. This marks the elevation of religion as the dominant power in the land, so that even the ruling court is under the influence of the priests of Ra.

The most famous pharaoh in this epoch is Khasekagmui, and he is placed as either the last King of this dynasty or the first King of the Third Dynasty. Pharaoh Khasekagmui is known because two of his statuettes have survived, saving for posterity the reality of the earliest pharaoh to date. He is further known for marrying a great royal lady named Nemaethapi or Hapenmaat. This marriage was significant as it united his royal line of princes with her line of sun-worshipping Kings. This gesture apparently pacified the entire country, and many peaceful years brought this dynasty to a conclusion. Pharaoh Khasekagmui not only leaves an inheritance of a practically indivisible, united Egypt with the powerful influence of the priesthood of Ra, but he is also credited with inspiring the great pyramid builders of the Third Dynasty, who in turn fostered the movement toward the greatest construction in stone during the Fourth Dynasty.

The dearth of information pertaining to the Third Dynasty gives us just as little knowledge as scholars have of the Second Dynasty, leaving our picture of the time with only a shadowy separation between the ending of the Second Dynasty and the beginning of the Third Dynasty. It must be remembered, however, that the classification of Kings into dynasties is a fabrication of scholars after the fact, and not a classification that the pharaohs themselves originated. So I feel that the great controversies concerning the beginnings and ends of dynasties is in reality "much ado over nothing." Anyway, Egyptologists still claim that mastabas evolved into pyramids during the shadowy period betwixt the dynasties. They justify their reasoning on the indication that the priests of Ra had developed strong political influence, possibly even ordaining the pharaohs into the ministry of the sun god.

It is quite conceivable that the high priests, attaining strong political influence, desired to proclaim their achievement of power through an emphatic statement. Perhaps this is how the pyramid evolved: as a macro-version of the pyramidion symbol of Ra, used by the priests as a sign of their influence over their Pharaoh, now in an enlarged version—a grave marker and tomb.

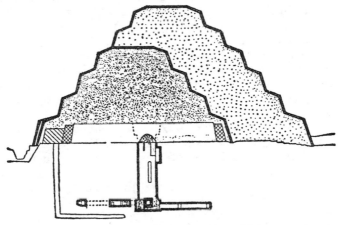

31. Section of the Step Pyramid

Several pharaohs out of the six ascribed to the Third Dynasty are elevated to greatness due to the discovery of their pyramid tombs. Step pyramids apparently are characteristic only of the Third Dynasty, and one of these—located at Sakkara—is accepted as the forerunner of the efforts from which the true pyramid evolved. The step pyramid is attributed to the second Pharaoh of the Third Dynasty. He was known by several different names, the more common ones being Thoser, Djoser, or Zoser.

It must be explained at this point why the Kings and

Pharaohs of Egypt are referred to by many different names and spellings. This is due to the Egyptologists' preference of either using their own translation of the glyph symbols accepted to represent that ruler, or their reticently adopting the historical documentation of the names. Name variations cause immense bewilderment to a student learning the history, legend, and mythology of ancient Egypt. Bewilderment quickly turns into total frustration when the fanciful patchwork of the lineage of rulers is studied, and then the student becomes painfully aware of the discordance of Egyptian historians. This results in either the continuing perpetuation of misnomers, or the introduction of new ones by the surviving student turned historian.

Taking this one step farther, the identification of Pharaohs of the earlier dynasties with particular pyramids is, in fact, only inferred from manuscripts no earlier than the Twelfth Dynasty, or on even more meager and deficient evidence. An example of such inference based on inadequate evidence is Zoser's identification with a particular step pyramid at Sakkara; while there is in fact no specific evidence of the pyramid pinpointing that it indeed belonged to Zoser!

Zoser's different names are translated "the Holy" or "God in the Flesh." It is presumed that Zoser's greatness was due to the achievements of Imhotep, his high priest. These two men are confusingly interchanged throughout manuscript translations and interpretations. Among the many titles of Imhotep are "the Hereditary Noble," "the High Priest of Heliopolis," "Chief Ritualist of King Zoser," "Vizier," "Overseer of Works," and "Architect." These titles seem to indicate that he was not a relative of the royal family, but achieved high status through his own genius. Legend regards him as the father of medicine as well as an accomplished astronomer and magician.

Zoser's step pyramid is a massive construction, rising to a height of 200 feet in 6 steps, with a base measuring 411 feet by 358 feet. Apparently, like the South

American pyramids, it underwent several changes of plan. The nucleus of the pyramid is considered to be a solid, square structure with an outer layer of dressed Tura limestone. This nucleus appears to have been a mastaba 26 feet high and about 207 feet square, aligned to the cardinal points. It is hard to believe that the degree of architectural perfection of this pyramid could have been achieved without having been preceded by a lengthy process of development. Yet no evidence exists of any large-scale employment of stone in any earlier construction. Because small blocks of stone were used in constructing the step pyramid, it is believed that the technique of quarrying and manipulating massive stone blocks may not yet have been mastered. Yet a mystery exists in the fact that the burial chamber in this step pyramid was plugged by a solid, 6-foot-long piece of granite weighing about 3 tons.

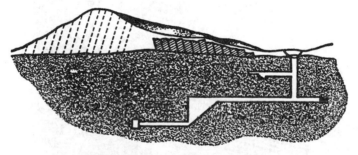

32. Section of the Layer Pyramid

The other pyramids of the Third Dynasty include those of Nagada and el-Kula, which are both four-stepped monuments; the pyramid of Zawiyet el-Aryan, which is not a true step pyramid, but rather a layered one; and the newest one unearthed in the mid-fifties, claimed to belong to Sekhem-Khet. Sekhem-Khet is considered the immediate successor of Zoser through the fact that Imhotep's name appears in red ink on the enclosure wall of the pyramid. However, this inscription does not necessarily signify that Imhotep was responsible for the planning and

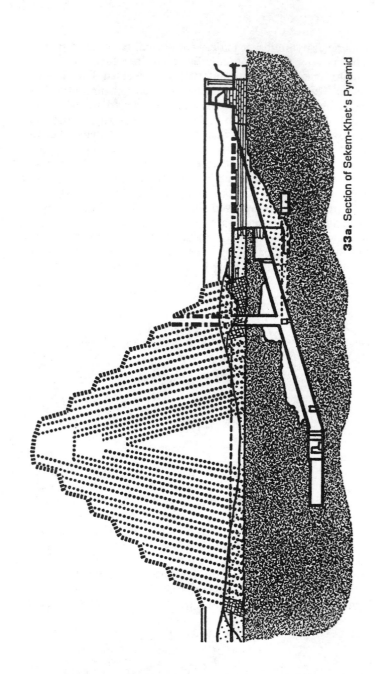

33a. Section of Sekem-Khet's Pyramid

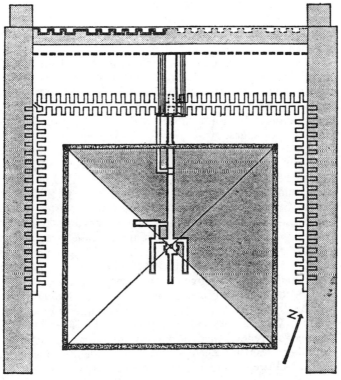

33b. Plan of Sekem-Khet's Pyramid

construction of this pyramid; it may simply signify a written remembrance of Imhotep, who by this time may have already been an ancient legend.

The discovery of this "new" pyramid, which showed no signs of forced entry, piqued the anticipation of the Egyptologists and made them confident that the interior would yield an untold number of artifacts and information. They did not anticipate finding "treasure" comparable to the incredibly rich deposits in King Tutankhamen's tomb; such richness in this Third Dynasty tomb could not be expected. King Tut reigned during a period of great conquests, in the Eighteenth Dynasty, which brought in enormous opulence never before enjoyed. The "treasure" in Sekem-Khet's pyramid was commensurate with that foreseen by the Egyptologists for a Third Dynasty structure, built some fifteen hundred years before Tutankhamen.

The pyramid contained stone bowls, dishes, and other vessels, along with golden bracelets, trinkets, ornaments, and other jewelry indicative of this dynasty. In addition, there were wooden boxes, beads, pottery jars, plates, cups, tables, and the most valuable item of all—an intact sarcophagus.

The sarcophagus had been carved from a single block of magnificent, pale gold, translucent alabaster. The opening is not conventional (at the top), but at the north end, sealed with a sliding alabaster panel. This five-hundred-pound panel remained intact with plaster in the joints, and as far as could be determined, no traces of forced opening were discernible. On top of the sarcophagus was found the decayed and crystallized fragmentary remains of a funerary wreath, made from some plant or shrub and roughly arranged in the form of a vee.

After much tedious effort, when the sliding panel was finally raised, the sarcophagus was found to be empty. Empty! It was beyond comprehension! The pyramid showed every evidence of having been used for burial, and there was not even a shred of evidence to suggest that it had been plundered by grave robbers.

What could be even the partial solution to the mystery of the missing mummy? The most acceptable suggestion is that this pyramid was actually the cenotaph, or the dummy tomb, designed for the symbolic burial of the *ka* (spirit) of the King. This burial ceremony for the ka is believed to have been designed and carried out as if a body were present. Therefore, because of the exact duplication of the ritual and procedures without any deviation whatsoever, it is impossible to distinguish between the symbolic burial site and the actual repository of the King's body.

Zoser's pyramid also contained a similar alabaster sarcophagus but with the conventional lid top. Interestingly, a second sarcophagus was found situated perpendicular to the first. The first sarcophagus was found empty, while the second one contained the residual remnants of a wooden coffin, and in the midst of the debris was found the skeleton of a child.

Throughout the long and arduous excavations of the pyramids credited to the Third Dynasty, no Pharaoh's body or mummy has ever been found. This has led some Egyptologists to believe that the pyramid was only intended to house the ka of the king, and that the real body was—and very likely still is—buried elsewhere. Egyptologists support this belief by the known fact that sets of tombs distantly separated belonged to the same Kings or Pharaohs. Although neither are pyramids, but rather cryptlike tombs under the desert sands, one contained the mummy while the second is substantiated as the tomb for the ka.

So little is really known about the religious customs that any conjecture is plausible and all are debatable. In fact, less is known about the religious aspect of the Pharaohs than about their individuality. The life, times, achievements, and identity of the Pharaohs are nebulous to varying degrees in the early dynastic periods.

The difficulty in developing a clear picture of the first three dynasties and their points of differentiation continues into the Fourth Dynasty. Here again, a point of controversy exists in deciding if Pharaoh Snephur, or Snofru, should be regarded as the first King of the Fourth Dynasty, or placed in the Third Dynasty. The consensus of opinion apparently favors Snofru as the last King of the Third Dynasty. Remarkably, Egyptologists credit three pyramids to this ruler: the pyramid at Meidum, the bent pyramid, and a third, known as either the Northern Stone Pyramid or simply the Pyramid of Dahshur. Each of the three pyramids has its individual characteristic, which strongly supports the theory that the evolution of pyramid-construction methods significantly reflects a philosophical and/or political change.

According to archaeologists, a significant alteration occurred in the design of the step pyramid at the turn of this dynasty. The steps of the pyramid were filled in, producing four smooth faces, forming what has become classically known as the "true" pyramid. Egyptologists believe that they have found the transition from the step pyramid to the true pyramid by investigating the badly damaged pyramid at Meidum.

In its present condition, this structure resembles a high, rectangular tower rather than a pyramid. This pyramid, about 30 miles south of Memphis, is apparently patterned after Zoser's. The pyramid at Meidum seems to have undergone several transformations during its construction. Experts have concluded that the pyramid was first built with two, three, and then four steps. After this stage it was enlarged to a seven-stepped structure, which was then enlarged to eight steps. The actual height it eventually reached is not known, but the inclination of the steps is approximately 75 degrees, and its base may have been 473 feet square. Evidently, the seven-step design was intended to be the finished pyramidal form. Other considerations suggest the eight-step pyramid as the final version. However, for reasons still unknown, the steps were filled in with local stone, and the entire structure was then covered with a smooth facing of Tura limestone. Thus, according to authorities, the step pyramid was transformed into a geometrically true pyramid.

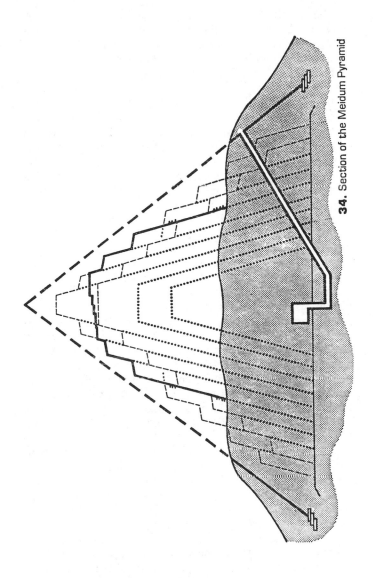

34. Section of the Meidum Pyramid

139

The possibility is very strong, based on records referring to several pyramids of Snofru, that not only was this pyramid at Meidum built by or for him, but also a group of two other pyramids, located 28 miles north of Meidum at Dahshur. One of these pyramids, popularly known as the bent pyramid, is also identified as the false, rhomboidal, blunted, or the South Stone Pyramid because of its relative location to the second of the group. The bent pyramid seems to have been initially planned as a geometrically true pyramid, but the builders changed the slope angle at the midpoint height of the pyramid. Hence the word "bent" is used to describe it. One reason postulated for the change in the angle of inclination from roughly 54 degrees, 31 minutes to 43 degrees, 21 minutes is that for some unknown reason it had to be hurriedly completed, so for the sake of efficacy the angle was decreased, thus proportionately decreasing construction time.

A better reason, however, derives from the Egyptians' basic theological philosophy that the pyramid shape had a deep religious significance. By developing the pyramidion symbol of Ra into the grave marker and tomb of the Pharaoh, as stated earlier, the high priests seemingly proclaimed the ultimate statement of their achievement of political influence through their religious power. As becomes apparent by analyzing the profile of the bent pyramid, the priesthood of Ra had at this stage acquired even greater political power. To signify their expanded status they applied a clever modification to the basic pyramid shape in order to accentuate the symbol of their sun god.

The impression one receives when viewing the bent pyramid is that of the Benben or pyramidion elevated on a pedestal. Thus the true reason for the bent pyramid's shape may in fact be the recording of the historical event for all in the land to see that the Ra priesthood had acquired and established a major increase in power. Confirmation of this theory may be punctuated by the second pyramid in the group at Dahshur, known as the Northern Stone Pyramid. This pyramid is nearly of the same angle of slope, 43 degrees, 36 minutes, as the top portion of the bent pyramid and may be the simple reiteration of the achievement of the engineers of the high priests of Ra.

It is reasonably clear that the sun-worshipping priests attained greater eminence during the reign of Snofru. Continuing this logic, it might be quite possible that this event spurred the impetus to "modernize" their symbol and that the pyramid at Meidum, possibly an early Third Dynasty step pyramid, was used as a full-scale model to test the feasibility of constructing a smooth-faced pyramid. If this were the case, the pyramid at Meidum probably had to be increased in height by adding the eighth step. This was necessary to prove their engineers' theory that the angle of inclination of the facing stones was all that was required for cohesion, without the necessity of cement bonding. This construction test, using an existing step pyramid during Snofru's reign, may be responsible for providing the erroneous clues that identify him with this pyramid at Meidum.

Once the engineers proved the feasibility of constructing a smooth-faced pyramid, they probably built the Northern Stone Pyramid next, but it turned out not to have the same effect—possibly due to the change, for some engineering reason, in the slope angle. The total engineering effort resulted in the pyramid of Snofru, and this Bent Pyramid exemplifies the perfect amalgamation of science and religion to produce a functional structure.

Regardless of whether Snofru is assigned to the end of the Third Dynasty or the beginning of the Fourth Dynasty, he is generally lauded as the founder of the Fourth Dynasty. The Fourth Dynasty is renowned for its burst of splendor in constructing the largest pyramid in Egypt—one of the Seven Wonders of the World. This structure is interchangeably referred to as the Great Pyramid of Giza or the Pyramid of Cheops—"Cheops" being the Greek form of "Khufu," who is thought to be the son and successor of Snofru's throne. However, Manetho claims that an intermediate Pharaoh between Snofru and Khufu reigned for a few decades.

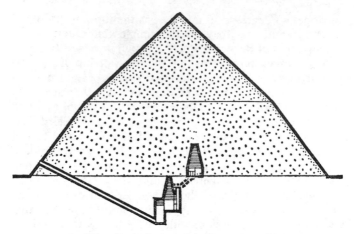

35a. East section of the Bent Pyramid

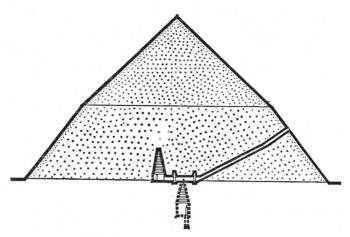

35b. South section of the Bent Pyramid

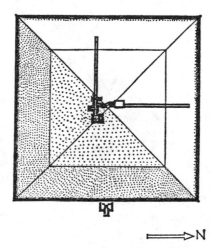

36a. Plan of the Bent Pyramid

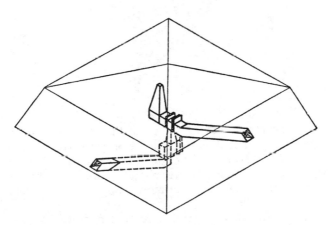

36b. Perspective of Bent Pyramid showing entrances and chambers

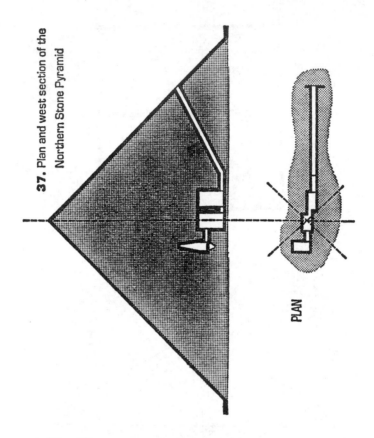

37. Plan and west section of the Northern Stone Pyramid

PLAN

The Westcar Papyrus indicates that Khufu was the son of Snofru, and apparently there is no doubt among Egyptologists that this is accurate. This papyrus is thought to date from the second intermediate period, about the Twelfth Dynasty, and may certainly be a copy of an older document.

Herodotus claims that Khufu was a cruel Pharaoh who locked up the temples of the gods; he decreed that it was unlawful for Egyptians to worship the gods because their total time should be spent in the service of the Pharaoh.

Manetho states that Khufu showed insolence toward the gods, and yet he is credited for writing a sacred book —now lost—that was regarded by Egyptians as a work of great importance. Even though later tradition regards Khufu as tyrannical, especially toward religion, he nonetheless was revered for many generations after his death. The mortuary service records almost twenty priests worshipping his spirit as late as the second succeeding dynasty. In fact, the worship of Khufu was reintroduced in the Twenty-sixth Dynasty—some two thousand years after his death!

The "facts" concerning Khufu's reign are only gleaned from much later dynasty myths and legends along with the writings of Manetho and Herodotus. From these records, Egyptologists confidently present him as a vigorous and powerful King, with his fame preserved by the singular achievement of constructing the largest pyramid in Egypt, surpassed by no other.

In actuality, contradiction is plainly evident in manuscripts discussing Khufu. Within the same manuscripts one can read that Khufu is wicked and impious, and then again he is hailed for his pietism in writing what was considered an important sacred book.

Different interpretations of ancient records contain minimal knowledge about Khufu and at best provide a sketchy profile of him. He reigned anywhere between twenty-three and sixty-three years in duration, had several wives, and sired many children. Several monuments throughout Egypt bear his name, which indicates he sponsored building projects. Archaeologists attribute several tombs to Khufu's family, his priests, and officials; however, inscriptions in these tombs do not detail any events of Khufu's reign, nor indicate his personality or character traits.

I suspect that the worship, and possibly deification, of Khufu for nearly two thousand years may be the testimonial to his true character. One is led to accept that he was really benevolent, because no evidence provided by Egyptian history substantiates the stories—as penned by classical authors—of Khufu's being an oppressive tyrant. There is more documentation alluding to his humanity, goodness, and religiousness than to his ruthlessness, cruelty, and despotism. In later dynasties, Khufu's name became a powerful charm, and was actually carved onto scarabs used as amulets. It is more reasonable to consider that Khufu was divine during his reign, and that his benevolence perpetuated his cult through successive millennia.

Some scholars argue quite convincingly, it is true, that Khufu was indeed a despot. He was hated by his subjects because he not only closed their temples, but also enslaved the entire nation to work on his building projects, especially his great tomb. Herodotus claims that Khufu was so despised by the people that in later dynasties the Egyptians were not very willing to mention his name. In addition, the pyramid was named after Philition, a shepherd grazing his cattle at the time of its construction. There is some evidence of a revolt by the Egyptians that brought about a concerted effort to eradicate evidence of Khufu throughout the land. This postulated revolt would explain, according to some scholars, the condition of the Great Pyramid at Giza—stripped of all statues, stellae, and ornamentations; defilement of the tomb was complete when the mummy itself was destroyed. The fervor of the revolt was not confined to Giza, but was widespread in Egypt. This theory may explain why so few records of Khufu are available.

The mortuary priests of Khufu obviously had to go into hiding during the revolt, to save their lives and, more importantly, to ensure the perpetuation of Khufu's existence for eternity, which was the specific duty of their office. These priests and their succession of apprentices not only promulgated knowledge of Khufu's existence, but also quite likely developed propaganda to counteract the aftermath of the revolt. The propaganda could have been so effective that by the Twenty-sixth Dynasty Khufu was worshiped as a demigod, and anything associated with him became a powerful charm.

On the other hand, both Manetho and Herodotus could have gotten their information concerning Khufu from a group of Egyptian priests having a quarrel with the Khufu priests, and the story they documented may be not at all true. Nonetheless, most of the records of these historians concerning Khufu and the Great Pyramid are considered accurate by classical Egyptologists. These Egyptologists are quite aware of the specific criticism that constantly accuses them of willingly accepting hearsay as fact.

As corroborated evidence to justify accepting the historians' statements, Egyptologists point to red ocher paint marks in the Great Pyramid as "confirmation" that Khufu built this pyramid. These markings are found on blocks comprising the walls of the five upper compartments in the King's Chamber. These upper compartments are considered stress-relieving spaces, possibly designed to circumvent the collapse of the ceiling under the weight of the pyramid. The markings are believed to have been painted on the blocks at the quarry site, and one of these quarry marks is zealously accepted as the glyph for Khufu's name.

This meager evidence is proof positive to Egyptologists that the Great Pyramid indeed belongs to Khufu. The fact that the Great Pyramid is devoid of carved or painted inscriptions, except for these quarry marks, raises suspicion regarding the Egyptologists' justification in positively identifying this pyramid. It could be that the quarry mark translated as the name of Khufu may actually be a mason's written incantation worshipping the creator of the universe. The quarry mark in question is read as Khnum-Khufu; it actually translates to "Khnum Protects," and is frequently found not only among pyramid quarry marks but especially at Sinai and in the quarry near Tell el-Amarna.

Khnum was the ram-headed god acknowledged by the Egyptians as the creator of the universe, and was

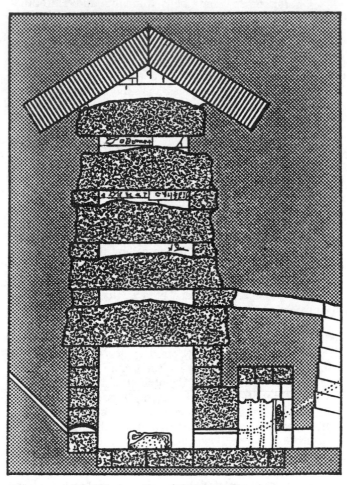

38. West section of the King's Chamber

also the specific deity for the city of Khufu's birth. This piece of information is extremely important when the dating of the Great Pyramid is analyzed in the next chapter, where we study the possibilities of the pyramid being many

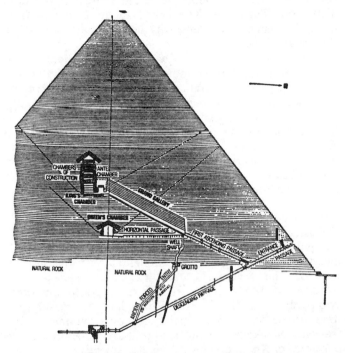

39. West section of the Great Pyramid

millennia older than the currently accepted date. It may simply be an absurd coincidence that, upon becoming Pharaoh, he took on or had conferred upon him the title of "Protector"—hence his name, Khufu.

In addition, his title very possibly incorporated the symbol for his birthplace—Khnum, or the Ram—and it is therefore quite logical for one of his newly acquired Nebti names to read Khnum-Khufu. However, Khufu's glyph symbol then would have been identical with the most revered incantation to the creator of the universe.

Because the phrase Khnum-Khufu was already designated to the ram-headed god, Khufu's Nebti name was in sacrilegious conflict with the liturgy to the most high God. Therefore, Khufu had to drop Khnum from his Nebti name, explaining why he is usually referred to simply as Khufu.

The obscurely located quarry mark, positioned so as not to be seen, further indicates the probability that it was a liturgical mark rather than the Pharaoh's symbol. This odd occurrence may be inadvertently misdirecting Egyptologists in assigning the Great Pyramid to Khufu.

The Great Pyramid could already have been an ancient structure in Khufu's time, as documented in an otherwise obscure, insignificantly regarded inscription called the Inventory Stele. The largest of the three pyramids comprising the Giza complex, the Great Pyramid, is already in existence when the story on the Stele takes place. According to the inscription, Khufu built his pyramid alongside the Great Pyramid, known then as the temple of the goddess Isis, and then he built another pyramid for his daughter, also alongside the temple. This curious inscription on the Inventory Stele may even indicate that Khafra and Menkeura, currently assigned to the other two pyramids at Giza, may not have had the treasury, the time, or the power to construct their own pyramids. Khafra and Menkeura might simply have taken over the pyramids of Khufu and his daughter, respectively.

For some inexplicable reason, Khafra, considered to be the son of Khufu, does not immediately succeed his father. Instead, his reign follows that of Dedefra or Radadef, who in every respect—outside of his pyramid and a portion of his statue—remains in obscurity.

Dedefra built his pyramid less than six miles north of the Great Pyramid, and it appears to have been finished in granite. Because of its ruinous state, it is considered and therefore called the Unfinished Pyramid at Abu Roash.

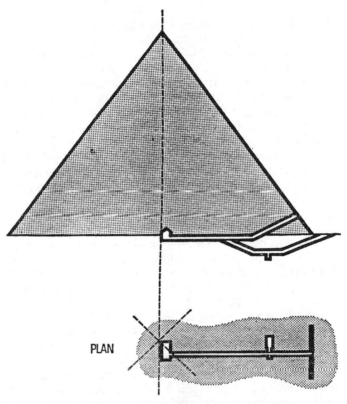

40. Plan and west section of the Pyramid of Khafre

The second largest pyramid at Giza is ascribed to Khafra or Chephren. It appears taller than the Great Pyramid because it is situated on slightly higher ground; its illusion of greater height is further enhanced by the steeper slope angle of its sides. Extremely little is known about Khafra, and in chronological sequence he is more or less accepted as the third Pharaoh in this dynasty. Khafra's name translates as "the sun god is his glory," and his pyramid is closely situated just to the southwest of the

151

Great Pyramid. Regardless of the implications interpreted from the inscription of the Inventory Stele, authorities completely discount its validity. Egyptologists expound as fact that Khafra actually built his pyramid; and they discredit the theory that the pyramid belonged to his father and he simply took it over. Herodotus claims that Khafra received the same condemnation as his father, Khufu, because Khafra continued his father's persecution of the gods and their worship.

The exterior of Khafra's pyramid is somewhat unique in two respects: It is faced with two different types of stone, and most of its facing is still intact. The outer casing remaining intact near the apex is Tura limestone, while the casing at the base is red granite.

It is thought that during the time of Khafra the Sphinx was carved from a monolith left as surplus by the builders of the Great Pyramid. The Sphinx is a recumbent lion with a human head. Although in disrepair, the symbol of royalty is well portrayed by the beard on its chin, the cobra on its forehead, and the royal headdress of the Pharaoh. When completed, the Sphinx probably had a covering of plaster, and was painted with royal colors. The altar and shrine between its paws is thought to have been constructed by the Romans.

The Sphinx is believed to have been dedicated to the four aspects of the sun god, which are: the rising sun, the setting sun, the apogee sun, and the creator sun. It is a colossal figure, nearly seventy feet high and over two hundred feet long; its weight is conservatively estimated to be hundreds—if not thousands—of tons. In ancient times, Egyptians referred to the Sphinx as simply *uh*, meaning "hewn thing"; and later generations referred to it as "the image of the rising sun god." It is believed that the face on the Sphinx was either intended to be that of Khafra or was rechisled during his reign to resemble him.

The question concerning whose face the Sphinx bears the likeness of becomes minor in comparison with other questions. One of the more important ones concerns

the existence of a deep quasitomb shaft in the middle of
its back. One answer suggests that the great mass of rock
initially contained the shaft before the Sphinx was carved.
A second answer proposes that the shaft was put in after
the Sphinx was carved, possibly in the quest for hidden

41. The Great Sphinx of Giza with granite altar
and the stele of Thutmose IV

treasure chambers. Third, it is contended that the shaft
was built in conjunction with the carving of the Sphinx.
The shaft is considered to have been designed to support
a giant ankh.

An equally persistent question, regarding the purpose

153

of the Sphinx, is also answerable in several ways. The first offers the mythology of the early Egyptians with a lion as the guardian of secret places. This mythology dates back to the Ra priests of On, who incorporated the lion as guardian of the underworld gates into their solar creed. The lion, symbolized by the Sphinx, retained its function as a sentinel, while the human features represent the sun god.

An inscription on a stele dating back to the time of Khafra depicts the Sphinx as saying: ". . . I protect the chapel of thy tomb. I guard thy sepulchral chamber. I ward off the intruding stranger. I hurl the foes to the ground and their weapons with them. I drive away the wicked one from the chapel of thy tomb. I destroy thine adversaries in their lurking place, blocking it that they come forth no more. . . ." Thus, simply stated, the Sphinx could be seen as performing a function equivalent to our contemporary scarecrow, warning trespassers that they are close to hallowed grounds.

The second suggested reason for the purpose of the Sphinx asserts that it was utilized as a gigantic altar, on and around which great ceremonial functions were performed.

A third answer is metaphysical in content, but more consistent with the mystery and wisdom of the Ra priests. Madame Blavatsky, in *The Secret Doctrine,* Vol. II, equates the Sphinx to the simorgh or the Persian roc, and the phoenix. She quotes from *Oriental Collections,* ii, 119:

> When the simorgh was asked her age, she informed Caherman that this world is very ancient, for it has been already seven times replenished with beings different from men, and seven times depopulated; that the age of the human race, in which we now are, is to endure seven thousand numbers, and that she herself had seen twelve of these revolutions, and knew not how many more she had to see.

This could very clearly indicate that the Sphinx represents the embodiment of the prophecy for the future, which could be the successive destruction and reproduction of the world—believed by many to be effected by a fiery deluge, followed in turn by a watery one. This then decisively establishes the prophecy of several cycles of death and revival.

An archaic speculation that is based on the writings of Lamblichus states that the Sphinx was the true admittance to the Great Pyramid. This Neoplatonic philosopher describes initiation ceremonies taking place in underground chambers having connection via passageway to the Great Pyramid. The entrance to these chambers is believed to be between the front paws of the Sphinx, and barred by a bronze door that could be opened only by a "master" who knew the operation of the secret lock. Within the Sphinx proper there is believed to be a network of labyrinthine passageways weaving through galleries and chambers, and ultimately linking with a subterranean chamber in the Great Pyramid.

Once gaining admission, the initiate must be guided through the labyrinth, in order to avoid wandering around ceaselessly and ultimately ending up at the beginning. The portal, with its bronze door, remains hidden; and evidence of its existence might be so obscured that it may never be found. Because of this, the generally accepted premise of the antagonists of this theory is that it does not exist.

There is more than mere speculation suggesting that chambers exist under the Sphinx and the Great Pyramid. The evidence of these chambers is deduced from a stele found near the Sphinx; the stele depicts a scribe following a priest possibly in a chamber under the structures. This stele projects its great importance because it is one of the rare drawings portraying perspective! This alone indicates very strongly that the chamber or chambers existed and are discoverable.

Many metaphysical schools propound that the priests of Ra instigated the erection of the Sphinx as a symbol of strength and intelligence. This priestcraft, knowing

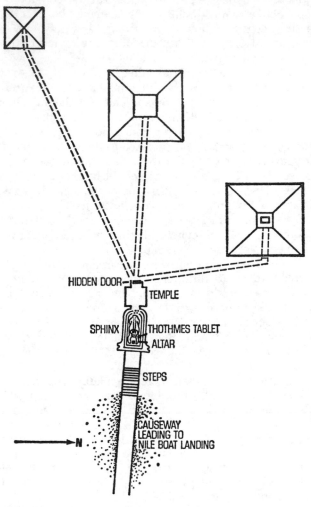

HIDDEN DOOR

TEMPLE

SPHINX

THOTHMES TABLET

ALTAR

STEPS

N

CAUSEWAY
LEADING TO
NILE BOAT LANDING

4'2. Plan of theorized passageways leading from the Sphinx
to the three pyramids at Giza

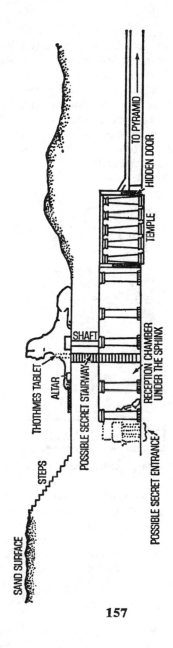

43. South section of theorized chambers and passageways beneath the Sphinx

157

that the male-female polarity was balanced in the gods, symbolized this truth in the Sphinx, with its half-masculine and half-feminine characteristics.

The mystique of the Sphinx originates in antiquity and is not a fabrication of our current millennium. It is exemplified in the dream of Tuthmosis IV of the Eighteenth Dynasty, and is recorded on a red-granite stele that is perched between the paws of the Sphinx. Deciphering the stone's inscription unfolds the story of why Tuthmosis gained ascension to the throne:

44. A stele portraying perspective

One day when he was still a prince, Tuthmosis decided to rest during a hunting expedition. He fell asleep in the shade of the Sphinx and had a dream in which the Sphinx promised to reward him with the double crown of Egypt if he were to clear the sand away and restore the majestic beauty of the Sphinx. The remainder of the inscription is too worn to relate just how the promise was fulfilled; but apparently it was, because Tuthmosis IV became Pharaoh; and a later dynasty erected the huge seven-by-twelve-foot stele to record this historical pact.

The word "Sphinx" was applied by the Greeks to the Egpytian monument because it resembled their own mythical monster. The Greek Sphinx is a female creature with a human head and breasts and the body of a lioness. However, the Arabs referred to the Egyptian Sphinx as the *Father* of Terror.

The successor of Khafra is Mycerinus or Menkeura, probably the brother of Khafra. This Pharaoh had a mild disposition, and it is said that he reopened the temples and permitted the people to once again worship their gods. He also devoted vast sums of money to the oracles, and made compensation to those men whom he felt had been unjustly dealt with by his predecessors. Menkeura is considered to have made the most just decisions of all Pharaohs before him. However, it is generally agreed that Menkeura's reign marks the decline from the level of achievement reached by his predecessors, and continues through to the end of the Egyptian dynasties. Although he was a good Pharaoh, he did not have complete control of the country's resources, as did his intrepid predecessors.

The decline is quite visible in Menkeura's pyramid—the smallest of the three in the Giza group. His is not only inferior to the other two in size, but also in the accuracy of construction.

Colonel Richard Howard-Vyse succeeded in entering the chambers of Menkeura's pyramid in 1837. He found parts of a wooden coffin in the upper chamber with an inscription that verified that it was Menkeura's burial chamber. He also found parts of a body wrapped in a course, yellow woolen fabric. In a lower chamber, Vyse found a magnificent, although empty, basalt sarcophagus. Colonel Vyse shipped the sarcophagus to England on a merchant vessel in 1838. The ship was lost with all hands in the Mediterranean, and the sarcophagus went down with the ship.

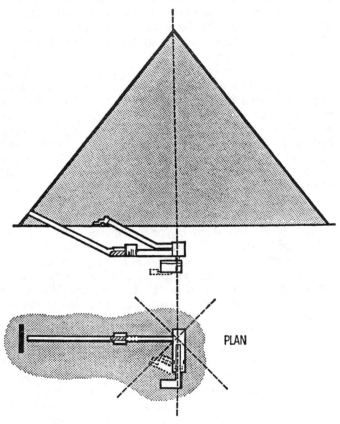

PLAN

45. Plan and east section of Menkeura's Pyramid

Archaeologists feel certain that the civilization of Egypt reached its apex during the Fourth Dynasty, under the combined reigns of Khufu and Khafra. These Pharaohs obviously mastered a beneficent manipulation of the land and the people. It is even suggested that the Egyptian civilization began an immediate decline from the moment Khafra died. Several Pharaohs are thought to succeed Menkeura, closing the Fourth Dynasty—which will forever be referred to as the Pyramid Dynasty.

By the time the Fifth Dynasty developed, religious decadence is plainly evident by deviation from the standard pyramid-shape tomb. The Fifth Dynasty shows a resumption of pyramid-building practices, but they were extremely inferior, and many are little more than mounds of rubble. However, the temples and mortuary buildings of this dynasty were lavishly decorated with great artistic quality.

Vertical columns with hieroglyphic inscription become a structural innovation within the chamber walls of the pyramid. The translation of these inscriptions first found in the pyramid of Unas is now known as the Pyramid Texts. Subsequent texts are again found in over a half-dozen pyramids of the Sixth Dynasty.

The purpose of the Pyramid Texts was to insure that the Pharaoh had a happy afterlife. Each text, translated from the individual pyramid, consists of a collection of spells rather than being a continuous narrative. Although the spells apparently are not arranged in any order, very few are found in every pyramid, and a total of more than seven hundred spells has been collected.

By the close of the Sixth Dynasty, the kingdom had fallen apart to such an extent that the Seventh and Eighth dynasties were considered the "Dark Ages" of Egypt, where complete anarchy prevailed, and most of the land was uncultivated during the chaos.

The end of the Ninth Dynasty brings forth the revivification of the kingdom, where many branches of the arts prospered, and impressive changes occur in the design of temples.

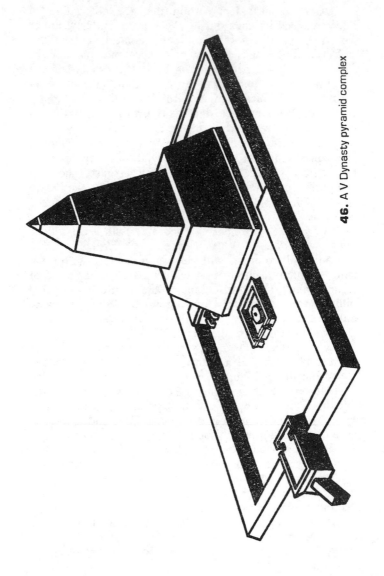

46. A V Dynasty pyramid complex

47. An XI-Dynasty pyramid complex

Throughout the remainder of dynastic Egypt, ending with the Thirty-first Dynasty, the use of pyramid tombs becomes increasingly popular; a person of far lesser rank than Pharaoh—as long as he could pay the price—constructed a pyramid tomb for himself. These pyramids, naturally, were inferior in quality and construction, and there were radical changes in their original design. Up until the Nineteenth Dynasty, the owner and his wife were buried in the chamber in their pyramid. By the Twentieth Dynasty, many generations of the same family occupied the same pyramid, and additional chambers were constructed when necessary.

The collapse of the Egyptian dynastic empire is thought to have been caused simultaneously by internal strife and invasions by surrounding countries.

Individual Pharaohs throughout various dynasties were able to acquire various levels of power and prestige based on their ability and inheritance. Religious influence and political control continually waxed and waned, with constant shift in the balance of power. Various Pharaohs are famous and remembered for their political administration, religious attitudes, conquests, and acquisitions, as well as for their ineptness, disastrous battle campaigns, and foreign entanglements.

A young Pharaoh by the name of Rathotis is considered to be the last Pharaoh of the Eighteenth Dynasty. His reign was somewhere between six and nine years, and his capacity as a Pharaoh is considered to be merely a rubber stamp for a reactionary movement that, at that time, was the real authority and control of Egypt.

This Pharaoh, who died at the age of nineteen, had an uneventful reign and would have remained obscure like most of his ancestors had his virtually intact tomb not been found.

The tomb of Rathotis was discovered in the famous Valley of the Kings, a valley where more than sixty royal personages were buried. His tomb remained basically undisturbed until November 4, 1922, when the vestibule to his tomb was discovered. Pharaoh Rathotis, better known as Tutankhamen, or King Tut, is world-famous. Tutankhamen's tomb, discovered by Howard Carter, was spared plundering because its entrance was further covered by rubble from the digging of a new tomb on the cliff over his.

Like the rest of the Kings buried in the valley, Tutankhamen's tomb was not found in a pyramid, as is popularly believed, but in a structure consisting of four underground chambers and a passageway dug below ground level.

Among the contents in his tomb was an interesting find—a wooden box standing near Tutankhamen's Canopic chest, containing two small coffins of wood. Inside each beautifully decorated wooden coffin was a coffin of solid gold. In each golden coffin there was a mummy of a prematurely born baby. The question is often raised as to whether or not these mummies belonged to Tutankhamen and his Queen Ankhesenpaaten. It is extremely likely that the babies were indeed theirs, because the Queen was of child-bearing age, they were married for a sufficient period of time, and, in addition, records indicate that they left no heirs.

The tomb of Tutankhamen yielded something far more important than priceless treasure and artifacts. His is the only known example of the magnificent splendor surrounding a Pharaoh and lavished upon him in death.

The wealth contained in the tomb of King Tut causes Egyptologists to lament about what has been lost to posterity from the pilfered tombs of the greater Pharaohs. However, the loss to posterity of tomb contents pales in importance when weighed against the disappearance of the tremendous knowledge, wisdom, and mystery that were responsible for the Golden Age of pyramid-building in the Fourth Dynasty. The metaphysical laws and principles possessed and taught by the original Ra priests are buried in obscurity through the culmination of predynastic Egypt along with its first four dynasties.

Instead of searching for treasure to satisfy our material desire, we must seek the more important treasure to satisfy our spiritual growth. If sufficient secrets are rediscovered, the prophecies that the Great Pyramid clearly states will be discernible to us, and we will be able to advance to our next level of evolvement. Some knowledge of where the secrets are, and how to recognize them, could very possibly be acquired by the thorough analysis of the measures comprising the Great Pyramid.

[7]

MILLIONS OF TONS, BILLIONS OF INCHES

Any theory dealing with the Great Pyramid attempts to either uncover the Pyramid's mystery and ultimately leads to the confirmation that the Pyramid underscores biblical truths and accuracies; or it endeavors to perpetuate the theory that the Great Pyramid was both a tomb for the burial of the Pharaoh as well as a monument to him. In the first case, measurements of the pyramid are used as proof of the theory; in the latter case, if and when the metrics are presented, it is done for purely factual purposes and conspicuously avoids any interpretation or correlation. In both cases, theories dealing with the Great Pyramid's meterology simultaneously leave the reader confounded and in awe. The awesomeness lies in the overall massive dimensions of the Pyramid and what it could all mean; while at the same time, the reader is bombarded by confounding lists and tables of dimensions, angles, and measurements that force him or her to simply gloss over, instead of wade through, them.

Ultimately, pyramid metrics must be dealt with in order to understand the reasons for the many proposed theories offered for the existence of the pyramid in Egypt.

Modern pyramid measurement and theory is historically accepted as dating from the last half of the eighteenth century. However, Professor John Greaves, an Oxford mathematician and astronomer of the early seventeenth century, is believed to have made the first distinct attempt to obtain correct measurements of the Great Pyramid. Professor Greaves, in his book *Pyramidographia* (1638), proposes his theory that the base measurement of the Great Pyramid was an intentional representation of the number of days in the year.

In the early 1760s, Nathaniel Davison, the British consul at Algiers, spent years investigating the Great Pyramid's interior, examining the various chambers and passageways.

French scientists and savants accompanying Napoleon's expedition to Egypt in 1797 also took measurements, and discovered two corner sockets of the pyramid. Subsequently, the other two corner sockets have been found, and it is now accepted that they were necessary in the pyramid's construction.

It was in 1799 that Captain Bouchard, a member of Bonaparte's expedition, found a 3½-by-2½-by-1-foot-thick basalt or diorite stele in the Rosetta branch of the Nile Delta region. This now famous Rosetta Stone records a trilingual decree thought to be proclaimed by Egyptian priests, issued at Memphis in the year 196 B.C., honoring Ptolemy V Epiphanes, King of Egypt from 205 B.C. to 182 B.C. It states, in brief, that he conferred great benefits upon the priests, set aside huge sums of money for the temples, gave tax rebates to the people, and performed engineering accomplishments for the irrigation system of Egypt.

This decree was simultaneously written in the Greek language, Egyptian hieroglyphs, and Enchorial or Demotic Egyptian. Demotic Egyptian became a new style of writing invented by scribes around 900 B.C., and is either an arbitrary or a conventional modification of the hieratic characters. The hieratic characters are a form of cursive writing developed from the degeneration of the pictorial character of hieroglyphics.

It should be noted that the two distinct forms of writing—hieroglyphs and hieratics—co-existed in Egypt well before 2600 B.C. Hieratics is considered to have had a subordinate position to hieroglyphs in that hieratics was used by scribes as a form of shorthand notation; the hieroglyphs were used more exclusively for religious documentation.

The credit for deciphering the hieroglyphs found on the Rosetta Stone is given to Jean-François Champollion, an Egyptologist. By 1824, Champollion had defined the hieroglyphic alphabet, established that Egyptians possibly made very frequent use of homophones, and demonstrated that vowels are indicated in many ways or omitted altogether. His decipherment became the foundation for the works of scholars in the reclamation of ancient Egyptian knowledge and information that otherwise would still lie hidden behind a meaningless, cryptic code.

Three famous men of Egyptology in the 1800s—Colonel Richard Howard-Vyse, Professor Piazzi Smyth, and Professor Sir W. M. Flinders Petrie—have contributed to the definitive measurements of the Great Pyramid.

The present overall, or perpendicular, height of the Pyramid is 450 feet, and it is conceived as originally having been as tall as 485 feet. The discrepancy in the height is either due to the erosion of the centuries or to the physical removal of its apical section. Its base covers 13.1 acres and is almost square, with each side averaging 755.5 feet in length. Although no two sides are absolutely identical in length, the difference between the shortest and longest side is only 7.9 inches. The entire structure, although slightly askew, is considered to have originally been oriented in perfect alignment with the four cardinal points.

The Pyramid is estimated to be constructed with as many as 2,500,000 blocks of hewn stone. Estimations concerning the weight of each block of stone range from

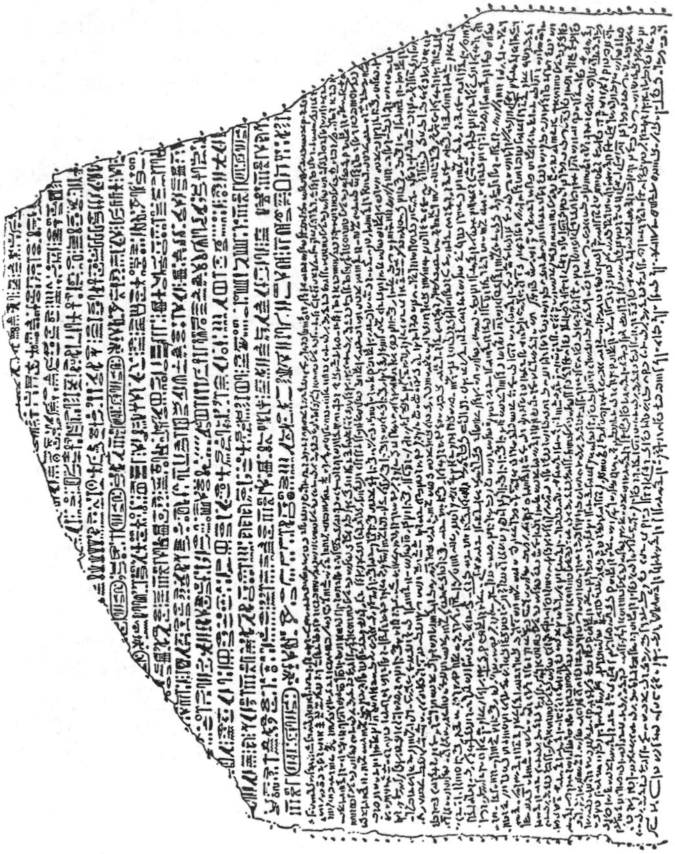

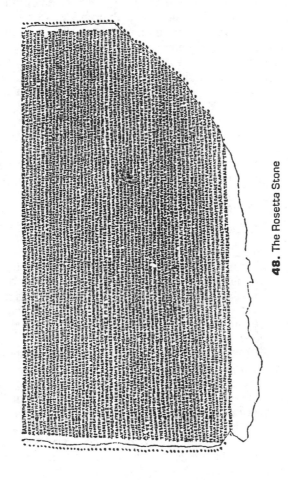

48. The Rosetta Stone

171

2 to 70 tons each, while the total weight of the entire Pyramid has been computed to be 5,273,834 tons. It is also thought that the center of its core consists of a nucleus of rocks whose size cannot be precisely determined.

It is believed that the entire Pyramid was originally faced with a casing of limestone cut from the Tura quarry. One of the few undisputed facts about the Great Pyramid's construction is that the perfectly worked casing stones, having a surface contact area of approximately 35 square feet, were so accurately cemented together that the joints between them have a separation of no more than .02 inch. This cement has such tenacity that fragments of casing stones exist, still being held together by the cement, although the rest of the blocks on either side have been destroyed. The entire casing of Tura limestone, with the exception of some pieces near the base, has been stripped by ensuing civilizations for the construction of their buildings. The casing stones rest on a platform slightly less than 17 inches thick, which in turn is on leveled natural rock of the Giza plateau. The platform projects a little over 16 inches beyond the casing stones.

The Pyramid has a limestone pavement surrounding it. This pavement or sidewalk, made of limestone, butts up level with the platform, and its existing width is less than 33.5 feet. On the east side of the Pyramid a basalt pavement begins where the limestone ends, and extends at least 90 feet to the east.

In 1859, John Taylor, a publisher and mathematician, in his book entitled *The Great Pyramid: Why Was It Built? And Who Built It?* proposed several theories based on the measurements of the Pyramid. One of Taylor's hypotheses was that the overall slope angle of each face of the pyramid was 51°51'14.3". He mathematically computed this angle from complex trigonometric calculations. Taylor is also credited with deciphering the figures of radishes, onions, and garlic used in hieratic writing as representing degrees, minutes, and seconds, respectively.

In the 1870s, Professor Piazzi Smyth, royal as-

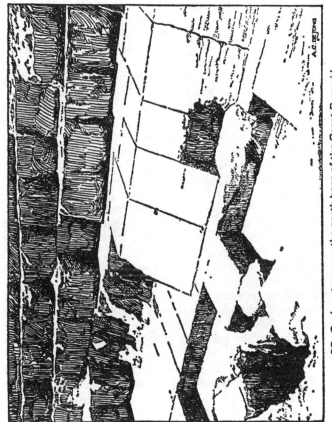

49. Casing stones on the north base of the Great Pyramid

tronomer of Scotland, confirmed this angle from a small, nearly complete casing stone with portions of all six originally worked sides. Professor Smyth considered it a most unique specimen, and in 1876 stated that it was: ". . . a completer example than is known at the present moment to exist anywhere else all the world over."

Waynman Dixon, a civil engineer, discovered this casing stone when digging into the rubbish mounds of the Great Pyramid. This discovery occurred during an Egyptian governmental project to acquire road-surface material, on which the Empress of France was to travel to visit the Pyramid in 1869. Mr. Dixon sent the stone for investigation to Piazzi Smyth, who found its ascending angle to be somewhere between 51°53'15" and 51°49' 55". The opportunity to analyze the angle of a casing stone in a laboratory setting allowed more accurate measurements, as opposed to those previously collected in the field from casing stones *in situ*. It must be kept in mind that because the Great Pyramid and its fragments are no longer in perfect condition, it is impossible to obtain precise numerical digits of linear and angular values. Hence, Professor Smyth accepted John Taylor's theoretical angle of 51°51'14.3" as an accurate mean.

When viewed from a distance, the Great Pyramid gives the impression of being preserved substantially intact. However, when viewed up close, one sees that it has suffered greatly from the elements and by the hands of the despoilers. It is estimated that a dozen or so courses below the capstone have been removed from the apex.

In the center line to the apex on the north face of the Pyramid is a large opening cut into the core, slightly below and to the right of the original entrance. Arab tradition explains that this aperture was made by Caliph Al Mamoun in the early part of the ninth century. His assault of the Pyramid on its north face confirms that traditional knowledge of entry into the Pyramid on the north side had remained accurate till his time. This forced entry into the Pyramid indicates that not only was the actual

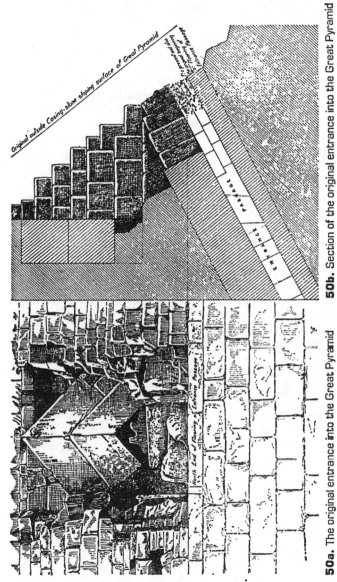

50a. The original entrance into the Great Pyramid

50b. Section of the original entrance into the Great Pyramid

175

door invisible when shut, but also that its true location had been forgotten.

Al Mamoun, Caliph of Bagdad, was the son of Haroun Al Raschid of Arabian Nights fame. In A.D. 820, with an army of workmen, Al Mamoun attempted to satisfy his quest for a fabled treasure secreted within the Pyramid. Among the many treasures listed in the tale, the ". . . instruments of iron . . . arms which rust not . . . and with glass which might be bended and yet not broken . . ." interested the Caliph most of all. His promise to pay his workmen only from the wealth stored in the Pyramid was the incentive for them to perform the rigorous and laborious task. But eventually the tunnelers became disenchanted; their motivation waned from the toil of digging 100 feet into the Pyramid without any discovery. Their discontent had them on the verge of giving up, when a distinct, muffled sound was heard and was surmised to be a large stone falling in a hollow place some distance past their tunnel!

It was, perhaps, a large block of stone that had fallen from the ceiling of the descending passageway leading from the original entrance. This stone might have fallen because it was dislodged by the vibrations of the excavation; or perhaps it was no accident, but providence was prepared to reveal one of its mysteries. It is hard to conceive, with the Pyramid so meticulously and substantially constructed, that a block of stone could have so easily and readily fallen out of its place. In any event, the workers were spurred on with rejuvenated cause to burrow toward the direction of the sound, and they finally broke through the wall surface and into the descending passageway.

Undoubtedly because the lower part of the descending passageway was blocked by that fallen ceiling stone, the Arabs explored upward and very likely found the method of opening the actual entrance door to the Pyramid. This door no longer is in existence, because it probably was carted away along with the casing stones when the Pyramid was stripped.

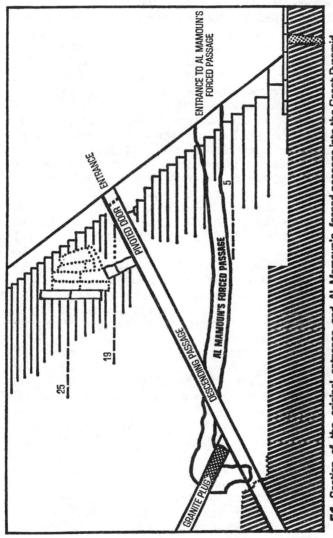

51. Section of the original entrance and Al Mamoun's forced passage into the Great Pyramid

Experts believe that the door was hung at the top of the entrance rather than at its side or bottom. It is also contended that the door, of such immense weight, was so well balanced that it could be easily pivoted out and upward, giving open access to the entrance passageway.

There is further reason to suspect that the ceiling stone fell not by accident, but by providence, because of what it revealed. The hole left by the stone clearly exposed another passageway in an ascending direction; but to the consternation of everyone, the ascending passageway was plugged by three huge granite blocks, each six feet long, wedged one behind the other. The disgruntled crew decided to burrow into the softer limestone and around the side of the plugs, rather than break their backs cracking them apart.

Once they got above the granite, they found the passageway still blocked, but this time only by limestone plugs, which they were able to break up and pull out. When they had finally cleared the ascending passageway, they proceeded along 110 feet of the unobstructed, though steeply inclined, highly polished white limestone passage. The workmen-turned-explorers emerged into a junction where a horizontal passage disappeared into the darkness, ultimately leading to what is now termed the Queen's Chamber.

Directly at this junction point, the explorers encountered a foreboding, well-like hole that is over 140 feet deep, which they felt vanished into the bowels of the Pyramid. Henceforth, this hole has been labeled the well shaft.

The explorers continued their ascent, no longer in an extremely cramped passageway, but now in one resembling a hall or gallery. It is about 6 feet wide, nearly 160 feet long, and 28 feet high, and its magnificence has earned it the title of the Grand Gallery.

At the end of the Grand Gallery the men had to surmount a 3-foot-high step, after which a low horizontal passage loomed out of the darkness. Stooping and

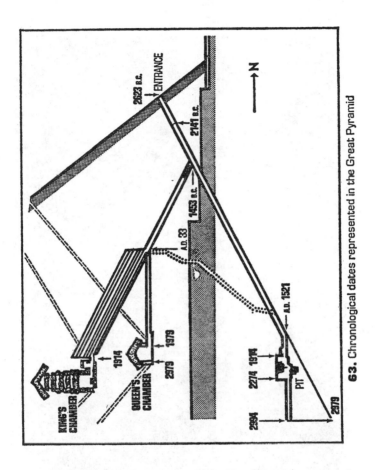

63. Chronological dates represented in the Great Pyramid

creeping through this, they entered a chamber approximately 34 feet long, 17 feet wide, and 19 feet high. This chamber (now the famous King's Chamber) was constructed using polished red granite blocks; and the walls, floor, and ceiling are at perfect right angles to each other. Much to the dismay of the Arabs, the chamber was thoroughly and absolutely barren save for ". . . an empty

179

53. Ascending view in the Grand Gallery

54. View of great step and passageway entrance leading to King's Chamber

55. West section of King's Chamber

stone chest without a lid" (now referred to as the sarcophagus or coffer).

Certainly the frustration level of Al Mamoun's workers had reached such a peak by now that they very probably scoured every accessible part of the Pyramid in a furious attempt to locate the treasure. The Caliph, in addition to being just as frustrated, was anxiously hopeful that his men would find the treasure tucked away in some nook or cranny; for he was afraid that if they did not, he would suffer the consequences at the hands of his crazed and angry workers. So, as an "insurance" plan in the face of the threat to his life and limb, Caliph Al Mamoun, in the dark of night, had part of his royal treasury buried in the masonry close to the end of their quarried passageway. The following morning he had to most assuredly convince his laborers to dig in that particular spot. Obviously they agreed, because they found the "planted" treasure, its appraised value amounting to exactly the sum that was owed to them for their many months of labor.

With his army of workmen satisfied, the Caliph returned to Bagdad, a disappointed but wiser man.

The preceding Arabian tradition is among the rarer ones accepted to be somewhat factual concerning stories about the Great Pyramid. In the tradition of their ancestors, Arabian writers have been known for conjuring up fabulous tales involving their Caliphs and the pyramids of the Giza complex. These notorious fables so obviously contain exaggeration of accomplishments that they are automatically discounted as fiction, even if they do contain a modicum of truth. What is undeniable in the Arabian story of Caliph Al Mamoun is that the environs of the Great Pyramid had been explored and were readily accessible in the ninth century; and most of what we know now was also known as late as A.D. 820.

The exterior and interior dimensions of height, width, length, and angulation of the Great Pyramid vary among authorities. The variations among measurements, ranging from feet to fractions of an inch, are a source of consternation; one is confused in attempting to derive the exact measurements of the Great Pyramid at the time of its completion. Its dilapidated condition, including many missing stones, is the primary reason for the discrepancy in the measurements.

Each Egyptologist taking measurements really has had no two distinct points between which to measure. For example, in determining the length of one of the Great Pyramid's base sides, some pyramidologists take into consideration an average thickness for the casing stones and therefore would add these amounts to the now existing base length. Other pyramidologists would measure the distance between the corner sockets, adding a considerable amount to the overall length; while still others theorize that the base of the Great Pyramid does not terminate or begin at the platform, but rather extends at least to the natural rock foundation of the Giza plateau, and perhaps even beyond that, causing an even more disparate base-length measurement.

In performing any linear measurements of length, width, and height, many an outstanding argument has developed into perpetuity because of the claims that the measuring device was not flush with, or aligned properly to, the end of the stone; and that the measurement over the course of great length was not perfectly perpendicular or parallel, and by the slight angulation of the measuring instrument, one was in effect measuring on a diagonal, thereby obtaining a larger value. Therefore, all measurements and angles mentioned in this book are based on either the more widely accepted values, or averages of them. They are intended to serve only as a guide in presenting theories, principles, and prophecies based on the metrics of the Great Pyramid. Mathematical computation based on given values will yield only approximate results to casually confirm what is presented here. In order to gain affirmation, one must go back to the original sources and wrestle with the mathematical manipulations of values used by them.

The first theory Mr. John Taylor made concerning

the Great Pyramid's measurement was that its overall height was twice that of the length of its base; and he hypothesized that this was directly correlated to the same relationship as that of the radius or diameter of a circle to its circumference. In both cases, the value of Pi is obtained, equaling 3.14159 . . . This value can be explained in another way—that is, the height of the pyramid is to twice its base length as 1 is to 3.14159 . . .

From this hypothesis, Taylor computed the slope angle of 51°51'14.3", which is commonly termed as the Pi angle. This Pi angle gives to the vertical height of the Pyramid the same ratio to its base as the radius of a circle is to its circumference. This value of Pi is shown to exist only in the Great Pyramid, and is found in no other pyramid of Egypt.

A series of questions arises as to the significance of this Pi value. Was it simply an act of coincidence, or was some genius at work in the design of the Great Pyramid? Was the genius expressing his or her wisdom and knowledge of Pi by incorporating it into the Pyramid's geometry, and therefore illustrating and embodying fundamental mathematical truth, without which the science and industry of today could not have evolved?

If the appearance of the value of Pi is mere coincidence, or a clever arithmetically computated correlation, then we should not expect to find this value reappearing within any other dimension of the Pyramid. However, it is indeed confirmed, not once, but many times. One confirmation of Pi is found in the cubic measurements of the granite leaf (discussed later on) in the antechamber leading to the King's Chamber. That is to say, height 48.57 inches times thickness 15.7 inches times width 41.2 inches, multiplied by 10,000, yields a very close approximation of the Pi value.

Another confirmation was determined by Piazzi Smyth. He derived it from the vertical height of the thirty-fifth building course divided by one tenth the horizontal distance, from this point, to the vertical axis of the Pyramid. He arrived at this computation by observing the thickness of the building stones. The Pyramid is built in horizontal courses of squared stones, and the thickness of these stones at the base is approximately 50 inches. As the height of the Pyramid increases in courses, the thickness of the building stones diminishes to 27 inches at the thirty-fifth level. There is then a sudden leap back to the 50-inch thickness at the thirty-sixth level, and the stones basically remain the same thickness along the remaining courses. Therefore, Smyth viewed this thirty-fifth course as an important indication, and when measuring the horizontal distance to the center line of the Pyramid from this thirty-fifth level, he found it to be 3652.42, or 10 times the number of days in a year.

Smyth also presented the confirmation of Pi as seen in the angular stones conspicuously protruding above the entranceway to the Pyramid. The stones are set apart from each other at an angle of 51°51'14.3", or the Pi angle.

Along with the value of Pi, another interesting value is apparently incorporated into the Pyramid. This is Phi (φ), better known as the Golden Section, which equals 1.6181818 . . . Phi, like Pi, cannot be arithmetically derived with great accuracy, and the proportions of the Pyramid incorporate the circumvention of complex calculations to arrive at a value for Phi.

It is recorded that the temple priests of Egypt informed Herodotus that the Pyramid was so designed that the area of any one of its faces was equal to the square of its height. Mathematicians have simplified the Pyramid's relationship by simply relating it to a right-angled triangle in which the base has a unit length of one, the height has a unit length of the square root of Phi, and its hypotenuse has a unit value of Phi (see Figure 56).

Mathematicians have also derived a useful formula demonstrating the relationship between Phi and Pi such that Pi is equal to 4 divided by the square root of Phi ($\pi = \dfrac{4}{\sqrt{\varphi}}$). Egyptologists have proven that the Egyptians fully understood the trigonometric properties of the 3-4-5

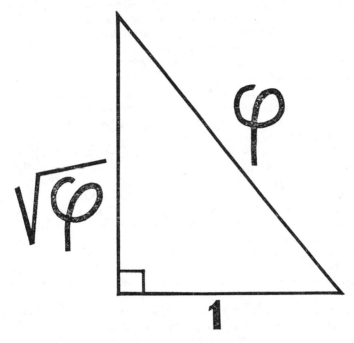

56. The Phi Angle

triangle from which can be extracted the valus of Pi and Phi. They also contend that many of the physical structures and artistic illustrations were designed and constructed with Pi and Phi purposefully included.

Interestingly, a well-known mathematician of the Middle Ages and a great Renaissance artist, engineer, etc., have incorporated the Golden Section in their works:

Leonardo Fibonacci was born in Italy around the twelfth century and had developed an additive series of numbers based on the equation of Phi + 1 = Phi squared ($\varphi + 1 = \varphi^2$). Known as the Fibonacci Series of Numbers (1, 2, 3, 5, 8, 13, 21, 34, etc.), it is a progression where each new number is the sum of the previous two, and their ratio comes closer and closer to the value of Phi.

The Fibonacci Series is typified in many natural formations, such as a great variety of seashells and antlers.

Leonardo da Vinci, the unparalleled genius of the sixteenth century, is credited with identifying the Phi proportion as the Golden Section, and some of his masterpieces were composed on its proportion.

Based on the knowledge that the proportions of the Great Pyramid define the value of Pi and Phi, Egyptologists got the idea to actively search for other possible correlations.

"The vertical height of the Pyramid multiplied by 10^9 equals the exact distance from the earth to the sun" is an oft-repeated and -written statement. As it turns out, however, this proportion is invalid for several reasons. First of all, to this very day, science still does not know for certainty what the exact distance is. Second, the trajectory of the earth is of an elliptical pattern around the sun, which means that at points along its path the earth will at times be closest to the sun and at other times will be at the farthest distance. Therefore, there cannot be an "exact" distance, but rather only a mean or average distance. Hence, to be accurate, the statement should be, "The vertical height of the Pyramid multiplied by 10^9, converted to miles, equals an approximate mean distance from the earth to the sun." This interesting correlation also has confirmation in other measurements of the Pyramid. However, Basil Stewart, writing in his book *The Witness of the Great Pyramid,* claims that the Pyramid's base plan, rather than its height, gives the mean sun distance, which he feels to be a truer value. Piazzi Smyth claims that the value can also be derived by either multiplying the height of the thirty-fifth building course by 10, or by taking the length of the antechamber and multiplying it by 100.

One of the confusion points in measurement of the Great Pyramid concerns the Pyramid or Sacred Cubit, and the Pyramid Inch. The development of the Pyramid Cubit and the Pyramid Inch was instituted by Professor

Piazzi Smyth as a standard unit to conform with Pi on the scale of the Great Pyramid. Through an elaborate process of logic, Professor Smyth determined that 999 Pyramid inches equals 1,000 regular or standard inches. Through the same elaborate process, he computed that the unit of measure used in the design and construction of the Pyramid was a cubit containing 25 Pyramid inches. For the sake of convenience, it would be best to assume, for the listing of measurements in this book, that a Pyramid inch is equal to a standard inch.

The Great Pyramid is geographically situated and oriented on the Thirtieth Parallel of latitude in Egypt, so as to have its apex at the central position from which an arc can be scribed, encompassing the whole Delta area. This Delta region is completely enclosed when the northwest and northeast diagonals of the Pyramid are extended to the arc. The Pyramid is also located on the meridian dividing the Delta into two equal parts. Professor Smyth points out that the position of the Pyramid indicates the center of the land mass of the earth.

It is contended by pyramidologists that the meridian (31° east of Greenwich) of the Great Pyramid is the most suitable zero of longitude for our globe. If the Great Pyramid is used as the center from which to draw two perpendicular lines on a map of the earth, the land mass and oceans are seen to be equitably distributed throughout the four quadrants. (See Figure 9.) The enigma of the Great Pyramid and its specific placement in Egypt naturally has caused brilliant minds to muse over its mass and external measurements for its relativity to that of the earth itself. Numerous mathematical analyses have been developed that show the Pyramid corresponding proportionately with earth, as well as showing correlations between earth and the solar system. Simply stated, pyramidologists believe that the Pyramid, in all its symbolism, represents *the laws* of the universe expressed geometrically.

An interesting collection of correlations to astronomy

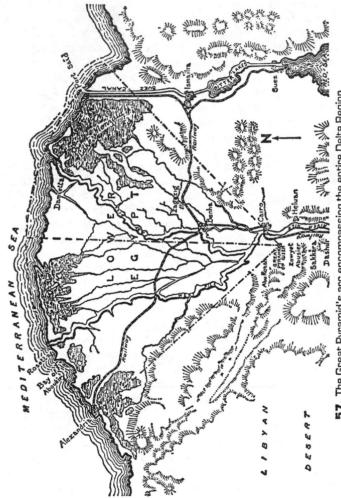

57. The Great Pyramid's arc encompassing the entire Delta Region

has been compiled since the late 1800s. A partial list of this collection is as follows:

1. Length of a base side (9,131 inches) divided by 25 inches or a cubit, equals 365.24, which are the days in a solar year.
2. The length of the King's Chamber plus half the length of the antechamber equals 365.24 inches.
3. A circle with the length of the antechamber (116.25 inches) for its diameter has a total circumference equaling 365.24 inches.
4. The width of the King's Chamber (206.066 inches) multiplied by the square root of Pi equals 365.24 inches.
5. Twice the length of the King's Chamber (2 times 412.12 inches) measured along the Grand Gallery's floor contains a vertical rise in that distance of 365.24 inches.
6. The total inch value of the base perimeter equals the number of days in a century.
7. The total inch value at the thirty-fifth-level perimeter equals the number of days in 80 solar years.
8. Twice the length of the base diagonal (2 times 12,913.26 inches) equals the number of years in the precession of the equinoxes and, in addition, equals the total inch value at the fiftieth-level perimeter.
9. Adding the length and the height of the King's Chamber, and dividing this value by its width, equals Pi.
10. Adding the length and width of the sarcophagus, or coffer, and dividing this value by its height, equals Pi.
11. One Great Pyramid face represents one curved quarter of the Northern Hemisphere.
12. The apex of the Great Pyramid corresponds to the North Pole, while the perimeter of its base correlates to the circumference of the equator.

191

13. The Great Pyramid is a perfect almanac register-
    ing the seasons of the year by functioning as a
    huge sun dial whose shadow indicates, among
    other things, the solstices and duration of the
    year.

French astronomer U. J. J. Leverrier, who discovered the planet Neptune by pure mathematical calculation, estimated the mean number of days in a solar year
to be 365.2421995949074 . . . while the figure computed from the Great Pyramid equals 365.24219866-
77311 . . . The overall difference between these two
values translates to approximately 0.08 second of a
year, which is slightly more than half an hour in one
cycle of the precession of the equinoxes—which is about
25,694 solar years.

Sir Joseph Norman Lockyer, an English astronomer,
mathematically computed the estimated number of days
in a lunar or a synodic month to equal 29.530588715.
The Great Pyramid indicates that the number of these
days equals 29.5305887150085. The difference is so extremely negligible that they can be considered to confirm
each other.

A curious contradiction exists regarding the Egyptian science of astronomy; even though some of the preceding points demonstrate the possibility that the Egyptians had firm knowledge of astronomy by designing it
into the dimensions of the Great Pyramid. Nonetheless,
Egyptians are thought to have been exceedingly backward
in astronomy; their meterology and division of seasons
in their system has convinced researchers that no true
system of cosmology could have originated among them.
These researchers indicate that Egyptian astronomy was
primitive. They substantiate this by explaining that the
Egyptian year was divided into three seasons: vegetation, harvest, and inundation. These seasons were each
4 months long, and had 30 days per month.

This contradiction apparently gives feasibility to an
old thought that states, "Even though the pyramids are in

Egypt, it does not mean they are of Egypt." Might this, therefore, clearly indicate that in Egypt there was a foreign influence that had superior knowledge, and that was responsible for the construction of the Great Pyramid? This is an extremely erudite question, and top priority must be given to find an answer. The answer is extremely significant, because it will bring about a definitive conclusion to many mysteries involving the Pyramid's existence.

The enigma of the Pyramid's existence in Egypt, with the postulations of its dimensions having cosmological interpretations, is paralleled by perhaps an even greater enigma once the internal structure is analyzed.

The entrance into the Pyramid is situated on the north face, slightly more than 55.5 feet above ground level, and approximately 23 feet left of the center. Thus the entranceway is situated on the nineteenth course of the existing 203 courses comprising the height of the Pyramid. The entrance becomes a descending passageway at an angle of 26°28′24″. The descending passageway is approximately 3.9 feet high and 3.4 feet wide, and travels a straight and true distance of a little over 343 feet. For about the first 25 per cent of its length, the passageway traverses through the Pyramid masonry, while the remaining 257-foot distance has been forced through the solid-rock foundation on which the Pyramid sits. The descending passageway then runs horizontally for 29 feet, where it finally opens into a subterranean chamber.

This chamber is roughly 100 feet below ground level, or the base of the Pyramid, and its area makes it the largest chamber in the Pyramid. It measures approximately 27 feet long, 46 feet wide, and 14 feet high. The roof and walls of this chamber are not too smooth, and in some places are uneven; but they are, nonetheless, square and level. In contrast, the floor is extremely crude and thought to have been left in an unfinished condition. Just before the horizontal portion of the descending passageway enters into the subterranean chamber, there is a small recess hewn out of its roof and west wall. Known as the little subterranean antechamber, it is surmised that the masons intended the subterranean chamber to begin at this point. Apparently changing their minds, the masons continued the passage a few feet longer, to where the subterranean chamber is now.

Entrance to the chamber is in the bottom east corner of the north wall. Directly in line with it on the south wall is another smaller, horizontal passageway only 29 inches square, measuring over 53 feet in length. This passageway is called the South Blind Passage, because it terminates abruptly, leading nowhere.

It is theorized that the Pyramid masons cut a shaft into the floor at the eastern part of the subterranean chamber. This shaft is 6.5 feet square, extending to a depth of 7 feet, at which point it becomes 4.5 feet square and runs 3.5 feet deeper. Colonel Vyse caused this shaft to be excavated to a depth of about 36 feet, in search of Cheops' sarcophagus. Vyse deepened this shaft because the writings of Herodotus mention the existence of a secret chamber in which Cheops is interred beneath the subterranean chamber. The excavation was originally intended to be 50 feet deeper, but was stopped when nothing was uncovered by the 36-foot depth. This shaft is now referred to as "The Pit," a term that has subsequently been used to designate the entire subterranean complex.

The most popular theory as to the function of the subterranean chamber is that it had originally been intended as the burial chamber. Possibly due to various reasons—one of which may have been a stifling and physically unbearable environment in which to excavate the necessary series of chambers, as well as the possibility of flooding—excavation may have been discontinued. The architect then might have had the revolutionary plan of forming the chambers and their passageways up into the very body of the Pyramid, and on different levels, rather than the contemporary underground plane. This would account for the unfinished appearance of the subterranean complex.

The possibility of work being abandoned provides us with a rational explanation of why the subterranean chamber gives the appearance of being upside down—that is, the upper portion of the walls and the roof are dressed, while the floor was left in a crude state. This would also explain the construction technique of the Great Pyramid masons, whereby upon excavating a large hollow area, they would then proceed to finish it by dressing the ceiling first, working down along each wall and finally dressing the floor. This reasoning is quite logical because more work would be entailed if the floor were finished first, causing the workers laborious removal of the rubbish cleared from the walls and ceiling.

Another possibility for the condition of the sub-terranean complex is worth mentioning. Apparently the genius of the Egyptian architects and builders of pharaonic tombs had been developed through the necessity of outwitting the tomb robbers, thus preventing them from gaining entrance to the sepulchered vaults containing the mummy and its treasures. By the time the Great Pyramid was constructed, the architects conceived the idea of deceiving the tomb robbers by expending the time, effort, and funds necessary to tunnel down into the bedrock and thereby excavate a rough chamber complex. This crudely finished room would thus appear to have been abandoned, and any tomb robbers gaining entry would then be misled into believing that the Pyramid was never completed internally, and that therefore no treasure or mummy existed.

The cleverness of the Great Pyramid masons is apparent in their concealing the entrance to the ascending passage in the ceiling of the descending passageway, nearly 100 feet from the entrance of the Pyramid. The ascending passageway has an angle of inclination equal to the angle of declination of the descending passageway, namely, 26°28′24″. The very first 18 feet of the ascending passageway's length is blocked up by three 6-foot-long granite plugs jammed one behind the other. These red granite blocks were probably cut out of boulder stones, and because of their intended purpose as plugs were not meticulously dressed.

There is a theory that claims that originally the granite plugs were actually spaced some distance one behind the other, and that several more limestone plugs of which we have no evidence today were spaced behind the granite plugs, extending the full length of the 125 or so feet of the ascending passageway. This theory develops from a bit of red granite cemented to the floor of the ascending passageway as found by Sir W. M. Flinders Petrie. He ascertained that this piece of granite about 2 feet distant fit the broken end of the third, or last, granite plug. In addition, Petrie saw a gap between the two granite plugs measuring approximately 4 inches. These limestone and granite plugs may have been jarred loose from their affixed point during an earthquake, causing them to slide one atop the other. The evidence for the limestone plugs develops from the previously mentioned story of Al Mamoun's workmen digging around the granite plugs, and then encountering limestone plugs, which they broke up into manageable-size pieces and removed.

The passageway above the granite plugs is approximately 3.5 feet wide by 3.75 feet high. It is lined with highly polished white limestone along its 110-foot length, where it terminates at a junction point.

At this junction a horizontal passageway, nearly 129 feet long and about 3.5 feet square, terminates at the bottom east corner of the north wall of the Queen's Chamber, which measures almost 19 feet long by a little more than 17 feet wide. It appears that the walls are limestone blocks that were once beautifully finished. The floor of the Queen's Chamber is roughly finished, as if a layer of polished stones were to have been laid upon it. This chamber is directly beneath the apex of the Pyramid, and level with the twenty-fifth course.

The ceiling of the chamber is constructed from sloping roof blocks at an approximate angle of 30°30′. The total

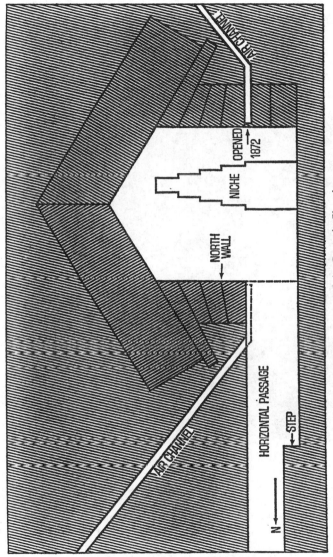

58. East section of the Queen's Chamber

AIR CHANNEL

ARCH TUNNEL

OPENED 1872

NICHE

NORTH WALL

HORIZONTAL PASSAGE

STEP

N

197

59. Interior view of the Queen's Chamber

height to the top of the ceiling ridge from the floor of
the Queen's Chamber is slightly over 20 feet. These roof
blocks overlap the width of the chamber, and extend
into the Pyramid's masonry more than 10 feet on either
side. They primarily act as cantilevers, reducing the
effective weight on the walls of the chamber by deflecting

the structural weight of the Pyramid's mass above the Queen's Chamber.

There is a recess in the eastern wall of the chamber called "The Niche." This niche is slightly more than 15 feet high, 5 feet wide at the base, and a little less than 3.5 feet deep in the wall. Its corbeled design of four overlappings reduces the width of the niche to 1.5 feet.

The most interesting feature of the Queen's Chamber are two air channels. Mr. Waynman Dixon originally discovered these air channels in 1872—one in the north wall and one in the south wall. They originally were not cut through the chamber walls, because a 5-inch-thick cover stone had to be broken to expose the mouth of each air channel. The air channels were each sculpted into a wall block and their mouth abruptly stopped, leaving 5 inches of thickness in the wall block. It is thought that these air channels had never been used, because there was no access to them from the Queen's Chamber. After the mouths of the air channels were opened by breaking through the wall blocks, they were found to be approximately 8½ by 8 inches rectangular. Both air channels run for a little over 6 feet before they angle upward toward the Pyramid faces.

Returning to the junction point, closer examination reveals that access to the passageway leading to the Queen's Chamber might have been covered by a portion of the floor of the Grand Gallery, which could have begun at the step terminating the ascending passageway. It is conjectured that when the entrance passage was constructed leading to a vertically descending shaft, which was excavated near the junction point, a portion of the Gallery flooring was removed, exposing the passageway to the Queen's Chamber. This vertical shaft has been termed "the Well" and has an opening of more than 3 feet in diameter.

John Greaves, in the seventeenth century, explored the well shaft and found notches opposite each other in the sides of the shaft. He descended about 60 feet, with the assistance of these notches, to where the shaft enlarges—now termed "the Grotto"—which is situated at exactly the first course.

Nearly a century later, Captain G. B. Caviglia, in analyzing the mysteries of the Well, accidentally unplugged it. He succeeded in descending 125 feet below the Grotto, where he found it to be plugged with mostly rocks and sand. Air was so scarce at that level that it was difficult to breathe, and candles constantly flickered.

Caviglia thought that the Well shaft and the descending passageway might intersect, so he decided to clear the descending passageway of deposits of rubble accumulated over the millennia. He thought that some of this rubble could be accounted for by the excavations of Al Mamoun's men, who dumped the stones down the descending passageway rather than carry them outside the Pyramid.

At a point about 50 feet before the descending passageway levels out, Caviglia noticed a small opening in the west wall of the descending passageway leading into a hole. His curiosity about the hole impelled him to dig deeepr into it. After digging a few feet, he became aware of the smell of sulphur, and it occurred to him that this might be from his attempt to clear the air in The Well shaft by previously having burned pieces of sulphur. Thus encouraged, he dug farther, dislodging the last portion of the blockage of the Well shaft, and as the rubbish was being cleared away, he indeed had not only excavated the Well shaft, but also found where it joined the descending passageway.

At the same time, Caviglia also uncovered another mystery to add to the already lengthening list of Great Pyramid mysteries. Who dug the Well shaft—and why? The most obvious theory for the purpose of the Well shaft was as a tunnel for tomb robbers. As plausible as this theory at first appears, experts are unable to readily accept it because of certain characteristics of the Well shaft.

The intersection of the Well shaft with the descending passageway—and at the other end, its junction with the horizontal passageway, ascending passageway, and Grand Gallery, along with its Grotto—indicate that the Well shaft could not have been dug by grave robbers, because it has been carefully constructed at these points.

The final branch at the junction point, the Grand Gallery, while at first glance appearing to be a chamber, on further analysis reveals itself as a mere continuation of the path established by the ascending passageway. The Grand Gallery travels nearly 160 feet along the same angle of inclination as the ascending passageway. It is almost 6 feet wide, and its 28-foot-high, corbeled structure gives it unparalleled magnificence. The distance between the walls is reduced to 3.5 feet in 7 overlapping steps containing a total of 36 polished limestone slabs.

The floor of the Gallery has a central passage about 2 feet wide. Along each wall is a ramp traveling the entire length of the Gallery. Each ramp is about 18 inches wide and 2 feet high, containing 27 alternately long and short oblong holes, or slots, on its top surface. These slots are between 8 and 11 inches deep, and three of the original slots are missing. The missing slots are thought to have been carved into a piece of dressed stone, covering the entrance to the horizontal passage of the Queen's Chamber. This stone may have been broken up and disposed of as rubble in previous centuries. The implications of the purpose of the Grand Gallery are many, and are discussed in the following chapter.

The Grand Gallery terminates at what is called the Great Step, which is a huge, 3-foot-high stone forming roughly a 6-by-8-foot platform. This Great Step is calculated to be centrally in line with the apex and the Queen's Chamber, and is positioned at the fiftieth course.

From the Great Step is a 3.5-foot-square, horizontal passageway just over 4 feet long, leading to a small room called "the Antechamber." The Antechamber is about 9.5 feet long, 5 feet wide, and 12.5 feet high. The walls in the interior are finished with polished red granite.

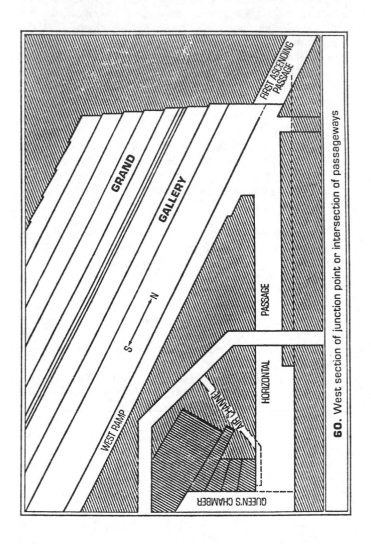

60. West section of junction point or intersection of passageways

Just 2 feet inside the Antechamber hangs a granite leaf, or slab, suspended 3.5 feet above the floor. It was first precisely described by Professor Greaves, who called it "the Granite Leaf" because the word "leaf" reminded him of a sliding door in the locks of canals.

The Granite Leaf is actually two stones, one above the other, which fit into grooves in each wall of the chamber. The grooves do not extend down to the floor, but rather stop approximately 3.5 feet above it. Each granite leaf is a slab approximately 5 feet wide, 2 feet high, and 16 inches thick. There is a space between the Granite Leaf and the north wall of the chamber of nearly 22 inches. The space between the ceiling of the chamber and the Granite Leaf is nearly 5 feet. Three other grooves along the walls of the chamber are 21.5 inches wide and extend into the floor of the chamber.

The construction of the Antechamber indicates to Egyptologists that it really was not a chamber, but rather a very complicated sliding-door system that completely blocked any possible entry into the "burial" chamber that lies beyond.

Ludwig Borchardt, a German Egyptologist around the turn of the century, developed an interesting idea that a pulley system could have been used to seal the entrance-way to the King's Chamber with huge granite slabs. A French Egyptologist, Georges Goyon, added his hypothesis of how the passage would be additionally plugged and sealed, to that of Borchardt's theory.

One interesting feature regarding the mysteries of the Pyramid is a small, projecting "boss" on the upper stone of the Granite Leaf. This boss is a small protrusion, 1 inch thick and horseshoe in shape. Could it have been intended to indicate the standard measure of the Pyramid mason's smallest unit of length—the Pyramid inch? The size of this boss, 5 inches by 5 inches equals 25, which is the exact number of Pyramid inches in a Pyramid cubit. Further confirmation is found in this theory by the fact that the boss is 1 inch to the side of the true center of the Granite Leaf, and that it is

5 inches above the joints between the leaves. The less venturesome experts explain away this boss as merely a projection left on the leaf for the purpose of lifting it; and similar projections are found on stones throughout the Pyramid.

Another low passageway leading from the Antechamber, exactly aligned with the passageway entering the Antechamber, and of the same 3.5-foot-square size, travels nearly 8.5 feet, where it opens into the King's Chamber. The length of the King's Chamber is slightly more than 17 feet, its width is twice its length, and its height is about 19 feet. The entire chamber is constructed of granite, and it has been computed as having a cubic volume twice that of the Queen's Chamber. The position of the King's Chamber within the Pyramid proper is about 30 feet south of the apex, and its length straddles the center line of the apex in proportionate ratio two-thirds east to one-third west.

There is a sarcophagus—also called a coffer or chest —near the corner of the west and north walls. Because of its unusual placement relative to sarcophogi in other pyramids, which are more centrally located within their chambers, it is the considered opinion of nearly all experts that the coffer had been moved at one time from its original position. Since there are no marks of any kind on the floor to indicate from where the coffer was moved, it is impossible to reposition it. It is judged that the coffer was carved out of one tremendous, red granite block, and hollowed out by chiseling and drilling. It was so perfectly created that, upon striking it with the hand, it still gives out a clear, bell-like sound.

The length of the coffer is situated along the width of the chamber. The external size of the coffer is about 7.5 feet long, slightly over 3 feet wide, and about 3.5 feet high; while the inside measurements are: length, about 6.5 feet, width, over 2 feet. Its internal depth is just under 3 feet, which indicates a thickness of its sides to be slightly less than .5 foot, and the thickness of the bottom is slightly more than .5 foot. The sarcophagus is

Elevation, looking West.

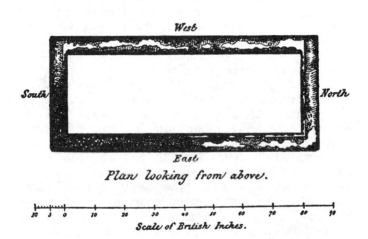

Plan looking from above.

Scale of British Inches.

61. The coffer

polished smooth, both inside and out, leaving it totally void of all hieroglyphs. However, some speculate that underneath the bottom surface a long hieroglyphic inscription will be found once the huge-tonnage weight can be sufficiently lifted to see the undersurface. A large piece of one of its corners has been cracked away. There is an indication of a ledge cut along the top edges of

205

the coffer; this implies that it had a lid at one time, which could have been slipped on from only one end, and fixated by three set pins. This lid seems to be lost forever. Some Egyptologists even assume that the coffer may at one time have been beautifully engraved, and to confirm Herodotus' writings that Khufu was a despised King, they postulate that the people may have stripped his Pyramid and polished his coffer smooth of all inscription, along with all the walls in the Pyramid, defiling his tomb as much as possible and thus eradicating any knowledge of him!

The ceiling of the King's Chamber is a series of five huge granite decks spaced one above the other, with a sixth and final deck constructed from sloping roof blocks similar to the ceiling of the Queen's Chamber. (See Figures 58, 59.) This multilayered ceiling construction is termed "the Chambers of Construction." It is possible that the specific construction of this ceiling was designed to greatly reduce the possibility of a cave-in from the immense weight above the King's Chamber.

Nathaniel Davison, in the summer of 1965, discovered and examined the lowermost Chamber of Construction. He was searching for secret galleries, passageways, or chambers within the Pyramid, and while he was at the top of the Grand Gallery he noticed echoes coming from somewhere overhead. Investigating what might have been responsible for the echo, he spotted a rectangular hole about 2 feet wide at the ceiling of the Gallery where it joined the wall. Accomplishing the herculean feat of reaching the nearly inaccessible hole, he climbed into it, crawling 25 feet to a chamber that was only slightly taller, but still not permitting him to stand. Its width and length later turned out to be the same as the King's Chamber. He investigated the floor of this squat chamber and noticed that it consisted of nine roughly hewn granite slabs, and he determined that he was actually on the ceiling beam of the King's Chamber.

He shortly made a second amazing discovery: The ceiling above his head consisted of another row of granite slabs similarly constructed as the one below. He found no treasure or signs of a secret passageway, but his effort was rewarded by having this space named "Davison's Chamber."

Captain Caviglia, apparently convinced that he would uncover a secret room, decided to tunnel through to the south wall of Davison's Chamber. It yielded no results and he simply gave up. His efforts were followed by those of Colonel Richard Howard-Vyse.

Colonel Vyse had the floor in front of the Niche in the Queen's Chamber dug up, and found nothing but an old basket. Refilling the hole, he had his workmen excavate the back wall of the Niche itself, which again yielded no discovery. Then the colonel decided to scrupulously investgiate Davison's Chamber, but his workmen could not effectively enlarge a crack found in the ceiling. Vyse used gunpowder, blasting his way upward, which gave them access to the second Chamber of Construction, directly above Davison's Chamber.

Analyzing this new chamber, Vyse found that the floor consisted of 8 blocks of granite, forming the ceiling of Davison's Chamber. The ceiling of the second chamber was constructed of 9 blocks of granite. Colonel Vyse decided to continue his trek upward, and found a third Chamber of Construction, with 9 granite ceiling blocks, a fourth Chamber of Construction, with 8 ceiling blocks, and a fifth and final Chamber of Construction. This final chamber did not have a flat ceiling, but a "ridge" roof consisting of 8 granite slabs, sloped to each other, forming a peak at the ceiling. All of the chambers have an approximate distance of 3 feet between them, except for the fifth chamber, which has a peaked ceiling allowing a person to stand. (See FIG. 38)

With the first Chamber of Construction setting a precedent in being named after Davison, its discoverer, Colonel Vyse, named the second, third, fourth, and fifth Chambers of Construction for General Arthur Wellington, Admiral Horatio Nelson, Lady Ann Arbuthnot, and Colonel Patrick Campbell, respectively.

Vyse also discovered the red ocher paint marks in the upper four Chambers of Construction, discussed in the previous chapter.

Colonel Vyse is credited with another remarkable discovery in regard to the two air vents in the King's Chamber. Although it was actually Professor John Greaves who identified the two 9-inch-wide openings in the north and south walls of the King's Chamber as possibly being air vents, these air channels were not completely verified until an assistant of Vyse located the ends of these vents on the respective faces of the Pyramid. Vyse was responsible for clearing these vents and allowing more fresh air to circulate in the King's Chamber.

Among all the discoveries and accomplishments of Colonel Vyse, the most significant find in the Pyramid —more valuable than any treasure, and causing the greatest astonishment and debate—was a large piece of wrought iron. John and Morton Edgar, in their book *Great Pyramid Passages,* state:

> It is significant to note, in this connection, that a piece of *wrought iron* was found in the Great Pyramid by one of Col. Howard Vyse's assistants, Mr. J. R. Hill, during the operations carried on at Gizeh in 1837. Mr. Hill found it embedded in the cement of an inner joint, while removing some of the masonry preparatory to clearing the southern air-channel of the King's Chamber. This piece of iron is probably the oldest specimen in existence; and Col. Howard Vyse was fully cognizant of the importance of the find. He forwarded it to the British Museum with the following certificates:
>
> "This is to certify, that the piece of iron found by me near the (outside) mouth of the air-passage, in the southern side of the Great Pyramid at Gizeh, on Friday, May 26th, was taken out by me from an inner joint, after having removed by blasting the two outer tiers of the stones of the present surface of the Pyramid; and that no joint or opening of any sort was connected with the above-mentioned joint, by which the iron

could have been placed in it after the original building of the Pyramid. I also showed the exact spot to Mr. Perring, on Saturday, June 24th.— J. R. Hill."

"To the above certificate of Mr. Hill, I can add, that since I saw the spot at the commencement of the blasting, there have been two tiers of stones removed, and that, if the piece of iron was found in the joint, pointed out to me by Mr. Hill, and which was covered by a larger stone partly remaining, it is impossible it could have been placed there since the building of the Pyramid. —J. S. Perring, C.E."

"We hereby certify, that we examined the place whence the iron in question was taken by Mr. Hill, and we are of opinion, that the iron must have been left in the joint during the building of the Pyramid, and that it could not have been inserted afterwards.—Ed. S. Andrews,— James Mash, C.E."

Because of its very rarity, some have been inclined to doubt the authenticity of this piece of iron; but Professor Flinders Petrie rightly defends it.—"The vouchers for it are very precise; and it has a cast of a nummulite on the rust of it, proving it to have been buried for ages beside a block of nummulitic limestone (which forms a large part of the core masonry of the Pyramid), and therefore to be certainly ancient. No reasonable doubt can therefore exist about its being a really genuine piece used by the Pyramid masons." The Scriptures make mention of artificers in iron, before the Deluge—Gen. 4:22.

The British Museum received this remarkable artifact and neglected it on the basis of its being the only piece of iron ever found, and consequently its significance was undervalued. But this singular piece— preserved for posterity because it had been encased in mortar for millennia, saved from oxidation and crumbling into dust—proves that iron was in existence during a time when Egypt was considered to only have been at the copper stage! The implication of this piece of iron could very well answer the long-standing question of the composition of tools required to work on the masonry.

As noted earlier, the coffer in the King's Chamber was found to have been carved out by means of chisel and drill. Petrie made mention of such telltale marks, as well as horizontal grinding lines. He feels that the masons used jeweled bronze saws, the existence of which he surmised from green stains in saw cuts and on grains of sand imbedded in the cuts. According to Petrie, it would only be a matter of a simple transition from a linear saw to a tubular drill bit up to 18 inches in diameter (the smallest hole found in granite is 2 inches in diameter). In addition, he further estimates that it would require approximately 1 ton or 2 tons of pressure on the drill bit to effectively drill a hole.

John and Morton Edgar were English ministers of the faith. In the early 1900s, during one of their several investigative trips to the Great Pyramid, they found numerous pieces of stone with as many as 2 large-diameter drill holes through them. The purpose of the granite stones with the many holes through them still lies beyond our comprehension, as does the ability of making these drill holes with jewel-tipped tubular drill bits. It would be more logical to consider the drilling and cutting devices to be jewel-tipped iron, because iron could bear the static force of 2 tons of pressure applied in the cutting process.

The question of copper vs. bronze vs. iron becomes another item in the list of Great Pyramid mysteries.

Judgment of each and every Great Pyramid mystery must be held in abeyance until irrefutable evidence is found; it is nothing more than an exercise in futility to theorize about what may have been. The majority of theories about the Great Pyramid put forth the argument that the Pyramid was specifically and purposely built by an ancient civilization, to record and document their knowledge and set forth prophecies, by which future man could advance and achieve the ultimate goal: universal wisdom.

{8}

CHAMBERS AND PASSAGEWAYS
TO THE FUTURE

The Great Pyramid, as a silent enigma in Egypt since recorded history, has continually awakened and sharpened the mind of scientist, philosopher, and layman alike. The relative correlations between the outer measurements of the Pyramid to our universe must naturally lead an inquiring mind to consider the possibility that the Pyramid's dimensions transcend mere coincidence.

Masoudi, an Arab historian circa A.D. 900, explains that the Pyramid was built to contain all the different arts and sciences known to the architects of the Pyramid: the knowledge of the stars and their cycles, the history and chronicle of times past, and predictions of things to come. He claims to have seen old records referring to the Pyramid as a carefully planned and carefully constructed monument, representing fundamental laws of nature, including a codex of the wisdom of the ancients.

Tantalized by Masoudi's statements, and coupled with the apparent significant relationship of the Pyramid's dimensions to a portion of the world's cosmology, investigators began to study the Great Pyramid more closely in the 1800s. If, for example, the relationship of

211

the Great Pyramid's dimensions to the world's astronomy were valid, there might even be a way of determining exactly when the Pyramid was constructed.

Sir John Herschel, son of Sir William Herschel, the discoverer of the planet Uranus, assumed in the early 1800s that the constructional phases of the Pyramid had to correlate with the position of the stars at the time in order for it to be perfectly aligned, and for its passageways and chambers within to be specifically oriented. His assumption was based on his theory that the descending passageway served as a sighting tube that was built to be in line with a polar star.

Sir John Herschel began to calculate to see if he could determine which polar star—and what date of that star—would be in line with the descending passageway. He determined that the descending passageway pointed to Alpha Draconis (or the Dragon Star), and that the date this occurred was 2170 B.C. The other date that Alpha Draconis would be in line with the passage angle was 3440 B.C. But 3440 B.C. did not "fit" in the estimation in the early 1800s that the Pyramid had been built about 4,000 years before. Therefore, Sir John and his supporters felt fairly confident that 2170 B.C. was the exact date of construction of the Pyramid, even though Egyptologists had set the building of the Pyramid to be between 4760 B.C. and 3360 B.C.

Piazzi Smyth, in viewing the then current disagreement between Sir John's date and that of the Egyptologists, considered the question with an inquiring mind. The application of logic, along with his extensive knowledge of astronomy, enabled him to confirm that the date of 2170 B.C. was, indeed, accurate. He questioned why the entrance to the passageway was aimed so low (26°) as to have only a relatively minor polar star, Alpha Draconis, aligned with it; and reasoned further that possibly the passageway was so designed as to align with *both* a minor and a major polar star simultaneously.

Piazzi Smyth made a logical assumption that there had to be a notable zodiacal or equatorial star aligned southward also. He found this to be the zodiacal group of stars called Pleiades, with its main star Alcyone, or Eta Tauri. According to Smyth, when Alcyone of the Pleiades was direcly at the apical point of the Pyramid, the Dragon Star was 12 polar hours ahead and perfectly aligned with the passageway. The exact relationship between these two stars occurs only once every 25,827 years—or one sidereal cycle. Therefore, according to Smyth, with this coincidence of the stars in the heavens in the autumn of 2170 B.C., the angle of the descending passageway was being constructed. At the present time, however, there is no confirmed date as to when construction of the Pyramid was begun, nor when it was completed. Not even carbon dating has proven satisfactory.

By the late 1800s a new branch of pyramidology was beginning to develop, which I call "pyramathology." It is a study of the significance of the Great Pyramid, using mathematical calculations. The pyramathologists start with certain unproven premises and seek to validate them through mathematical extrapolations of measurements in the Great Pyramid.

Although this system has precipitated numerous frauds and hoaxes, it can also yield insights into both the history and the construction of the Great Pyramid. For example, I question the assumption that the Pyramid was constructed in the Fourth Dynasty, and instead look to a much earlier construction date, based on evidence that even in the Fourth Dynasty the Egyptians considered the Great Pyramid to be an ancient marvel (the Inventory Stele—see Chapter 6). Coupled with Herschel's conclusion on the zodiacal relationship between the two stars, Alpha Draconis and Eta Tauri, necessary in aligning the angle of the descending passageway—and in turn perfectly aligning the base of the Pyramid—it is reasonable to assume that the Pyramid was built prior to the Fourth Dynasty. Applying pyramathology and the direct statements of the ancient Egyptians, we can see that the passageway was not constructed in 2170 B.C., as is commonly theorized, but was actually constructed in 27,997 B.C., which is exactly one sidereal cycle removed from 2170 B.C., when the two stars were previously aligned.

Other pyramathologists may argue this point further, and fix the date at the second, third, fourth, or more sidereal cycle removed from 2170 B.C.—which would gives the dates of 53,824 B.C.; 79,651 B.C.; and 105,478 B.C. At this point it is really impossible to argue the dating, for any date is actually a moot question whose answer awaits specific factual evidence as proof. Nothing less can ever be accepted. Nevertheless, the pyramathologists pressed onward, seeking additional confirmation within the structure of the Pyramid that they could point to as "factual" truth.

The length of the sidereal cycle, calculated or approximated along several principles, varies between 25,000 years and 26,000 years. The pyramathologists, on the other hand, applying John Taylor's principle of 1 Pyramid inch equaling 1 year, arrived at a sidereal cycle of 25,826.52 years. This figure was derived by measuring the diagonal of the base of the Pyramid at 12,913.26 inches. Since the Pyramid has two diagonals, they doubled it, thereby indicating the Egyptian knowledge of the sidereal year, called "the grand chronological dial of the Great Pyramid."

Professor Hamilton L. Smith showed that the perimeter of the Great Pyramid at the level of the King's Chamber equaled approximately 25,827 inches, verifying that the builders of the Pyramid built into its geometry many redundancies, to insure the fact that the key points would not be overlooked.

Professor Smith further relates that if the vertical height of 5,813 inches of the Pyramid is proportionate to the sun distance, then the vertical height from the King's Chamber level to the apex, 4,110 inches, proportionately indicates the radius of the circle of the precession of the equinoxes in years.

In noticing how the metrics of the Pyramid related

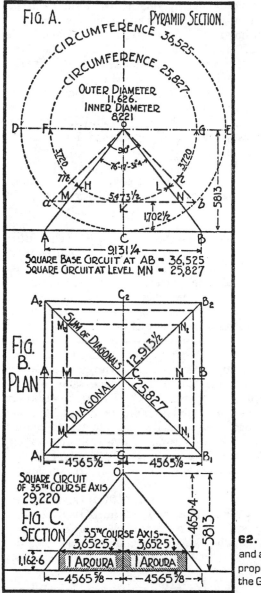

62. Geometrical and astronomical proportions of the Great Pyramid

to astrological times, the pyramathologists mused if the Pyramid may also relate to sacred and prophetic times.

An Englishman, Mr. Charles Casey, in communicating with Piazzi Smyth, stated: ". . . unless the Great Pyramid can be shown to be Messianic, as well as fraught with superhuman science and design, its 'sacred' claim is a thing with no blood in it . . ." This challenge gave Smyth the impetus to more specifically derive dates from the internal metrics of the Pyramid, to "prove" that even though the Pyramid was built by human hands it was really divinely inspired.

Through a complicated system of logic and philosophical thought, many pyramathologists had concluded that the junction point of the ascending passageway, the Grand Gallery, the Well mouth, and the Queen's Chamber passageway signified the year A.D. 1. Measuring back down the ascending passageway, and still back farther, up the descending passageway toward the main entrance —a total of 2,170 inches—Smyth found marks on the walls of the descending passageway. These marks are simply lines ruled at right angles to the floor, from top to bottom. These lines in themselves were originally unnoticed until this measurement was made, because in the immediate vicinity there are two joints perpendicular to the passageway, and also two vertical joints. Piazzi Smyth interpreted these joints as intending to draw attention to the importance of the scored lines. This, then, was the 2170 B.C. date long sought for confirmation. However, fixing the date at the junction point to be A.D. 1 rested solely on the fact that scholars in the nineteenth century had the Nativity occurring at that date; while the Nativity is now considered to have occurred in 4 B.C. due to finer chronological measurements. With this revamping of chronological dating totally unrelated to pyramidology, the pyramathologists of the early 1900s reviewed the dating at the junction point, and redefined it to be about A.D. 30. Hence, in the light of revised chronological dating, a group of pyramathologists believe that a date of about 2141 B.C. is more precise than 2170 B.C. In fact, they

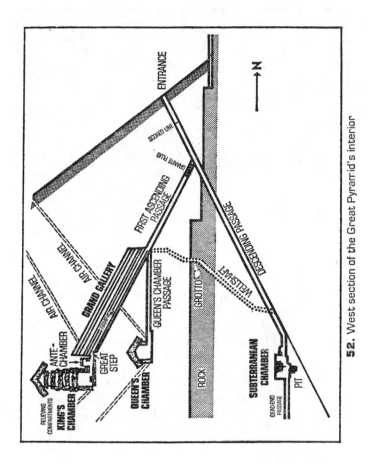

52. West section of the Great Pyramid's interior

claim that the scored lines are the datum line for the midday of March 21, 2141 B.C.!

Measuring the distance back up along the descending passage, from the scored lines to the entrance, indicates the summer of the year 2623 B.C., which is interpreted to be the year in which construction of the Great Pyramid

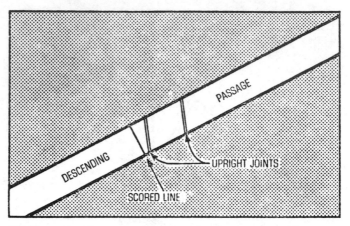

64. The scored line and upright joints of the descending passageway

began. This, then, has become the distinctive point of the interpreted symbolism: Every inch into the pyramid along the passageways and chambers reveals either a successive year into the future or into the past.

The basic platform on which the pyramathologists stand in accepting that the Pyramid represents a Bible of stone is that the results of the dimensions of the Pyramid's interior follow a historical sequence that is clear-cut and that requires no interpretation.

Mr. Adam Rutherford, in the first volume of a five-volume set of works called *Pyramidology,* states: "An ancient Egyptian tradition says 'The plans were let down from heaven,' or as we would say today, they were Divinely inspired."

Robert Menzies of Edinburgh, Scotland, is credited with discovering the Christian, or Messianic, interpretation of the Great Pyramid. It was Menzies' philosophy that the passageways and chambers in the Great Pyramid were the secrets of God's plan and its progression through the ages. He claimed in 1865 that the passage system is a chronological representation of Scripture prophecy, with the Grand Gallery denoting the Christian dispensation; the ascending passage representing the Mosaic dispensation; while the other passages typified nontrue religions, or paganism, or simply human histories and nothing more.

However, long before the time of Menzies there was already identification of the Great Pyramid with biblical prophecy. Scripture scholars had already indicated that the Bible revealed the essential purpose of the Great Pyramid in Egypt. Many verses in the Bible contain allegorical references to the Pyramid, which pyramathologists accept as proof that the Pyramid is a Bible in stone, and that Christ's Messianic mission was foretold at least 22 centuries before His birth.

The key verse, around whose philosophy the pyramathologists base their belief that the pyramid is a Bible in stone, is Isaiah 19:19:

> In that day shall there be an altar to the Lord in the midst of the land of Egypt, and a pillar at the border thereof to the Lord.

The interpretation of the word "pillar" is translated from the word *mastaba,* which could be equated to the word "monument"; therefore it is deemed that Isaiah talks about the "monument" in Egypt, which is identified as the Great Pyramid.

The word "altar" is also interpreted as meaning "monument," because there are two types of altars mentioned in Scripture—altars of sacrifice and altars of witness. Appropriately, pyramathologists have accepted the words "altar" and "pillar" to be representative of the word "monument," which in turn is equated to the Great Pyramid. Pyramathologists argue that Isaiah is discussing one and the same building, rather than two different edifices.

The above-quoted verse can be logically read as an altar constructed somewhere in the middle of Egypt; and an entirely different monument, or pillar, constructed at the border of Egypt. The pyramathologists contend that this interpretation is not correct, for there is really no contradiction involved in considering the two structures mentioned in the verse as being one and the same. Their remarkable position cannot really be effectively argued against, because the Great Pyramid apparently does sit in the center—or the political and economic part—of Egypt; and yet at the same time, its physical and geographical location does place the Pyramid at the border of Egypt, where the sands of the Sahara Desert extend many hundreds of miles to the west, across the African continent.

Another allegorical reference involves Jesus Christ and the Pyramid, further implicating the divinity of the structure. This is found in Ephesians 2:20:

> And are built upon the foundation of the apostles and prophets,
> Jesus Christ himself being the chief cornerstone.

In fact, there are quite a few scriptural text references to Jesus Christ as the living cornerstone, foundation stone, top stone, or capstone, and the Pyramid itself, whether allegorical or not.

For further research enlightenment of Scripture that are believed to relate in some way to the Pyramid, I refer you to the following texts in Scripture: Psalms 118:22; Isaiah 28:16; Romans 9:33; Isaiah 8:14–15; Matthew 21:42–44; Mark 12:10–11; Luke 20:17–18; Acts 4:11; 1 Peter 2:4–8; Job 38:4–6; and Zechariah 4:7.

The strong possibility that the Bible reveals the essential purpose of the Pyramid, and that the Pyramid is a Bible of stone, gave birth to an entirely new concept in attempting to understand what is now called the divine plan of the ages. Accordingly, pyramathologists believe that the infinite wisdom of God is portrayed with a few simple passageways and chambers, and that the Great Pyramid's symbolical features and important time marks indicate the plan of salvation and the various dispensations of mankind from beginning to end. These pyramathologists have read into and defined the symbolism of the passageways and chambers of the Great Pyramid.

John and Morton Edgar, in their book *Great Pyramid Passages,* have clearly defined the internal symbolism of the Great Pyramid. In their résumé of proofs:

1. The descending passageway is the world on its downward course to the pit of destruction (subterranean chamber). The pit symbolizes Gehenna—the condition of death from which there will be no awakening. The entire complex represents the plane of Adamic condemnation to death.

2. The ascending passageway symbolizes the Law Dispensation of the Israelites. This Dispensation is a divine period of 1,647 years, during which the whole nation of Israel was subject to the Law. This time period began at the Exodus from Egypt in early 1615 B.C., when the Passover was first observed, and ended with the Crucifixion of Christ in early A.D. 33.

   The ascending passageway also symbolizes the Law Covenant which offered eternal life on the human plane with earthly blessings, rather than offering a blessed spiritual life with a heavenly inheritance. 33½ inches before the end of the ascending passageway would indicate the Death and Resurrection of Christ, ending the Law Dispensation and beginning the Gospel Dispensation.

   The Divine Law blocking the way of life which the Law Covenant offered to the Israelites is believed represented by the granite plugs completely blocking the entrance to the ascending passage. Thus, the granite plugs have become the symbol of the Divine Law.

3. The horizontal passage leading to the Queen's Chamber symbolizes life on the human perfection plane, as it is thought to be at the end of Jesus Christ's millennial reign, with the Queen's Chamber indicating the upper planes of the life of human perfection at the time of restitution with only the possibility, but not certainty, of everlasting life.

Thus, the complex of the Queen's Chamber and its horizontal passage represents the plane of the perfect human nature, which enables individuals to obey the perfect law of God and, by continuing to do so, live forever as human beings.

4. The Well is considered the hell and the death stage. It symbolizes Hades, with the condition of death from which there will be an awakening—as represented by the Death and Resurrection of Jesus Christ. The Well's shaft represents the only way to life and immortality, because the ascending passageway is blocked by the granite plugs.

5. The Grand Gallery symbolically becomes the Gospel Dispensation, which is the dispensation of grace heralding the advent of the Saviour.

6. The King's Chamber becomes the symbol of immortality, with the possession of the divine nature making death an impossibility. It is the heavenly inheritance of those who have responded to the invitation of God and make a covenant with Him to follow in the path of Jesus Christ of sacrifice unto death.

The Antechamber leading into the King's Chamber represents the School of Christ. This is the School of Consecration unto death, into which are accepted those who heed the calling and in turn are accepted by Him.

7. The Grand Gallery, Antechamber, and King's Chamber represent the highest level of spiritual attainment, and are equated as having the same significance as the Court, Holy, and Most Holy of the Tabernacle.

The Edgars believe that the aforementioned symbolisms are punctuated by the use of granite in both the King's Chamber and the Grand Gallery. They also postulate that the use of granite symbolizes spiritual and divine things or beings, while the use of other stone symbolizes merely human things or beings.

Mr. Adam Rutherford, considered by many to be the greatest pyramidologist, founded the Institute of Pyramidology—the only institute of its kind in the world

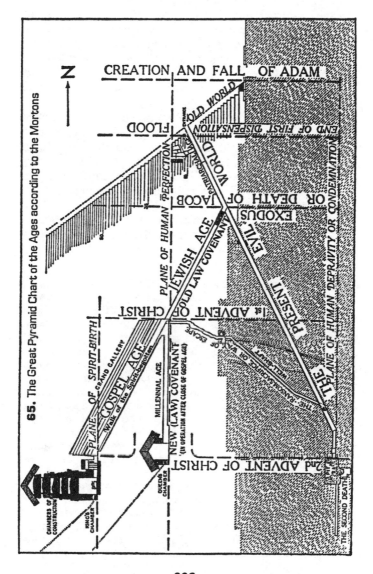

65. The Great Pyramid Chart of the Ages according to the Mortons

223

—in London in 1940. By 1941 the Institute expanded to the international scale with the publication of *Pyramidology Magazine.* The Institute's objective is to advance knowledge and research in pyramidology in all its branches. Its main aim is to make more widely known, all over the world, the great divine revelation enshrined in the Great Pyramid in all its aspects—scientific, prophetic, and religious.

Mr. Rutherford states: "Pyramidology is the science which co-ordinates, combines, and unifies science and religion, and is thus the meeting place of the two. When the Great Pyramid is properly understood and universally studied, false religions and erroneous scientific theories will alike vanish, and true religion and true science will be demonstrated to be harmonious."

In Volume I of his five-volume work on pyramidology, Mr. Rutherford introduces the elements of pyramidology and defines its terms:

> Pyramidology is a new science and therefore, right at the outset of this work, it is well to give definitions of terms. In our day of modern research it has been discovered that the Great Pyramid of Giza in Egypt is something more than just a great tomb of a Pharaoh. This colossal monument of antiquity has been found to portray the Christian religion upon a scientific basis in a manner most appropriate to our present scientific age. Pyramidology is the science that deals with the Great Pyramid's scientific demonstration of biblical truth, true Christianity and the divine plan respecting humanity on this planet. One who is skilled in this science is therefore defined as a pyramidologist. But it is necessary clearly to distinguish between a pyramidologist and a pyramidist. A pyramidist is an Egyptologist who specialises in the study of the pyramids of Egypt, or in other words, a specialist on the Egyptian pyramids from the archaeological standpoint. Hence we find some people who have a good knowledge of pyramidology know little or nothing about Egyptology. On the other hand, an Egyptologist, or even a pyramidist, may know nothing about pyramidology. An expert

pyramidologist, however, knows the Great Pyramid in all its aspects, including the Egyptological, even though his knowledge of Egyptology in general may not be very wide. Apart from a few builders' marks, which include a dating and the cartouche of Khufu (the Pharaoh in whose reign the Great Pyramid was erected), there are no hieroglyphics in the Great Pyramid. Hence to become a pyramidologist, a knowledge of hieroglyphics is not required, whereas it is essential for all Egyptologists including pyramidists to be able to read hieroglyphics proficiently. In some cases, the walls of subterranean chambers of other pyramids are thickly covered with hieroglyphic texts—as, for instance, in the Pyramid of Unas at Saqqara, which was built approximately two centuries after the Great Pyramid. These Pyramid Texts, as they are called, are entirely wanting in the Great Pyramid.

Mr. Rutherford was going to contribute a chapter to this book, but his untimely passing over to the other side has not made it possible. However, his son, Mr. James Rutherford, carries on as vice president of the Institute of Pyramidology, and anyone wishing further details or full particulars of the Institute's activities and publications should write to him at the following address:

Secretary
Institute of Pyramidology
31 Station Road, Harpenden
Hertfordshire, AL5 4XB
England

All of the dates symbolized by the internal dimensions of the Great Pyramid are readily found by simple linear measurements. The start of the Pyramid's construction, as seen earlier, is recorded at 2523 B.C., which is at the entrance point. The birth, death, and resurrection of Jesus Christ are also pinpointed, according to Figure 66. The creation of Adam is interpreted from the Pyramid by John and Morton Edgar to be the year 4128.25 B.C., while the date Adam fell from perfection

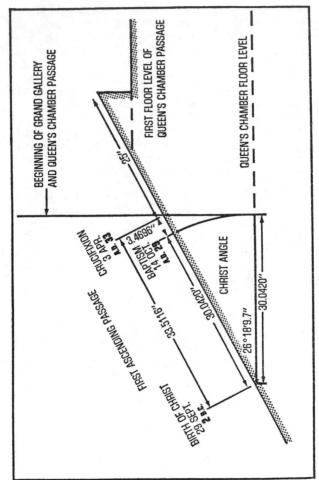

66. The Christ Angle in the Great Pyramid

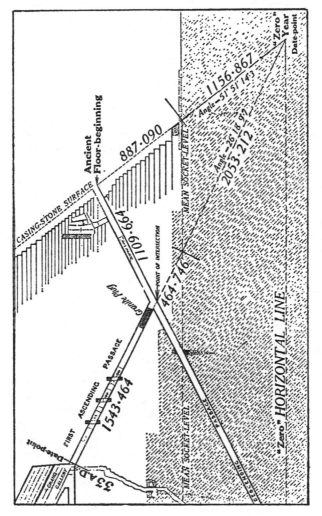

67. Determining the "zero" year date

is interpreted to be 4126 B.C. Adam Rutherford dates the founding of the house of Adam to be 5407 B.C. Interestingly, the year preceding Adam's creation is termed by pyramidologists the "zero" year. It is considered prehistoric because this year is just before the advent of man on earth. This zero year was expected to be found within the Pyramid, but this point is apparently not physically marked within the Pyramid's passage system.

However, in the early 1900s, Mr. Macdonald, a Scotsman residing in England, suggested that the zero year might be determined by the intersection formed by extending the outer casing stone surface line along with extending the line of the floor of the ascending passageway. This purely geometric intersection occurs at a point in the rock foundation below the face of the Pyramid, directly in line with the casing stone surface. This point has been accepted as appropriate to mark the zero year because it is definitely related to the Pyramid; and it is sufficiently removed from the passage system to indicate that this year is not within the history of mankind. If the Egyptians who so elaborately developed the measurements in the Pyramid would have considered the zero year as an element in their equations, it would have been represented in the stones themselves. Consequently, it seems highly unlikely that the zero year was significant for the Egyptians.

The correlation of biblical events to linear inch measurements within the Pyramid has been demonstrated to be accurate and is accepted by the pyramathologists even though there are discrepancies. John and Morton Edgar list their chronology of events in diagram form, while Adam Rutherford lists his chronology of events in table form (see page 229).

Chart VI
Summary of the Chronology*

B.C.	
5407	House of Adam founded (autumnal equinox)
5177	House of Seth (birth of founder)
4972	House of Enos
4782	House of Cainan
4612	House of Mahalaleel
4447	House of Jared
4285	House of Enoch
4120	House of Methuselah
3933	House of Lamech
3745	House of Noah
3265	120 years of grace began
3245	House of Japheth
3243	House of Shem
3145	The Flood (October 31)
3143	House of Arphaxad (spring)
3008	House of Selah (Samaritan)
2878	House of (H)eber
2744	House of Peleg
2623	Work on the Great Pyramid began
2614	House of Reu
2482	House of Serug
2352	House of Nahor
2273	House of Terah
2143	Birth of Abram (Abraham)
2068	Death of Terah
2068	Abraham entered Canaan
2043	Birth of Isaac
1983	Birth of Jacob (Israel)
1893	Birth of Joseph
1883	The Israelites entered Canaan

*According to Adam Rutherford in *Pyramidology*, Book IV.

CONTINUED

1883	Abrahamic Covenant confirmed
1876	Joseph sold into Egypt
1863	Joseph made vizier in Egypt
1854	The Israelites left Canaan
1853	and arrived in Egypt
1836	Death of Jacob
1783	Death of Joseph
1533	Birth of Moses
1453	The Exodus of the Israelites from Egypt
1453	Giving of the Law on Mount Sinai
1452	Erection of the Tabernacle
1413	Death of Moses
1413	Joshua leader
1413	2½ tribes receive land east of Jordan
1413	Israelites cross the River Jordan
1413–1388	Joshua (and the Elders) rule
1413	Fall of Jericho
1407	2½ more tribes receive their land
1405–1404	Jubilee. Division of the land to remaining 7 tribes (50th autumnal year from 1454–1453)
1388–1380	Chushan-rishathaim, King of Mesopotamia, rules Israel
1380–1340	Othniel, judge
1340–1322	Eglon, King of Moab, rules Israel
1322–1242	Ehud, judge
1242	Shamgar, judge
1242–1202	Deborah (with Barak), judges
1242–1222	Canaanite Oppression (20 years)
1222	Conquest of Canaanites complete
1209–1202	Midian Oppression (7 years)
1202–1162	Gideon, judge
1162–1159	King Abimelech, usurper (3 years)
1159–1136	Tola, judge (23 years)
1136–1114	Jair, judge (22 years)

1132–1114	Ammonite Oppression (18 years)
1114–1108	Jephthah, judge (6 years)
1109–1069	(Eli, ecclesiastical judge, 40 years)
1108–1101	Iban, judge (7 years)
1108–1068	Philistine Oppression (40 years)
1101–1091	Elon, judge (10 years)
1091–1083	Abdon, judge (8 years)
1083–1069	No civil ruler (Eli still ecclesiastical judge)
1069–1058	Samuel, judge, alone (11½ years)
1058–1039	Saul, joint King with Samuel, judge (18½ years)
1039–1018	Saul, King, alone (21½ years)
1018–1011	David, King of Judah only (7½ years)
1013–1011	Ishbosheth, King of Israel only
1011–978	David, King of all Israel and Judah (33 years)
978–938	Solomon, King of all Israel and Judah
974–968	Temple erected at Jerusalem
938	Division of the Kingdom into Israel and Judah

The dates given below are those of the regnal years (not the accession years) of the Kings. The regnal years began with Nisan (spring) in Israel, but with Tishri (autumn) in Judah.

Kings of Judah	Kings of Israel
B.C.	B.C.
938–921 Rehoboam	938–916 Jeroboam I
921–918 Abijah	916–914 Nadab
	914–892 Baasha
918–915 Abijah/Asa	892–890 Baasha/Elah
915–877 Asa	890–888 Elah
	888–886 Zimri/Tibni/ Omri
	886–879 Omri
877–874 Asa/Jehoshaphat	879–874 Omri/Ahab

CONTINUED

874–852	Jehoshaphat	874–857	Ahab
		857–855	Ahab/Ahaziah
		855–852	Ahab/Jehoram
852–844	Jehoram	852–850	Ahaziah/ Jehoram
844–843	Ahaziah	850–843	Jehoram
843	Jehu slew both Ahaziah of Judah and Jehoram of Israel		
843–837	Athaliah	843–815	Jehu
837–797	Joash	815–800	Jehoahaz
797–791	Amaziah	800–798	Jehoahaz/ Jehoash
791–768	Amaziah/Uzziah	798–793	Jehoash
768–751	Uzziah	793–782	Jehoash/ Jeroboam II
751–739	Uzziah/Jotham	782–752	Jeroboam II Zechariah (6 months) Shallum (1 month)
739–735	Jotham		
735–731	Jotham/Ahaz		
731–728	Ahaz		
728–715	Ahaz/Hezekiah		
715–695	Hezekiah	751–741	Menahem
695–686	Hezekiah/ Manasseh	741–739	Pekahiah
		739–731	Pekah
686–640	Manasseh	731–722	Hoshea
640–638	Amon	722	Fall of Samaria Monarchy ends in Israel
638–607	Josiah Jehoahaz (3 months)		
606–595	Jehoiakim Jehoiachin (3 months)	670	Deportation of Israel to Assyria completed
595–585	Zedekiah		
585	Fall of Jerusalem Monarchy ends in Judah		

585	Deportation of the Jews to Babylon completed
580	Jews in Egypt deported to Babylon
572	Vision of Ezekiel's Temple
572–571	Last recorded Jubilee (but not observed)
559	Jehoiachin released from prison in Bablyon
537	Fall of Babylon after 70 years of domination, 607–537 (often erroneously given as 609–539) Persia becomes the dominating empire
534	First return of Jews from Babylon to the Holy Land 70 years after beginning of the Captivity in 604 B.C. Sabbatic cycles reinstated
520	Rebuilding of Temple at Jerusalem began Termination of 70 years' Divine Indignation on Judah (590–520)
515	Temple at Jerusalem rebuilt and dedicated 70 years after Temple was destroyed in 585
458	Second Return of Jews from Babylon to the Holy Land Restoration of Jerusalem and rebuilding of the city wall but subsequently partly destroyed by enemies.
445	Nehemiah came to Jerusalem, restored damage, and completed the city wall in 52 days
433	Nehemiah revisited Persia (last dated event in the Old Testament)
409	Restoration of Jerusalem completed; end of first 7 "weeks" (49 years) of Daniel's 70 weeks' prophecy
331	Battle of Arbela; end of Persian domination Greece (Macedonia) becomes the dominating empire

CONTINUED

68.

Determining specific points within the Pyramid to corroborate biblical events has been a relatively difficult task, but it is considered easy compared to the attempts of determining events yet to unfold in the history of mankind, as prophesied by the overall internal measurements of the Pyramid.

The 1-year-to-1-inch scale is apparently valid up to the end of the Grand Gallery. Beyond the south end wall of the Grand Gallery, 1 Pyramid inch no longer equals 1 year, and there was every indication that the length of time had to be shortened.

Mr. William Reeve of Toronto, Canada, published a pamphlet in 1909 suggesting that the time measurement of the Pyramid be shortened to 1 inch equaling 1 month, as the unit of measure to be used starting at the end of the Grand Gallery. The final date that is clearly marked in the King's Chamber by continuing measurements in this manner is August 20, 1953. However, this is not the end of recorded time as measured from within the Pyramid.

In the early 1900s the measurements of the Pyramid had been interpreted as prophesying the dates significant to World Wars I and II, along with other important political, economic, world, etc., events. Therefore, it had been anticipated that a great circumstance in history was going to occur, significantly altering the future of the world, commencing in 1953. Indeed, this may very well have begun, but not as obviously as anticipated. According to the interpretation of several pyramathologists, we are currently passing through a "phase of ending," which is correlated to the "period of cleansing sanctuary" as mentioned in Daniel 8:13–19.

The actual end of the Pyramid's recorded time falls between July 1992 and September 2001. This measurement was developed by extending a vertical line from the end of the King's Chamber to where it intersects with the subterranean chamber complex, and measuring from this intersection point to the termination of the blind passageway. However, there are significant argu-

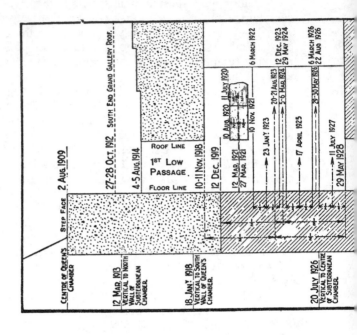

ments opposing all prophetic dates from the internal
dimensions of the Pyramid.

Any mathematician will attest to the fact that the
multiplication of a number by a constant value will equal
any amount by simply manipulating the value of the
constant figure. For example, taking one's birth date—for
example, September 27, 1937—and adding up its
numerical digits, 9 + 27 + 1937, equals the two-digit or
complex number, 20. This birth date number of 20,
when multiplied by 2,000,000 times 12—the number of
zodiacal signs—equals 480,000,000, which just so
happens to be the population of the Americas in 1967.
Although this is a singularly simple example, it is exactly
this that the proponents of classical anthropology,
archaeology, and Egyptology point to as mere manipula-

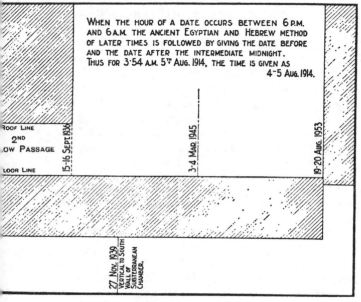

WHEN THE HOUR OF A DATE OCCURS BETWEEN 6 P.M. AND 6 A.M. THE ANCIENT EGYPTIAN AND HEBREW METHOD OF LATER TIMES IS FOLLOWED BY GIVING THE DATE BEFORE AND THE DATE AFTER THE INTERMEDIATE MIDNIGHT. THUS FOR 3·54 A.M. 5ᵀᴴ AUG. 1914, THE TIME IS GIVEN AS 4⁻5 AUG. 1914.

ROOF LINE
2ND
LOW PASSAGE

FLOOR LINE

15-16 SEPT 1936

3-4 MAR. 1945

19-20 AUG. 1953

27 NOV. 1939
VERTICAL TO SOUTH
WALL OF
SUBTERRANEAN
CHAMBER.

69. Specific Dates derived from the Great Step to the far wall of the King's Chamber

tion of evidence to prove the existence of something that does not really exist.

These scholars claim that the dimensions of other pyramids in Egypt can also be finagled so that the perimeter will yield the number of days in a solar year, the height will be relative to the sun distance, and so forth. Their argument is very strong indeed, and one can only arrive at a conclusion after weighing the evidence in the light of one's general faith.

The conclusion that the pyramid has a relationship to the world onto which it was constructed, which in turn indicates the world's relationship to the astronomy of the cosmos, is legitimate logic and cannot ever be rejected. One can never be faulted for believing that the Great Pyramid was more than a mere tomb, just as one

237

cannot be faulted for believing that the Great Pyramid was nothing more than a mere tomb. For ultimately, the Pyramid remains one of man's greatest accomplishments and awe-inspiring works.

However, is the Pyramid really prophesying either the physical destruction of the world, or simply a drastic change in man's relationship to man by the turn of the century? Only time will tell. But we can, nonetheless, continue to monitor the progressing prophecies until then, in order to determine the accuracy of the interpretations.

Metaphysicians are well aware that individuals can effectively reduce the impact of this point if the world's people collectively strive to bring about a constructive change rather than a destructive one. Therefore, let each one of us take the responsibility for what we can contribute toward that fated date, bringing about a rebirth rather than a terminal death.

Nonetheless, the abrupt end of time prophesied by the Pyramid indicates the completion of one gigantic cycle and the start of a new one, for which the internal dimensions of the Pyramid start afresh. The Pyramid will once again prophesy all significant dates and events taking place in this new cycle; for the Pyramid itself is a glyph expressing the laws of genesis, which in turn determine our history.

By all standards of logic derived from the data of the Pyramid, one is channeled to conclude that the builders did indeed construct into this edifice a codex of their wisdom and, therefore, their prophecies.

Throughout all recorded history, oracles and gifted individuals have successfully prophesied great moments and events of time. In the next chapter we will see who some of these gifted individuals were, what they have prophesied, how this all relates to the prophecies depicted in the Great Pyramid, and what the specific prophecies are as recorded in the Great Pyramid.

[9]

WHISPERS FROM THE PAST — THE KEY TO TOMORROW

Symbolism has been used for expressing and recording prophecies throughout time, and is the key to unlocking the prophecies of the Great Pyramid.

The use of ciphers has its origin with the beginning of mankind. Ciphers hide the truth or truths in many different and subtle manners. The knowledge of the ancient mysteries was never revealed to the layman except through the media of symbols.

Symbolism fulfilled both the need to conceal sacred truths from the uninitiated and to offer a language for those qualified to understand it. Formless divine priciples are always represented by symbols.

Most clearly, symbolism is the language by which nature expresses itself. The wise penetrate the veil of symbolism with respect, and with a clarity of vision meditate upon reality. The ignorant, on the other hand, being unable to differentiate between the true and the false, envision only a universe of strange signs and figures.

The schools of the ancient mysteries each evolved their own sacred ciphers whose secrets were known only by the initiates and never spoken except in the inner sanctum. The masters considered it a sacrilege to discuss the sacred divine truths of eternal nature in the language of the profane.

By definition, a secret or sacred science needs to be incorporated by a cipher or sacred language. This sacred or hermetic cipher is thought to be incorporated into the Great Pyramid. Through the ages, symbolic ciphers have been established in various forms such as literal and spoken, pictorial, numerical, musical, and acroamatic (which are parables and allegories considered to be the most subtle of all ciphers), as well as arbitrary, code, and miscellaneous ciphers.

The spoken cipher is what we are most familiar with, furnishing a fascinating form of developing the acuteness of the mental facilities. The most famous spoken ciphers or prophecies are those of the oracles recorded in early Greek history, such as those of Delphi, Dodona, Trophonius, and Latona.

The oracles of Delphi were either messages or answers to questions that were recorded by five holy men. Then they were given to the philosophers of the oracle, whose duty was to interpret and apply them. Afterward, the statements were delivered to poets, who translated them into lyrics and odes for the use of the masses.

The Delphi oracles were transmitted through virgins called Pythia. Virgins were used probably because they were more sensitive and their emotional nature responded more quickly and completely; and more importantly, they were able to devote themselves with an undivided mind. A Pythia was seated on a tripod, or three-legged stool, which straddled over a fissure. This fissure was usually found in a cave from which exhilarating and intoxicating gaseous fumes exuded. Under the influence of the gaseous "high," the virgin developed an altered state of consciousness in which she verbalized the words of the prophecies.

Nostradamus, a sixteenth-century prophet, used a small tripod made of brass. He placed what is commonly believed to be a bowl of water on it, and—using a wand pointed over the center of the water—acquired his prophecies through divination.

Nostradamus was born Michel de Nostredame in St. Remy de Provence, France, at noontime on December 14, 1503. His family was converted from Judaism to Catholicism when he was about nine years old.

The most influential book among his various scientific studies was *De Mysteriis Egyptorum,* published at Lyons in 1547. Nostradamus wrote his prophecies in booklet form, called *Centuries* because he intended to have one hundred four-line verses—called quatrains— in each. He planned to have ten centuries, yielding a total of one thousand quatrains of prophecy. However, for some unknown reason, *Centuries 7* is incomplete, with only forty-two quatrains.

Nostradamus lived during the time of the Inquisition, when it was common practice for the Church to mete out torture and death for alleged heresies against Catholicism. He read and interpreted many occult books, which he claimed to have burned later as a possible attempt to misdirect Church leaders. In order not to be prosecuted for heresy for being a magician, it is obvious that Nostradamus wrote his verses in a cipher using several languages. These were usually the archaic forms of French, Greek, Latin, and Italian, combined within the same sentence. Nostradamus states that he deliberately wrote the prophecies with distorted time sequences in order that their secrets would only be understood by the initiate. Hence, his *Centuries* can be translated in many different ways, causing much confusion concerning correct interpretation and chronology of his prophecies.

Great ages seem to produce, along with mighty accomplishments in the arts and sciences, penetrating visions from their prophets. It is interesting to note that Nostradamus (1503–66) was contemporary with Michelangelo (1475–1564) and Leonardo de Vinci (1452–1519), and it is quite possible that all three men acquired arcane knowledge from the same source or sources.

Erika Cheetham, in her book *The Prophecies of Nostradamus,* first published in Great Britain in 1973, has done a fine job in penetrating prophecies long considered to be impenetrable, and her literal translations are extremely enlightening. According to her translation of the first *Century*'s quatrains 1 and 2 (I, 1, 2), Nostradamus secreted himself alone in his study at night. He placed something on his brass tripod and sprayed the hem of his clothes and his feet with water. A small light came out of the void and Nostradamus placed the wand in his hand in the middle of the legs of the tripod. He heard a voice and he sensed a God seated in the room with him.

I believe the object placed on top of the tripod to be a crystal, rather than a bowl of water so classically interpreted. The picture I envision from this scene is virtually identical to that described by Dr. Ray Brown when he found the crystal ball in the inundated pyramid in the Bermuda Triangle. (See Chapter 10.) In both descriptions a pedestal holds an object; and a wand or a rod is in close proximity to that object.

Nostradamus' predictions for the turn of the century of the year 2000 parallels, in many ways, those interpreted from the Great Pyramid. The cipher he used when dating the prophecies was based on astrological signs, with which he was extremely familiar.

The picture I interpret from his *Centuries* is that of a great catastrophe followed by a war, with smaller wars ensuing; then a time period of long peace; and finally another war. The secret of his quatrains within each *Century* is not necessarily sequential or chronological in nature. Therefore, the following story, which I have pieced together, indicates the *Century* and verse upon which my statements are based.

In his prophecies, Nostradamus states that we are in the last or final seven-thousand-year period that began in A.D. 1555 (I, 48). This final seven-thousand-year cycle contains a great war, and at the end of the cycle the dead will come out of their graves (X, 74). This great war will occur around the year 2000, and its nuclear holocaust may precipitate forty years of rain followed by forty years of drought (I, 16–17). The forty years of rain might be responsible for tremendous flooding occurring in the Middle East. This flooding will be so vast as to inundate Portugal, Spain, France, Switzerland, and Italy (III, 12 and VII, 16).

In the beginning of 1981 two leaders, possibly Arabs, will become prominent political and military figures, and their symbolic colors will be blue for one country and white for the other (II, 2 and IX, 73). These two leaders will become friends and possibly unite, creating an even greater power (II, 89). Around 1987 these two principal leaders will either war with each other or go to war together, invading Egypt, Iran, and Turkey (IV, 25; V, 25; and VI, 80).

Between now and the year 2000, a new land will be seen in the Middle East near Syria, Jordan, and Israel; and the administration of this new country will be among those perishing at the turn of the century (III, 97). Another new land is seen to develop in the other hemisphere during this time, whose capital Nostradamus refers to as the new city. It will be visited by a foreign official. His presence will be treacherous to the new land because he wants to capture it; it results in war and the city's water supply is poisoned with sulfur. All of this is compounded by earthquakes damaging the new city, resulting from volcanic eruptions occurring on April 10 (IX, 93; X, 49; VI, 97; I, 87; IX, 83; and VI, 5).

Around September 1995, as these two wars escalate, great changes to the earth will be foretold by looking toward heaven. Having become accustomed to a relatively long period of peace before the beginning of the next war, man will not be able to comprehend the ensuing devastation, and will blame God for the destruction that results, especially in the west (I, 59, and I, 91).

About September of 1999, either a meteor or a comet will collide with the earth, simultaneously occurring with the outbreak of the great war that is heinously nuclear in content (II, 46, 62, 91 and X, 72). The nuclear war is prophesied to continue through the year

2044, with its first blast lasting a week, and nuclear fall-out engulfing the globe for about nine months (V, 90; II, 41; and VI, 5). The war's holocaust is definitely nuclear, because Nostradamus envisioned heat like that of the sun partially cooking fish, and people eating them because of a food shortage (II, 3).

While the wars are further developing, the Mongolian power will re-establish itself, led by some European-born leader (X, 72 and X, 75).

The nuclear explosion precipitates a Vatican decision to relocate away from the boundaries of Rome. When this occurs, a Pope who significantly departs from the behavioral norms of his office will probably reside at the new site of the Vatican. Decades before the Vatican is moved, there is a schism among the cardinals to elect a Pope, and the gossip against this new Pope will cause irrevocable injury to the Church (II, 41; III, 65; and V, 46). The future of the Vatican is foreseen by Nostradamus in that Pope Paul VI is the second of five Popes who will come and go within a quarter-century timespan. The sixth and final Pope will be extremely progressive and will not be too agreeable to the Italians (V, 92 and VIII, 46).

Shortly before or after the death of Pope Paul VI, three brothers will be born who will be responsible for the start of the great nuclear war (VIII, 17 and 46). Nostradamus clearly foresees the birth of the three brothers, along with a shift in world power brought about by their administration (VIII, 97).

A heavily armamented fleet of submarines will appear near Italy, conveying the commander responsible for the war. This man travels inland, afflicting everyone in his path (II, 5 and 29). Along with the ravaging of the cities, towns, and villages, war will principally engulf the countries of France, Italy, and Spain, causing great nuclear fallout (II, 4 and III, 75).

Most of the world's land mass will become uninhabitable, and war is perpetuated over the acquisition of habitable land. The two previously closely united Arab leaders either fight each other to one's death, or one is killed (II, 95). The remaining brother avenges the other's death, and he is responsible for uniting France and England for a very long period of time (X, 26).

In midyear 2002, a new administrator will be born who will be responsible for bringing peace following the war, for a long duration (VI, 24). During the early days of the great war, the East will attack the West two times—losing, but also weakening the West through their sea battles. In this time of turmoil, a man born under the signs of Cancer, Aquarius, and Aries will initiate a new religion whose day of rest will be Thursday, and his power will greatly affect the East.

During this regime, the world will experience either the coldest winter in recorded history, or a polar shift (I, 50 and X, 71). Another man will be born who will be a prophet taking Monday as the day of rest, and he will be responsible for freeing a great nation (II, 28). An anti-Christ also appears on the scene; this anti-Christ will also later wound and murder the three brothers during a twenty-seven-year war (VIII, 77 and IX, 36).

Nostradamus' predictions for the turn of the century appear to be quite sobering, yet, with all that he prophesies, the world does not end; instead, it will continue to the year 8555. He allays our fears by prophesying events dated beyond 2044.

Trips to the moon are foreseen by Nostradamus, possibly for agricultural purposes. Perhaps new fruit will be developed by these astroagriculturists as a result of these excursions (IX, 65).

Early in the year 2769, the outbreak of war will once again occur; and furthermore, around midyear 3755 an earthquake, or some catastrophe, may result in a possible polar shift (VIII, 48 and X, 67).

Edgar Cayce, known as America's "Sleeping Prophet," somewhat confirms the prophecies of Nostradamus. Cayce prophesied that he would reincarnate in the year 1998, and help bring about the new age. Then he will return once again, as seen in one of his prophetic dreams,

245

and he will be born again in A.D. 2100, after the upheaval.

He recounts the dream of his being born again in Nebraska in A.D. 2100. In his journeys he traveled in a long, cigar-shaped metal ship that moved at high speeds through the air. Cayce saw that New York had been destroyed and was being rebuilt; Alabama was partly under water; and Norfolk, Virginia, had become an immense seaport. Industries were scattered throughout the country rather than being centralized in cities. Houses were made of glass. Nebraska had become America's West Coast. He predicted great upheavals affecting millions of people, beginning in 1968 and continuing through 1998.

The year 1998 is given in a number of readings. By that time the world will have seen much drastic change and upheaval of both a geologic and a social nature. The new lands spoken of by Nostradamus may be the lands Cayce foresees as appearing all over the world. Poseidia will be the first portion of Atlantis to rise again in the Atlantic; while in the Pacific, lands will appear as well. The greater portion of Japan will be inundated. The South Pacific, the Mediterranean, and the Aetna area will have rising and sinking of lands. The upper portion of Europe will be changed so that the battlefields of World War II will be oceans, seas, and bays.

The continent of America will experience major and minor degrees of physical reshaping. The North Atlantic seaboard will not be as disturbed as the West Coast. Los Angeles and San Francisco will be destroyed before New York. Portions of New York State and maybe all of New York City will disappear.

The central portion of the United States will also feel its share of physical change, while the southern portions of the Carolinas and Georgia will disappear. This will be the earliest of all. According to Cayce, the waters of the Great Lakes will empty into the Gulf of Mexico. The areas of the Great Lakes and the southern portions

246

of Nevada will experience an inundation caused by earthquakes. And according to him, "safe lands" will be those found in or around the southern and eastern portion of Canada, Illinois, Indiana, sections of Ohio, Norfolk, and Virginia Beach.

The Arctic and Antarctic also will be touched by upheavals from eruptions of volcanoes brought about by the shifting of the poles.

Unquestionably the sea lanes will also be affected, especially near Davis Strait. The sea lanes of Libya, Syria, and Egypt will be affected, according to Cayce, along with the straits of Australia, the Persian Gulf, and the Indian Ocean.

In general, Cayce foresaw land disappearing into the northern waters of Greenland. South America will be shaken up from the uppermost portion to the end, and all this, according to Cayce, will occur around the year 2000 to 2001. He also cautions that while it may appear that extremely high land would be a safe place to retreat to during this time of catastrophe, many will be fooled because this land will sink far below the surface of the water.

From the late 1960s to the mid-1970s many countries in all corners of our world have experienced devastating earthquakes, which very possibly portend the predicted future of Edgar Cayce. His numerous predictions have been validly proven in more than enough instances to indicate the reality and the exactness of his prophecies.

I believe that prophecy and prediction are part of our lives, our world, and our universe. They are phenomena that at the very least contain truths that cannot be denied and have found a place in every age.

Hidden among the hieroglyphic writings of Egyptians are prophetic statements that corroborate the prophecies of the Great Pyramid as well as those of the famous and also the unknown seers. For example, an Egyptian papyrus entitled *The Admonitions of a Prophet* is dated to be before the Sixth Dynasty. In it, the fifth poem contains an interesting statement. One translation of this section reads:

> Behold, wherefore seeketh he? A timid man is not distinguished from one that is violent; he will bring coolness upon the heat. It is said: He is the herdsman of all men. No evil is in his heart. His herd is diminished, and yet he hath spent the day in order to tend them. . . .
>
> Ah, but had he perceived their nature in the first generation; then would he have smitten down evil; he would have stretched forth the arm against it and destroyed the seed thereof and their inheritance.
>
> There is no pilot in their time. Where is he today? Doth he sleep then? Behold, his might is not seen. When we were thrown into mourning, I found thee not. . . .

Another translation of the same text is:

> Lo, why does he seek to fashion men, when the timid is not distinguished from the violent? If he would bring coolness upon the heat, one would say: "He is the herdsman of all; there is no evil in his heart. His herds are few, but he spends the day herding them." There is fire in their hearts; if only he had perceived their nature in the first generation! Then he would have smitten the evil, stretched but his arm against it, would have destroyed their seed and their heirs!
>
> There is no pilot in their hour. Where is he today? Is he asleep? Lo, his power is not seen! If we had been fed, I would not have found you, one would not have summoned me. . . .

The above translations, although varying considerably in some parts, both have what may be considered to be broad interpretations of a prophecy concerning the coming of a savior.

Another papyrus entitled *The Prophecy of Neferrohu,* dating from the same period, contains an interesting statement toward the end:

> Be glad, ye people of his time! The son of a man of high degree will make himself a name for all eternity. They that would work mischief and devise hos-

tility, they have subdued their mouthings for fear of him. The Asiatics shall fall before his carnage, and the Libyans shall fall before his flame. The foes succumb to his onset, and the rebels to his might. The royal serpent that is on his forehead, it pacifieth for him the rebels. And Right shall come again into its place, and Iniquity, that is cast forth. He will rejoice who shall behold this, and who shall then serve the king. A man of learning shall pour out water for me when he seeth that what I have spoken is fulfilled.

The other translation reads:

Rejoice, O people of his time, the son of man will make his name for all eternity! The evil-minded, the treason-plotters, they suppress their speech in fear of him; Asiatics will fall to his sword, Libyans will fall to his claim, rebels to his wrath, traitors to his might, as the serpent on his brow subdues the rebels for him.

Then Order will return to its seat, while chaos is driven away. Rejoice he who may behold, he who may attend the king! And he who is wise will libate for me when he sees fulfilled what I have spoken!

Contemporary hieroglyphics translators believe that the interpretation of these two texts can only refer to a Pharaoh of the times, rather than herald a savior. Nonetheless, the above passages do resemble Old Testament phraseology, a fact that lends support to the theory that the manuscripts comprising part of the Bible are modified versions of earlier Egyptian writings.

Interpretations of prophecies have to be done very carefully in order to distinguish what is yet to come from what has already occurred. In fact, interpretation of any esoteric material must be guided by intuition.

All the marks and dates delineated within the passageways and chambers of the Great Pyramid have apparently been designed into the internal structure of the Pyramid so as to highlight dates of events or recurrences of cycles. However, it must be kept in mind that the Pyramid prophecies work in the opposite direction from which prophecy generally proceeds.

249

A verbal prophecy usually states the event that is to occur, but cannot date it precisely; whereas the Pyramid indicates dates, but not what the events occurring on those dates will be. For example, the final date by general agreement indicated by the measurements within the Great Pyramid is September 2001; but no one knows what event will make that date significant.

During World War I, pyramathologists looked more closely to the dates outlined by the measurements within the Great Pyramid. They became convinced that a chronograph of history was more precisely defined than had been realized. Constructional features between the dates 1914 and 1918 indicated a topographical design that they interpreted to mean "The Great War." In projecting to future dates, the pyramathologists discovered a period between 1936 and 1945 that they interpreted to be another era of trial and tribulation similar to that of World War I.

One is never certain as to what the date signifies, in reality, until the actual event occurs and is known; the date simply means that something universally important or necessary in man's existence will occur.

The fact that the last date measurable within the confines of the pyramid is September 2001 does not at all—as stated earlier—mean that the world is coming to an end, but simply that the cycle would be starting anew.

Rodolfo Benavides, of Mexico City, Mexico, presents prophetic material that appears in his continually updated editions of his book *Dramatic Prophecies of the Great Pyramid.* This material is interpreted from symbolism of the Great Pyramid as well as original prophecies obtained from pure inspiration of the Pyramid. In brief, Benavides claims that the period from 1977 to 1982 could contain cataclysm for the world, with the possibility of the earth's axis shifting. A large, cold planet will be approaching Earth, whose encounter might result in the birth of a new moon, the body of which is ripped from our planet.

For the period from 1982 to 1987, Benavides

interprets heavier rainfall. Polar ice caps will melt and possibly disappear completely, causing the world's water level to rise as much as sixty feet.

Benavides prophesies the period of 1987 to September 2001 as one in which madness and confusion run rampant, eventually heralding a return to normalcy, new environment, new climate, new philosophy, and a new Messiah. He envisions up to 70 per cent of the world's population to have been destroyed by this; and that by September 17, 2001, when the trumpeter signals Yom Kippur, the new era will begin without a Jewish nation or congregation.

The Instituto Raymundo Lulio in Mexico City, Mexico, is a small occultist center composed of spiritualists, and in the early 1940s it prophesied future events of a rapidly increasing catastrophe gaining momentum from 1970. The world's bodies of water will signal a cataclysm years before with tidal waves, earthquakes, and other great forces. However, the people who understand the crisis occurring at that time will be able to save themselves.

According to these prophecies, China will not be ready to participate in a war in the early 1970s, but if war is postponed to later on toward the end of the century, China will participate and be quite capable of destroying the world. Other spiritualistic centers around the world seem to generally confer with this basic fire-and-brimstone forecast.

All the aforementioned prophecies are very reminiscent of the New Testament Scriptures in the last chapter of the second general Epistle of Peter—in which he speaks of a catastrophe bringing about a new heaven and a new earth.

The tremendous preoccupation of certain pyramidologists since the late 1800s with the Great Pyramid as a Bible in stone is more easily understood when one realizes the basis of their belief. The ancient manuscripts comprising the Old Testament, and the later ones incorporated into the New Testament, make the Bible student

251

believe that the writers of these manuscripts were extremely prophetic. Some say that the Bible is the divinely inspired Word of God and that the writer is an instrument through which these prophecies were expressed; whereas others claim that the writers themselves were the prophets who could foresee the future.

Whichever the case may be, the pyramidologists, in the symbolism of the Great Pyramid, had become awe-inspired in believing that the conception and construction of the pyramid was only done through the divine inspiration of the Almighty. They sought to prove that the Bible and the Great Pyramid were equal to each other.

The Great Pyramid has come to be seen as representing the planet earth, with the missing capstone as Jesus Christ, the Savior and Messiah to come. The internal passageways and chambers of the Pyramid have been defined as the soul's progression through earthly life. The direction of travel within the interior of the Pyramid is symbolically equated. Any downward, eastward, or leftward travel signifies degeneration, negation, and descent into hell; whereas upward, westward, or rightward paths symbolize enlightenment and immortality. In addition, traveling to the south signifies the soul passing through time, and northbound is the soul's return to physical existence. Horizontal passages symbolize a level of attainment, and a deviation from them will elevate the individual to a different level, either positive or negative, depending on the course of the deviation.

The chambers themselves symbolize the conclusion or final decision. The level of the Queen's Chamber is thought of as the plane of life and its potential enlightenment; whereas the subterranean chamber level indicates death with its unenlightened mortality. The King's Chamber represents the ultimate—that is, union with the divine.

Just as one's faith is augmented by the knowledge of the Bible through reading and understanding, so the pyramidologists believe that the Great Pyramid is the physical representation of the path man's free will could choose to travel. Through this reasoning that the Pyramid is a Bible in stone, the pyramidologists-turned-pyramathologists have interpreted certain events from the symbolism of the Great Pyramid in relation to the clearly evident dates.

One must take care not to confuse prediction with prophecy. Prediction is a learned talent, which is developed after observing the previous track record of occurrences. Definite laws can be formulated that indicate the regulation of the rule and order of subsequent events to follow, which simply means that a visible trend will clearly indicate the end result. In the stock market, for example, it is quite well known that the price cannot steadily increase without expecting a drop in the price of the stock. The weather, too, is a predicted phenomenon. Weather forecasters are able to foresee the condition of the weather for the week or the weekend based on the environmental conditions and patterns around the world.

Psychics, spiritualists, and mediums predict more than they prophesy. Many predictions are misunderstood as prophecy, and when the anticipated event or condition does not come to pass, one becomes disenchanted with that person's prophetic ability. Prophecy is an inspired phenomenon occurring sporadically in the lives of ordinary people.

I am led to believe more and more that the prophecies interpreted from the Great Pyramid are not prophecies but rather predictions based on historical trends, coupled with prophetic statements contained in old manuscripts. Even now, pyramathologists are "updating" the prophecies of the Great Pyramid based on the matching of previous events with past dates in the Pyramid. This supposedly gives these pyramidologists more accuracy in decoding the prophecies of future events and their dates.

This to me is nothing more than the ability of prediction in disguise, for when an individual becomes quite adept at predicting, the subtleness of the predictions are interpreted as prophecies. However, there is truth in the statistical correlation of the greater the accuracy of the prediction the more close the individual is to prophesying, for prophecy is always 100 per cent accurate, whereas predictions are never 100 per cent accurate.

Since the late 1940s, numerous pyramidologists have reviewed and re-evaluated the dates within the Great Pyramid, and the latest date recorded by Rutherford is the year 2979 (see Fig. 63). The most current predictions based on the Great Pyramid are as follows:

1979 to 1991—The world will be turned on its side because a cataclysm will alter the earth's axis. There will be major changes in the climate of the world. A new spiritual influence will infiltrate and enlighten the world's leaders. Lands will rise and sink because of war, and cataclysms will be brought on by rain.

1995 to 2025—A new human society with a purely spiritual allegiance will have been formed, "the Kingdom of the Spirit." Natural eruptions, electrical storms, and other natural disturbances will have become a way of life. From now till the turn of the century civilization will continue to decline, reaching its final collapse around 2025, at which time a new civilized society will become established.

2034—A sign of the Messiah's appearance emblazoned in the sky.

2040—The long-awaited Messiah returns incarnated in a physical body.

2055 to 2080—Materialistic progress reawakens with expanded growth of prosperity and achievement.

> *2080 to 2115*—New spiritual expansiveness with mankind's consciousness raised to new heights.
>
> *circa 2116*—Passing of incarnated Messiah, who incarnates again around 2135 and again a third time around 2265.

The symbolic data interpreted from the Great Pyramid are so complex that they allow many variations. Many individuals regard the interpretations as inconsistent and very scarce in detail. As stated before, the Pyramid only reveals specific dates of future, unknown, and possibly unfathomable events. Human intervention to predict occurrences for these dates may turn out to be not realistic or accurate; but on the other hand, who knows until the Pyramid date arrives?

The apparent perfect agreement, as proposed by pyramathologists, between the Bible and the Great Pyramid is based on the lack of dates in the Bible and the Pyramid's exclusivity of dates. The eloquent dissertations formulated within the past century proposing the Great Pyramid to be a Bible in stone is an appealing theory, especially to the biblical exegetes and ordinary Sunday Christians. The concept that the Bible and the Great Pyramid are interrelated is a fascinating possibility. Is the Bible the best possible link to the code of the ancients? The correlation of the metrics of the Great Pyramid and the Bible seem to conform quite readily, as seen in the previous chapter, and it appears that the Great Pyramid prophesied events as written in the Bible —or does it? Those of us who are armchair theologians and are capable of siding with either the pro or the con in a religious debate, are aware of the many conflicts and numerous contradictions within the Scriptures that comprise the Bible. The canonists, however, believe that armchair theologians are incapable of good theology. They believe rather that good theology is rooted in "sound" textual analysis and the utilization of modern methods of interpretation.

Hollywood has added to the confusion concerning

truths of the Bible. Many a bet has been won in taverns and living rooms about the story of Samson and Delilah, where Samson's strength is lost when his hair is cut short. Now everyone assumes that Delilah actually cut Samson's hair, because the movie shows it that way. This is not true. Consulting the King James Version of the Bible, Judges 16:19 relates what really occurred:

> And she made him sleep upon her knees; and she called for a man, and she caused him to shave off the seven locks of his head; and she began to afflict him, and his strength went from him.

Then there are the misconceptions ingrained in us through various misteachings and misinterpretations that we acquire in the whole of our maturation process. In addition, religious teaching, as with *any* instruction, stresses only those points that are beneficial to the topic and the ideas presented. One should question history as it is taught by any religion, knowing that numerous alterations to history have been prepared and designed to conceal facts and mislead the unwary.

If the Great Pyramid is a Bible in stone, it seems logical to look at the Bible itself and its history to see exactly how accurate or true the Bible is. Proponents of the "Pyramid as a Bible in stone" theory base their theory on the premise, never questioned or analyzed, and upon which they build all else, that the Bible is, in fact, absolute truth, and that it must be read literally. This fundamentalist view is in many ways out of step with the esoteric, and in turn Egyptian view that spiritual truths are conveyed by symbol and allegory, and are not meant to be read literally, but have a double meaning.

What if the Bible cannot sufficiently substantiate the proof required? That is what must be established before one accepts the dogmatic correlation between the Bible and the Pyramid as proposed by scholars. Keep in mind that the Pyramid as a Bible in stone is not an accepted *fact;* it is only a proposed theory with a number of scholarly dissertations backing it.

We should be aware that all the Pyramid scholars refer to the King James Version of the Bible, which, according to canonical scholars, has long ago been rejected as not being the best translation available. They use in its place the Revised Standard Version and even the Jerusalem Bible because they believe them to be more reliable.

The many different versions of "the Bible" of all the world's religions indicate the differences in the doctrines of those religions. The "Bible," or the "book" of each religion, will contain only those manuscripts that are most acceptable to those particular religions. In 1926, a most unusual and unique book was translated into English, and published for the first time. Entitled *The Lost Books of the Bible and the Forgotten Books of Eden*, it is a collection of apocryphal writings that have been shrouded in silence for centuries, but nonetheless are an important part of our religious heritage.

Dr. Frank Crane, in his Introduction to *The Lost Books of the Bible*, states that "The Bible is a growth" and that few people realize that it was not written by one person, but is an edited collection of manuscripts written by many people from many lands. We would need to become biblical scholars to know how this collection of manuscripts grew into the Bible, and why manuscripts were either accepted or rejected for inclusion. The Church asks us to accept as "Bible" those manuscripts selected by some remote council of the Church, and reject as apocryphal all others.

But sometimes it is more satisfying for us to reach our own conclusion based on examination of all the available evidence. It is also understandable that the manuscripts comprising the Bible are considered to be far superior in value to those purposely left out. One's examination of Gospel and non-Gospel texts must be undertaken within the redactional nature of their composition. In order to have an intelligent awareness of the writings of one's religion, one must consider the books

257

of the Scriptures in its authorized versions as well as those Scriptures eliminated by various councils.

Dr. Crane also states that the Church council cannot claim that the Bible was compiled by individuals qualified to do so. Although lives of the compilers of the Bible are, with rare exception, unknown, we are nevertheless asked to accept their conclusions.

Of the many manuscripts eliminated from the Bible, *The Lost Gospel According to Peter* is the most intriguing. It is a translation of a Greek parchment codex found in 1886, and has over twenty variations of detail from the canonical editions, some of which raise very interesting questions. These discrepancies can be pinpointed by reading *The Lost Books of the Bible and the Forgotten Books of Eden* and comparing them to the four canonical Gospels. For example:

In Matthew 27:24 Pilate washed his hands of the death of Jesus, giving Jesus over to the multitude; but Peter's version claims that Herod actually gave the execution order.

Instead of Jesus saying, "My God, my God, why hast Thou forsaken me?" (Matthew 27:46 and Mark 15:34), Peter's version is: "And the Lord cried out, saying, 'My Power, my Power, thou hast forsaken me.' " (Peter 13).

In addition to the fantastic wording of "My Power, my Power . . ." varying from "My God, my God . . . ," there is the astounding variation of the resurrection of Jesus in Peter 9, 10, and 11:

> And in the night in which the Lord's day was drawing on, as the soldiers kept guard two by two in a watch, there was a great voice in the heaven; and they saw the heavens opened, and two men descend from thence with great light and approach the tomb. And that stone which was put at the door rolled of itself and made way in part; and the tomb was opened, and both the young men entered in.
>
> When therefore those soldiers saw it, they awakened the centurion (Petronius) and the elders; for they too

were hard by keeping guard. And as they declared what things they had seen, again they see three men come forth from the tomb, and two of them supporting one, and a cross following them; and of the two the head reached unto the heaven, but the head of him who was led by them overpassed the heavens. And they heard a voice from the heavens, saying, Thou hast preached to them that sleep. And a response was heard from the cross, Yea.

They therefore considered one with another whether to go away and shew these things to Pilate. And while they yet thought thereon, the heavens again are seen to open, and a certain man to descend and enter into the sepulchre. When the centurion and they that were with him saw these things, they hastened in the night to Pilate, leaving the tomb which they were watching, and declared all things which they had seen, being greatly distressed and saying, Truly he was the Son of God. . . .

An important point to keep sight of with respect to Christ's resurrection is whether Jesus' rising from the dead justifies the ascription of divine attributes. His resurrection may not, in fact, set him apart from all other men, because it cannot be defined in what form this resurrection actually took place. The many accounts include both extremes of the actual resurrection, from seeing the corpse of Jesus to simply the visions beheld by witnesses of Christ.

Being raised from the dead back to life in that era seemed not to be so incredible as it does in our minds. In the New Testament there is reference to many raisings of the dead. It is said that Jesus raised at least three people from the dead (John 11:44; Luke 7:15, 8:55; Mark 5:42), and that he told the two disciples of John the Baptist to report that they had seen the dead being raised up.

Hebrews 11:35 makes a reference to Old Testament resurrections of the dead in a manner that seems to have been a natural occurrence:

There were women, too, who recovered their dead children, brought back to life.

These manuscripts seem to suggest that Jesus may not have been in a unique category simply because he was raised from the dead, especially when one reads St. Matthew 27:52, 53, where bodies of many saints arose from open graves and went into the holy city and were seen by many. However, the original understanding of Jesus' resurrection is impossible to determine, for the event appears to have only been proclaimed, not narrated, by people who were evangelists and not historians. Indeed, it is uncertain whether anyone actually witnessed Jesus' resurrection.

It is also important to note the basic radical distinction between "resurrection," applicable only to Jesus Christ, and "resuscitation," applying to other revivals. Resurrection involves the transformation and spiritualization of a corporeal body, whereas revivification implies no such changes.

There are some variations between the different texts of the Gospels according to Saints Matthew, Mark, Luke, and John. Religious doctrine justifies these differences as being the expressions of different functions, each Gospel having been written with a distinct community in mind, in a distinct time and place.

The Lost Gospel According to Peter could conceivably once have been held in as much esteem as the other four. St. Peter's record is only a fragment of an entire work, the rest of which is no longer extant.

Many metaphysicians and Gnostics contend that besides a difficulty in accounting for the resurrection of Christ, religion has had even greater difficulty explaining Christ's statement on the cross. Could the deletion of St. Peter's Gospel be due to his quoting Christ as saying: "My power, my power, thou hast forsaken me"? This simple statement, the metaphysicians feel, indicates the possibility of a "power" within all people, and not only in Christ. Could this "power," capable of being learned by anyone, have been learned by Christ—as the metaphysicians believe—in the Pyramid, during his unrecorded life prior to his public ministry?

In the western Esoteric tradition, there are a number of philosophers who indicate that Jesus spent time in Egypt.

There is an extraordinary account by Paul Sédir of Jesus' visit to the Great Pyramid based on this tradition.

In his book *Initiations* (1967), Sédir states:

> One evening our exiles visited the Pyramids. The sun was sinking low and in the shadow of those enormous triangles of stone, the fires of the Bedouins' tents grew red.
>
> While his father and mother talked, the little Jesus, in the shelter of a rock, seemed to be amusing himself by tracing some lines in the sand with a reed. Then he ran to the oldest of the Bedouins and led him to his work, just as all children do when they have built some fragile wonder. But, as soon as the old man with an impassive face looked at the drawing, he became pale and leaned quickly over the confused geometry. In its large isosceles triangle he discovered the plan of the inside construction of the Pyramid: the crypt, the rooms of the King and the Queen, the passageways, the pits, in brief—everything. But those nomads were the only ones who knew the secrets of those structures. Inheritors of the antediluvian traditions, they knew that the Pyramid, together with the Sphinx, was one of the stoney books in which the patriarchs deposited all the keys of their knowledge. The geodesic position of the Pyramid, its orientation, exterior and interior measurements, the angularities of its edges and passageways, the position of its rooms, all give the elements of general and earthly astronomy, geography, sociology, laws and political, philosophical and religious history, as well as those of physiology and psychology.

While the pyramidologists ascribe many correlations between Jesus Christ and the physical structure of the Pyramid and verify Christ's existence by the delineation of various dates within the Pyramid, it must be pointed out that certain sects believe that Jesus never really existed at all!

In the minds of most people, Jesus Christ did in fact exist, to give us the example of what a human being, par excellence, should or could be. This is the case even though secular history has minimal testimony for the life of Jesus or of the early Christian Church.

According to Gerald Massey in his *Egyptian Book of the Dead* and *The Mysteries of Amenta,* Book IV of *Ancient Egypt the Light of the World* published in 1907, the *Sun Book Helio Biblia* of the ancient sun worshippers seems to be the basis for Christianity's Holy Bible. Massey states that Christianity is nothing more than a revised version of an ancient world's primeval sun worship. He claims that these sun worshippers migrated to Egypt from Atlantis. Interestingly, sun worshippers are even referred to in Ezekiel 8:16.

Massey further states that Christianity and Hinduism appear to be linked together. The Hindu word for "sun" is *kris,* which seems to have evolved into the name "Christianity"; and the Hindu "Krishna" has close relationship with our "Christ."

Massey tells an interesting story concerning the origin of Christ and the Church. Massey writes that nearly a hundred years before the supposed birth of Jesus, there were two strong sun religions flourishing. The sun god of the West was called "Hesus" and the sun god of the East was called "Kristos." Over the centuries, these two religions were in such strong competition with each other that there was rioting in Rome even then. Massey elucidates in his book that Emperor Constantine felt that the struggle between these sects was reaching a dangerous level, and he ordered the convening of a great religious council in Nicea, a city in the Roman province of Bithynia, a country in Asia Minor. This Nicean Council not only convened under Constantine's orders, but was actually directed by him in A.D. 325.

Massey alleges that eighteen hundred high priests

comprised the Nicean Council. They were to determine which religion should prevail—that of the East, known as "Hindu Krishna"; that of the West, known as "Druidic Hesus"; or a combination of both. If the two were joined, then there should be a new, united name—"Hesus Kristos"!

According to Massey, Constantine moved to combine the two sects, and ordered a vote on the matter. When only three hundred voted in favor of Constantine, he had the Roman guard evict those who opposed the motion and exiled the leader of the opposition. This action led to the unanimous agreement to combine the two religions and creat a whole new doctrine. Thus, according to Massey, began the Christian Church.

To support this scheme, the wealth of the Roman Empire was used to erect a new capital, called Constantinople, under the direction of Constantine. To make the new city completely Christian, churches were built in every quarter and all sun worship was forbidden. Massey also states that the name "Jesus Christ" was unknown until after the Nicean Council adjourned, for before that time it appeared in no writings.

The Council, in creating a new religion, also created a huge problem for it. A figurehead had to be found, much like Moses is to the Jews, whom the newly formed Christians could emulate. Massey writes that this figurehead was Apollonius Tyaneus, born of wealthy parents around A.D. 2. Thoroughly educated in the sciences and philosophy, Apollonius traveled extensively to the far reaches of the world, learning the religious practices of other civilizations, to the extent that he became a very profound mystic. Apollonius had acquired such tremendous mental powers through his experiences with other religions that he was not only able to see the future, but also is credited with raising a woman from the dead.

Gerald Massey states that scant evidence exists regarding the life of Apollonius Tyaneus, but even more scant is the evidence regarding the life of the Gospel Jesus. Apparently only a total of fifty hours of Jesus' life can be accounted for in the Scriptures! Theologians quite effectively argue against the statements of Gerald Massey, pointing out that the fundamental basis for the Christian Holy Bible is rooted in Jewish tradition, but there is, as Massey claims, the possibility that the Jewish tradition hails from the *Helio Biblia*.

When the Dead Sea Scrolls were found, it was hoped that more light would be shed on the life of Jesus. Instead, they renewed arguments among theologians, deepened conflicts within related fields of study, and, very surprisingly, increased the possibility that the Christian Church had been fabricated and that Jesus may not have actually existed.

The Dead Sea Scrolls consist of manuscripts written on material such as animal hide, copper, and papyrus. Texts were written in Hebrew dialects, Aramaic, and Greek. The word "manuscript" does not necessarily mean an original document. In fact, it actually refers to a document written by hand. Most manuscripts are actually a single transcription resulting from a long series of earlier copyings. In most cases, scholars may not know if a manuscript is an original or one in a series of copies that extend back several centuries to their origin in a unique text.

According to A. Powell Davies in his book *The Meaning of the Dead Sea Scrolls,* published in 1956, dating of manuscripts not only uses evidence uncovered by archaeology at the site of the texts, but relies more upon paleography, the systematic study of ancient writings. Expert paleographers encounter numerous problems in translation along with dating. Within the scrolls themselves there is an evolution of writing. Paleographers are faced with continuously changing alphabets; variations from the base line in the placement of the words; and in the case of Hebrew, the lack of vowels. Ancient Hebrew was only written as an aid to memory, to sufficiently remind the reader of what was already familiar to him.

For example, the word "Jehovah" evolves from

"Yahowah," which when written in ancient Hebrew is actually "Yhwh." An Israelite was not allowed to speak the sacred name of Yhwh; instead, when this word was encountered they substituted either "Elohim" or "Adonai."

Yhwh was the Israelites' God of War, and was also apparently their principal God. The meaning of "Lord of Hosts" may derive from the fact that the Israelites were henotheists rather than monotheists, and that Yhwh was specially related to their other gods.

The Dead Sea Scrolls are believed to have been written by the Quamran Sect, which in turn is thought to have originated from the Essene community.

The Quamran Sect existed several centuries before Christianity, and its organization suggests close relationships to the early Christian Church. This sect had Scriptures which the Christians used to compose their own texts. If the Christians borrowed from these texts, it is also possible that the Dead Sea Scrolls could have been borrowed from much older Scriptures. Conceivably the philosophy in the Dead Sea Scrolls may be much older than we imagine today.

Around the second century B.C., there were quite a number of religious sects differing from each other in their doctrines. The Essenes were considered a solitary sect and the most saintly of all. There was no particular city in which they lived, they were travelers, they owned no property, and they donated earnings to a collective fund that assisted in providing for other traveling members. Their duty was to help the needy and the poor. Like the Egyptians centuries before, the Essenes worshipped the sun, to which they prayed at dawn.

The Essenes followed a doctrine of life commanded by natural law. They wore white garments and bathed in cold water, which to them was a sacred form of purification. They also believed in angels, and took an oath never to reveal their names.

The ritual of the sacred meal that the Essenes practiced consisted of the gathering of ten or twelve members of the sect before a priest, according to their rank. The table was set with bread and wine, and the priest pronounced a blessing by stretching his hand over the bread and wine.

The Essenes believed in a Teacher of Righteousness, along with a Prophet or Messiah to come. Massey points out that the fabled existence of Jesus drew its inspiration from the Essene teaching, in the hopes of becoming more plausible and acceptable to the people of that time already familiar with the doctrine of the Essenes.

The word "Christ" is not the name of a person, but of an office, the office of an "Anointed One"— usually a priest or a King. To indicate that Prophet and Messiah were one in the form of Jesus, the Gospels refer to him as "Jesus" when relating his ministry; the Acts and the Epistles refer to him as King by saying "The Lord Jesus," "Christ Jesus," and "The Lord Jesus Christ." Little is actually said of Jesus the Teacher, and it was Christ the (King) Savior who was Lord of the Christians. The decision to formalize Christ as the Savior God was done later by majority vote at the Nicean Council in A.D. 325.

Theologians have known for quite a while that there are important similarities between the Essenes and the Christians, and also that the lay individual's concept of the origin of Christianity is not based on history as much as on theology. Christianity is certainly indebted to other religions during its infancy.

Scholars concede that it is historically impossible to learn where or when Jesus was born. If he was born in Bethlehem, was it really the Bethlehem in Judea? Or the one in Galilee? There is no record of the "slaughter of the infants" to substantiate the story in the Gospels. The great historian Josephus, who details very specifically the crimes of King Herod, fails to even allude to this slaughter.

During the time that Jesus was believed to have lived, there was no city called Nazareth. Neither is it mentioned in the Old Testament or the Talmud. Josephus never mentions Nazareth. Possibly "Nazareth" is a synonym for all of Galilee, which would mean that "Nazarenes" is identical to "Galileans." "Nazarene" may also have meant a religious sect whose doctrine revolved around watching for or believing in a Messiah. Hence, "Jesus of Nazareth" may only mean "a Jesus of a particular religious community."

Many religious cults prior to the Christians had deities—such as Mithras, Adonis, and Osiris—who were considered the "Redeemer of Mankind." The Mithric first day, or the winter solstice, was known as the Day of the Conquering Sun. It is this birthday of Mithras, the twenty-fifth of December, that was chosen by the Christians to be the birthday of Jesus.

According to Gerald Massey, the story of the Savior is drawn and elaborated from the vegetation myth. The concept of the Virgin and Son originates from the goddess Earth, who is virginal every spring; the fruits are her son, born to die in order to renew the cycle once again.

The seasonal earth cycles have a parallel in the cycles of heaven. Sirius, the star of the East, signals the new birth of the sun simultaneously with the rising constellation, Virgo. Consequently, the idea of the virgin from the sun was easily transposed from Virgo passing through the horizon.

The Earth myth, merged with the Heaven myth, mingled with memories of ancient men, developed into the saga of the coming of the Redeemer.

Egyptian mysteries deal with the creative action. The mother earth as the producer is symbolized by Isis. The Earth, impregnated by the rays of the Sun (God), brings forth fruit, symbolized as the child Horus sitting on the lap of Isis, as depicted in various Egyptian scenes. This was the origin of the Virgin and Child of Christianity. They existed long before in Egypt, Babylonia, India, Assyria, and developed from even older civilizations.

Massey further contends that Christianity stumbled in its early formulation of theological doctrines. It turned simple functions into mysterious actions, causing severe problems for a maturing world, failing to adequately follow through with the principles of creative action, and attempting to stop the cycle of creativity with the death of Jesus.

Ancient masters of religion, scientists in their own right, taught the philosophy of reincarnation, based on the creation cycle. Their premise was the scientific postulate that something *must* derive from something else. This

70. Child Horus on the lap of Isis

"something else" must contain all the qualities that it imparts to that "something" and, in its due course, has to return to the source of its origin. This is the basic law of the creative cycle. The masters would not have taught the creation as modern religions interpret the Bible; rather, they taught the doctrine of transmutation, in which the terrestrial world is but a reflection of the astral, celestial, or spiritual world.

In First Corinthians 15:40, Paul definitely refers to

268

two bodies, the terrestrial and celestial—indicating he knew there were two worlds. The great secret between things eternal and things temporal are clearly presented by Paul. Temporal things, including the universal planetary system, are created, lasting for an undetermined time, but their end is certain according to the laws of creation. On the other hand, the eternal—the celestial body—being uncreated, has never had a beginning and therefore can never have an ending. It is this eternal spirit, embodied in the human form of flesh, that is reincarnated endlessly.

The story of Horus, the son of Osiris—who suffered, died, was buried, and who rose again from the dead—is clearly plagiarized by the Christians in their story of Jesus. Horus dying bodily and resurrecting in divine spirit symbolized what the Christians state as the "resurrection and life." Horus simply stands for a spirit, (and all human spirits), the divine offspring of the uncreated; not for any particular historical character possessing miraculous powers.

The Bible as constructed by Christianity raises many questions, rather than merely supplying answers, as was originally intended by the founding fathers. For example, if Jesus were actually baptized by his cousin, John the Baptist, where did John get the doctrine that he was preaching? It is known that some of Jesus' disciples were drawn from John's following—which indicates that John and Jesus had parallel influences from a common religious order such as the Essenes.

The doctrines and teachings of Jesus, whether divinely inspired or not, can be traced to the religious sects of his time. Indeed, the basic foundation of Jesus' philosophy is present not only in Judaism of that time, but is also discernible in numerous other religious movements.

The blessing pronounced by the priest at the ritual of the sacred meal of the Essenes contained the statement that the bread and wine were the body and blood of God. Jesus deviated from the prescribed script for the

269

sacred meal by stating that the bread and wine were his body and blood:

> And as they were eating, Jesus took bread, and blessed it, and brake it, and gave it to the disciples, and said, Take, eat; this is my body.
>
> And he took the cup, and gave thanks, and gave it to them, saying, Drink you all of it;
>
> For this is my blood of the new testament, which is shed for many for the remission of sins.
>
> But I say unto you, I will not drink henceforth of this fruit of the vine, until that day when I drink it new with you in my Father's kingdom.
>
> Matthew 26: 26–29

According to A. Powell Davies, with this slight alteration of the script Jesus announced himself as the Messiah (See also Mark 14:22–25 and Luke 22:19, 20).

During his imprisonment, John the Baptist sent messengers to Jesus asking whether it was true that Jesus was the prophet heralding the Messiah, or the Messiah himself. Jesus scarcely gave an answer; all that is known is that whatever answer was given was worded in guarded language.

Jesus later explained to some of his disciples that John the Baptist was the prophet Elijah and that he, Jesus, was actually the Messiah, as he subsequently reconfirms at the "last supper." Jesus requested that these few disciples keep this statement secret, but Peter blurted it out and the rest of the disciples heard it. This seems to be the secret Judas betrayed to the authorities, which they needed in order to prosecute Jesus.

This was not the first occasion that Jesus acknowledged that he was the Christ or the Messiah. He states it quite clearly in Matthew 16:15–17, and in John 4:25–26, to cite a few.

Regarding the title "Messiah," biblical exegetes consider the following points that they believe rule out Jesus' thinking of himself as such:

1. The redactional nature of the infancy narrative.
2. Jesus' ordering silence (Mark 8:29).
3. Jesus' refusal to answer the question, instead quoting a passage about the suffering Son of Man.
4. Jesus' nonacceptance of the title other than in a Samaritan context (John 4:25–26).
5. The question that concerns the exegetes is not whether Jesus considered himself the Messiah, but what his understanding of such a personage was.
6. Any Messiahism is attributable more to the theology of the early Church than to Jesus himself.

Albert Schweitzer, according to Davies, believes that Jesus could have so strongly identified himself with being the Messiah that he actually could have sought death to prove that he was the Son of God. Judas may not have needed "thirty pieces of silver" for informing the authorities concerning Jesus' whereabouts. Rather, Judas may have also deeply believed that Jesus was the Messiah, and helped him carry out the plan that would bring about Jesus' acknowledgment as the Messiah. Afterward, upon seeing that Jesus actually died and that the action did not bring on the messianic kingdom, perhaps Judas hung himself in disillusionment rather than remorse.

An additional conflict to ponder is the possibility that Mary did not remain a virgin, as the Scriptures lead us to believe. There is also evidence to show that Jesus had a brother called James the Just. He could have been a blood brother, or simply a brother in the Essene order. This James had his own twelve disciples and apparently had no association with Jesus. After Jesus' death, Peter, James, and John chose James the Just as bishop of the Jerusalem Church. In addition, James the Just continued his own theological teachings following Moses' law, and looking for a messiah!

271

Biblical scholars do not believe that the Dead Sea Scrolls present problems to the world's religions because they believe that rather than polarizing theologians, the Scrolls are actually bringing some of the Christian churches closer.

The books of the Bible—both the New and especially Old Testaments—being translations of manuscripts that were derived from earlier copying efforts, are in fact highly vulnerable to criticism. How accurate were the copiers of the manuscripts that were finally translated into the Bible? Was there simply copying, or was interpretation involved too? Could the translators of the Bible have included interpretations they felt as necessary for the needs of their people and the times? These questions and many others may never be resolved properly in the light of current evidence.

Basically what we have to go upon is the consensus arrived at by scholars, a supposedly informed opinion group, and accepted by seminarians. This view of the Bible is in turn given a seal of approval by theology when in agreement with it and held as the equivalent of history.

The circular reasoning that the pyramidologists use to "prove" that the Pyramid is a Bible in stone is that the Bible and Pyramid enshrine the same eternal truth; one in words, the other in stone. The Pyramid is a Bible in stone; the Bible is the Pyramid in words. The Pyramid is truth in structural form; the Bible is truth in literary form.

If the truth of the Bible is questioned, then its relation to the Pyramid must also be questioned. Obviously this does not mean that there is no historical truth in the Bible. For example, Heinrich Schliemann, in the late nineteenth century, discovered the site of the city of Troy based on his interpretations of the Bible.

There are people who say that the Bible is just a story book; in the same respect, others say that the Great Pyramid is simply an exceptional architectural feat. However, I feel that the main point is going unnoticed because scholars are embroiled in the task of establishing accuracy, rather than acknowledging the underlying principles of these two cultural masterpieces.

It seems apparent that the builders of the Pyramid, as well as the authors of the various biblical manuscripts, lived in a time of cyclical crisis. Their understanding of time as perpetual revolutions of great ages, each with similar and special qualities, being born, disappearing, then new ages manifesting, was based not on a linear progression of time, but instead on a system of the constant evolution of great cycles and events.

Chaos was considered at hand when physical upheavals or religious and social disorders occurred. To them a cycle would be concluded in either a consuming fire or a flood. Then a new cycle would begin with the birth of a new world, and the relationship of macrocosm and microcosm would once again be ordered.

Extant biblical and related manuscripts, whether altered or not, indicate correlations with architectural and other scientific and mystical concepts embodied in the Great Pyramid.

In the Bible and the Great Pyramid are found the keys to the sciences of astronomy, astrology, theology, archaeology, meteorology, and chronology, to name but a few of the more important segments. No one today can dispute the possibility of divine intervention in any or all of these systems of knowledge. Ask most scientists with an original discovery if there is a possibility that divine inspiration was involved in their thoughts and they will most likely not deny it. Einstein and others give ample testimony to this.

If we accept that the Bible and the Pyramid are based on the knowledge of ancient divinely inspired masters, and both were originally intended to fulfill the needs of the civilizations of those times and offer a cosmic guidebook to future man, then indeed there is a harmony between the Bible and the Pyramid.

Both the Bible and the Pyramid reflect a myth of man that includes all the properties and events of any given time. Their decipherment leads to a knowledge of man's becoming, his purpose on earth, and a spiritual direction for his future. Obviously, within such an immense view of time, and for that matter, earth evolution, parallels with historical events are bound to occur. But the real meaning of these two ancient testimonies to divinity lies not in the mere history of human events, but in the history and evolution of consciousness.

The coincidence of the metrics of the Pyramid with biblical events and their interpretations by pyramidologists is highly suspect. One of the pyramidologists was actually found at work cutting down a stone in order for its measurement to fit his theory. Others give the various chambers and passageways symbolical titles, which then can be more easily associated with biblical events, such as calling the pit the "Chamber of Chaos." And all of them combined then proceed to search for a crack, a seam, anything that will attest to their proposed chronology. Every one of them seems to arbitrarily pick points of reference or departure in order to make their chronology fit. They count backward, forward, along the walls and ceilings to prove the exactness of the Pyramid and its chronology.

In reading about the chronological interpretation of the biblical pyramidologists, besides learning that there is disagreement among them, one discovers that they continually change the unit of measure to coincide with their theory more closely. The changes have varied from one inch equaling one year to one inch equaling one day.

The search for a biblical chronology in the Pyramid, and in fact a search for a historical view of the Bible, seems at best a futile effort. Rather, the proportions of the Pyramid can and have spoken directly to men of each generation and given them the inspiration to search for the meaning and direction of life, and in so doing

274

discover the secret codes within the sacred measures of the Great Pyramid.

That there is a code in the Pyramid is undeniable, and it may well be that one of the secrets of it lies in the energy produced in the pyramidal shape itself. Pyramidal energies exuding from, and felt within, scale-model replicas of Cheops' Pyramid have been established as real, functional forces through thousands of experiments performed since the late 1960s.

The key to the prophecies of the Pyramid lies in gaining from its code divinely inspired visions of the future and the ability to apply them to the present. Both the Bible and the Pyramid disclose the keys to the nature of time. They rather give the secret language from which man can read the present moment and discover his place within the larger progression of earth evolution.

[10]

THE MYSTERIOUS CRYSTAL—
A MESSAGE FROM ATLANTIS?

In the early 1970s, when the energies of the Great Pyramid were rediscovered, an inundated group of ancient structures, possibly a portion of the fabled land of Atlantis, was being explored in the Caribbean. This underwater city has a pyramidal structure whose size has not yet been determined, which yielded a very important key to the possible decoding of the knowledge of the ancients.

This key is an incredible quartz crystal. When you look at the 3.5-inch-diameter crystal ball, you immediately see three large pyramids and several small ones deep inside the center. They are there not because you have to look hard and imagine them, but because the flaws within the quartz are so ingeniously formed as to produce pyramidal shapes.

Dr. Ray Brown, a naturopath, discovered the crystal near the Bahama Islands in 1970. In his own words, Dr. Brown relates his thrilling and chilling story of his remarkable find:

"In the summer of 1968, a group of ten or twelve professional divers and myself set out to search for

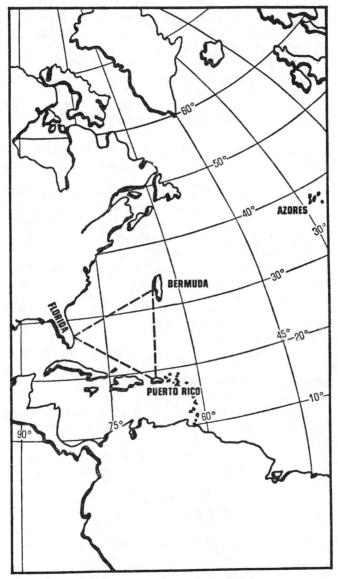

71. Aerial View of the Bermuda Triangle

sunken treasure ships in the area of the Bahamas. We had some very sophisticated equipment, which made it possible for us to make the discoveries which later led into the Atlantean crystal discovery.

"We used a magnetometer, which senses any interference with the return, magnetically, of a signal. Anything that is ferrous warps this returning signal, and therefore we are able to determine that there is a metallic substance under the water. This would then merit further investigation.

"We used an airlift device to move the sand underwater at these sites in our investigation, as we looked for buried ships.

"Our explorations led us from the shores of Cuba and the Cay Sal banks, and later we returned to this area to help make movies for Jacques Cousteau's television series. One of them concerned the 'Blue Holes' of the Bahamas, which is about gigantic areas where fresh water comes up right in the middle of the ocean. There are huge ponds and eruptions of fresh water, some of them in circles with 5-mile diameters. The sea will rise as much as three feet above the normal surface, with this huge current of underwater fresh water arising in the middle of the salt water.

"This area is known as the Bermuda Triangle. There are things that happen in this area that are 'different,' and I have had some experiences here myself which only I can judge.

"Our underwater work drew us in a wide circle, exploring the outer islands from Grand Bahama Island down to the Dutch Antilles and Antigua and Martinique. The smaller islands are just beautiful, with their customs and traditions from the early 1800s virtually unchanged today.

"After working all summer in 1968 digging holes in an area off a physical flaw in the earth called the Great Tongue of the Ocean, off the Bari Islands southeast of Bimini, our group had discovered a vast area of magnetic readings. They were so numerous that we were very excited. We figured we had found the Plate fleet that had gone down in 1733. The Plate fleet was a large fleet of Spanish galleons that went down at one time. There are single ships in this group that have as much as 12 billion dollars' worth of gold, at today's value!

"We worked all summer digging holes in a vast mountain of sand on a plane off the Tongue. The Tongue is an area that has a depth of about 35 feet and drops sharply down a wall to 12,000 feet.

"This wall is strange. About 70 feet down, the fish are disoriented. When you reach about 35–40 feet, you are weightless underwater. You are naturally buoyant at that point—not going up or down. The fish think that the wall is the floor, and they swim up and down the wall. The plants grow straight out.

"The fish in the Bahamas are a sight you must see to appreciate; they are of incredible colors—every tiny little creature is beautiful. And when you look out from this wall you just see space in every direction—a deep beautiful blue color, going off until it dims out.

"We dug many hundred holes during the summer, all over the area. We marked the holes by taking a magnetometer reading first from the air, then dropping weights with floats over the area. Then we would take diving crews in and begin digging holes down 30–40 feet in the sand, looking for what was making these magnetometer readings. The area was about 15 miles by 5 miles wide, containing not solid readings, but maybe a few hundred feet apart.

"At the end of the summer, after spending about a million and a half dollars and finding nothing, the group was exhausted, the money was exhausted, and the crew broke up, each going his own way.

"In 1970 we put together a new crew of people to explore the area. One day, while making a movie off Miami, I became so involved in watching an interesting sequence of events between a diver, a lobster, and an eel that I forgot it was time for me to return to the surface. I tried to help the diver instead. And I ran out of air!

"At this time I was an experienced diver, and I didn't have an air reserve. I knew enough to always be on the surface before my air ran out. But this time, the tank emptied out when I still had about 100 feet to go.

"On the way up, I didn't know that there was a Fort Lauderdale tour boat over this area. I couldn't hold my breath any longer, and decided to risk surfacing alongside of the boat. As I broke the surface—I don't even think I had time to take a gulp of air—another craft, a 35-foot sport fishing boat, ran over me.

"I could see the twin props coming at me. This was all in slow motion—many people report that in a moment of danger, things seem to slow down. I knew that I was dying.

"My first reaction was panic—fear! The force of impact drove me down into the water some 40 feet.

"It seemed that at the point I leveled out, all fear left me. There was a deep stillness inside me—very peaceful. At that point I was aware that my body was not breathing. It didn't have to—the shock had stunned it, and everything was shut off.

"I looked below me and I could see a jewel fish. I was thrilled by the sight of this beautiful little fish, and it was as though something inside me focused on it. It was like we were communicating. There were no words—the fish didn't talk to me in words that I can repeat to you; but it was an acknowledgment, like, 'Hello. I know who you are.' It was very peaceful.

"I could see all around me, in every direction, and this visual experience expanded outward at a slow rate in a circle; and at each point there was pure acknowledgment of any life form that this circle touched. It touched plankton; it touched sea fans; it touched fish, of course; and so forth.

"There was an intense awareness of exactly, in the finest detail, everything about that creature, its life, its past, and its ancestry; there was complete understanding

of all things to do with that life form. As this awareness expanded, it was hard to contain the beautiful feeling
that I had. It kept expanding . . . growing . . . I always
wanted to know what was way down in the Gulf Stream
and I got to see it very vividly.

"At no point during this whole time did I ever lose
consciousness—I was fully awake. This circle-expanding
eventually wrapped entirely around the planet, and at
points it began to overlap itself in little diamond-shapes.
These were very intense, and there seemed to be awareness of all points at the same time, but intense awareness
at these diamond-shaped points of concentration.

"After circling the globe several times the awareness,
maybe tiring of running through the earth life-forms,
seemed to explode and burst outward.

"I felt at that moment a great release, and my consciousness was going in all directions through space,
leaving the planet and touching and seeing this planetary
system, then going outward through the galaxy and the
universe, and through other universes and galaxies and
other systems beyond what our imaginations could conceive.

"There were places where there were life forms
similar to ours; there were other places where there were
life forms not similar to ours. But at all points I was
aware.

"Going through this beautiful experience, there
wasn't an awareness of time—it went on and on and on.
I was drawn back from the experience by being aware
that my body was being grabbed hold of. I felt myself
being pushed through the water and I was pushed up
on the back of the boat that had run over me. I was
flown to Fort Lauderdale on a helicopter.

"The paramedics were telling each other, 'He's dead.
There's nothing there.' And I was very much aware and
tried to talk to them, to tell them, 'I'm okay—I'm alive!'
—but nothing was happening. They used a respirator on
me, and all of a sudden the body decided to 'turn on'
again and I started breathing.

"I spent the afternoon in the hospital. It was hard for the doctors to understand . . . the time I had left the boat to the time I was brought to the surface was 2½ to 3½ hours—the stories vary. Some people say that the time I was without air was anywhere from 50 minutes to 2 hours. I don't really know. But that's a long time to hold your breath! I'm a doctor—I know you can't live without air. However, this happened.

"This experience was to change my entire life. I feel that the moments that I have in my clinic and in my work are borrowed time—they are not mine. I don't know if I have some great destiny.

"This experience opened the gate that, in the next several weeks, brought into focus the event of discovering this crystal.

"We went ahead with our schedule to explore the large area in the Bahamas which we had discovered in 1968. It's interesting that Edgar Cayce predicted that there would be a discovery in 1968 of an ancient civilization known as Atlantis. I can't prove that the ruins we discovered were Atlantean, but they were in the right place, and it was an ancient civilization.

"I will describe some of the buildings and things that are there, and I think soon you'll be able to see pictures; we don't have any, but author Peter Tompkins and some of the people who are in the area searching, will be there at the right time and you will see, I'm sure, evidence that these ruins exist.

"I'm not the original discoverer of this underwater city; there are others whom we've talked to who have been able to observe it many years before we were there.

"In returning to this area, we struck out through the Bari Islands. There was a violent storm, and we had to stop at one of the nearest islands until it was over. We lost much of our gear during the storm, but as soon as it was over, we decided to get into the water.

"Out in the water it was very murky. As soon as we got over our 'ruin' area we found that the water, even though murky, revealed the outlines of buildings—everywhere that we drove the boat, back and forth, we could see the shape of structures underneath us! We picked a spot, threw the anchor over, and our divers—like in a panic—were in the water.

"There were five of us. I was the last in the water. It's a good idea to pair up with another diver when you're in a lonely area, and I could see a pair of fins ahead of me through the murk every once in a while, and tried to follow them. In trying to catch up I became exhausted and had to stop. I rested on a piece of coral, trying to set my bearings.

"I could see the golden sunlight filtering through the murky water, sparkling, and I could see all this light coming behind the shape of a pyramid. I just sat looking at it—because it *couldn't* be there—and I didn't want it to go away. The sun was directly behind the pyramid, with the light shining out in all directions with this sparkly effect. It was like somebody had painted this fantastic picture. I kept thinking, if only I had a camera! If I could capture this moment, it would be the most beautiful sight that man had ever laid eyes on. It was absolutely spectacular! It was better than any sunset that nature had ever provided for me to view. It was just fantastic! It had color—it had a beautiful feeling to it.

"All at once I came back to 'myself' and realized that this—whatever it is—is real. It has to be. So rather than just sitting and looking at it, I decided to get over to it.

"Not all of the pyramid was exposed from the ocean floor, but just part of it. I could see about 90 feet of the structure, and from its shape it appeared to be equal to the Egyptian pyramids, if not larger.

"The surface of this pyramid was mirrorlike. It was stone, but they were very highly polished stones, and the workmanship was fantastic. The surface stones were polished and fit together so tightly that I would imagine you would have a hard time fitting a razor blade between them. There's no way you could imagine that humans could put together such beautifully, tight-fitting stones.

There were beveled surfaces on the edges of the stones; they did not butt together smoothly.

"I swam around the cap. The water was surging and it was a little dangerous near the top.

"I circled the cap three times. On the way down the third pass, I came across an opening. On my passes around before there was no opening—I know that I was intensely looking at this structure. I don't have any explanation as to how this opening was there and not there —I'm just explaining it as I remember it.

"The first thought I had was, if there is an opening, there must be a door. I looked carefully around the area and there was nothing. It was just an opening. No door; nothing that I could see slid open.

"Curiosity got the better of me, and I went inside. Going down a hall straight away from the opening, it opened into a singular room. This room would be on the upper part of the pyramid if you were looking at the structure whole, out of the water. It was approximately halfway down in the exposed area.

"The room was rectangular shaped, and the top was pyramid-shaped. From the peak in the room was a metallic rod, approximately 3 inches in diameter. It appeared to be gold—but apparently it was not.

"In the center of the room was a stand, carved, stone, and on top of it was a flat breastwork plate with scrolling ends. On top of that were two metallic hands, human size. Inside the hands was the crystal. Directly above it was the metallic rod from the ceiling, pointing straight at the crystal. On the end of the rod was a faceted red stone coming to a sharp point.

"Around this structure were seven large chairs, one slightly elevated on a stone platform above the others. I swam up to the ceiling and put my feet against the edge and tried to pry the metal rod loose. I was sure it was gold. It didn't move. I knew that I was going to need help to remove this treasure.

"Knowing that the other divers would only have half tanks of air left and would not want to dive again, I decided to bring something back to the boat to prove to them that there was something worthwhile down here. I took my knife and scraped the rod to get filings to put into my glove. But instead of filings coming off, I ruined the edge of my knife. That knife is as hard a metal as we know how to make—tempered steel. And it didn't make a scratch on the rod!

"Next, I settled down to the floor area and sat on the large chair. It had a comfortable shape, with arms. After resting a moment, my eyes were drawn back to the crystal, radiating a form of brilliance there. I was looking for anything in the room that was loose to take back as evidence of this experience, because in the back of my mind I kept thinking, 'Is this real? It's so beautiful, maybe this is all my imagination.' I reached between the hands and the crystal moved—it was loose! I reached in and picked it out.

"The metal hands were bronze-colored, but on the inside they were gold-colored, similar to the rod; and on the inside it also appeared black, like it had been burned by some flame or high energy, and it was a little frightening to pick up this stone. If it could burn this metal, what would it do to me? I picked it up and nothing happened.

"I stopped for a moment; there was a moment's peace. And all at once there was a voice—not an audible one, and yet it was coming very loud, but inside, and through the structure itself around me. Sort of radiating, yet it was a voice, instructing me: 'You came, and you have what you came for. Now leave, and don't come back.'

"Interestingly, in returning to the surface and getting onto the boat, the other divers all had a similar experience. All had felt this same impression—or voice. Each one of the divers had artifacts of some sort. Some were strange-looking devices similar to a small pocket calculator with a window, but no switches. We never did figure out what made them work. We don't know what they are.

285

"Since that time, I'm the only one left alive of that group. Each one of the other divers has died in the water in the Bermuda Triangle somewhere. I've been diving since in the Triangle, but not in that area. I won't go in the water in that area!

"But hopefully some of the people who are filming will be there at the right time, when the structures are free of the sand that moved for us that day because of the storm, and will be able to film for you the underwater city.

"The buildings were a mixture of Egyptian-type, some similar to those found in ancient South America, although the pyramid was smooth-edged and not stepped; and there were many dome-shaped buildings. I spent all of my time at the pyramid, and only from a distance observed the other structures.

"On the return home, a strange feeling came over all the divers. We seemed to feel isolated from one another and didn't feel like talking much. We only met a few times after that day. There was no bond between us from that moment on, although there should have been.

"It was five years before I felt safe in displaying the crystal to the public. And we have this crystal that came out of this experience.

"Whether I truly died in preparation to get this crystal, I don't know; you have to judge for yourself. I feel differently today; my mind, my thinking is much different.

"The crystal itself is a phenomenal thing. We've exposed it publicly five times, and it is displayed at no other time. Many people have claimed many things around the crystal. We're researching the effects and the phenomena that occur around it.

"People have claimed to be healed; we have people that see, feel things. I don't think that we have had more than a half dozen people who have ever come up to the crystal, placed their hands over it, and not felt the ionic wind that comes off of it.

"The crystal is quartz. As a gem it was appraised

72. The famous Pyramid crystal found by Dr. Ray Brown

in 1970 at $20,000. Today, as a gem, it's worth a little more. But of course it is priceless for what it really is.

"It is a perfect sphere. Of course it has to have been cut; quartz crystals don't form spherically.

"It has a flaw in it. In the center of it, out of smoky quartz naturally formed, is a nearly perfect pyramid, and if you look at it you will see three pyramids, one stacked behind the other; and in the alpha state there is a fourth pyramid that appears behind the three.

"If you look at it from the side, you see that the

pyramid shape is formed from thousands of little grid lines, similar to electronic grids, in the smoky quartz. It is observable in the shape of a pyramid just from the front side; from the sides you see the grid lines. There are pyramids within pyramids within pyramids, upside down, sideways, all ways, but the main pyramid structures are forward and straight ahead."

Anyone hearing Dr. Brown recount his spectacular story of becoming the guardian of the Atlantean crystal immediately has dozens of questions to ask. I've included the ones that shed more knowledge on this beautiful gem recovered from the pyramid:

Q.: Exactly where is the site of these ruins?
A.: I cannot give you the latitude and longitude—I don't have it in my head. But I can mark it on a map for you. It's very near the tip of the Tongue of the Ocean, pointing in a straight line to the larger islands in the Bari Islands chain, some 20 miles from the shelf edge, dropping into the Tongue. It's a long way from any particular large land mass; Andros Island on one side; the nearest habitable place of any size is Bimini.

Q.: What was the depth the sand was uncovered to, to reveal the pyramid?
A.: At the base of the pyramid, about 120 feet. There was about 90 feet of the pyramid exposed through that. It continued on down. The surfaces of anything left underwater are covered with algae and a slime of animal materials. In the room there was no growth of any kind. Everything was absolutely spotless, and the surface of the pyramid was as shiny and spotless as if you were looking at a highly polished mirror. It was a white stone. Above water it must have appeared from a distance as a gigantic piece of white marble. It would have been just magnificent!

Q.: Where was the opening in the pyramid?

A.: On a center line right in the exact middle. I believe that the rod came right from the cap. The cap, by the way, appeared to be lapis.

Q.: If the doorway remained open, wouldn't sand fill the room?

A.: Yes, if it remained open, when the sand filled in, it would fill the room, I'm sure. But whatever opened I'm sure closed at some point. I didn't observe it close, but I assume that if I went around and couldn't see a hole or opening, and then found one, whatever made it open would also make it close.

Q.: Was there any sand in the room?

A.: There was no evidence of sand in the room. The floor was white stone. I was impressed at how clean and clear everything was.

Q.: What happened to the opening in the pyramid when you left?

A.: As long as I could observe, the opening remained open. I didn't see any form of door. I looked inside, I felt the edges of the stone, and there was nothing. That's a mystery.

Q.: Do you believe that the walls were solid?

A.: I don't have any way of knowing. I assume they were. Everything appeared to be quite heavy and made of solid stone. The hallway going in some 30 feet was solid stones, and I assumed that the whole pyramid would be solid.

Q.: What was the source of light within the room inside the pyramid?

A.: I do not know. There was no source like a light bulb, but everything was light. In my excitement, I had left my diving light on the boat.

Q.: Was there any connection between the rod and the crystal?

A.: No. There was a space of maybe 4 feet between the end of the red stone and the crystal itself. The crystal appeared to have been used as some device as part of a ceremony that this pyramid was used for.

Q.: What was the metal rod?

A.: I don't really know what it was, but I believe it was gold, apparently treated with some type of hardening process.

The Ancient Americans had a process by which they tempered copper, and I know that there is a reward by several metal companies that want to know how they tempered copper to have a hardness above that of case-hardened steel. We haven't yet learned their secret.

Q.: Which direction were the chairs facing?

A.: I had some orientation from my watch setting, but in the room I didn't observe compass settings to tell you which direction which chairs were facing. They were sort of circular around this pedestal.

Q.: What are some physical properties of the crystal?

A.: It is quartz, although there is something strange about this stone. It has a peculiar metallic property above that of quartz. You can tell by light refraction that it is quartz, but it is half again as heavy as quartz should be by weight. Perhaps it is the metallic form in the grid lines in it that's metal rather than quartz.

Q.: What is your experience when you touch the crystal?

A.: When it's first uncovered, nothing spectacular happens; but after a few minutes it picks up energy and it takes off . . . if you place your hands above it, you'll feel hot and cold layers as observable as anything you've ever felt. You can feel the ions shooting up from the crystal and it tingles. The closer you are to the crystal, the weaker the energy; the farther above it, the stronger it gets.

Q.: What is some of your experience with the stone?

A.: Many times when I'm around the stone I return to my experience out of the body. I go look at things in a very conscious, alert way. The other things are rather hard to describe. I can go see what I need to see to correct the problem I'm working on. Other people who have passed near the crystal have written and told me they have had similar experiences in problem-solving.

We've observed this stone giving light off all by itself at times. We've been able to feel things. We've had readings by psychics all over the country, and all of the readings have been consistent in that they claim that the stone is a phenomenal thing for the planet, and that it is a device that will magnify thought and energy of any form many, many times. They claim it can be dangerous and good.

Tiny little chips in computers do phenomenal things—they're made of crystals. We know that crystals do have electronic qualities. Whether the little grid lines around this thing are of that nature remains to be seen. We have people who claim to be cured of illnesses when near the crystal.

Q.: Do you believe in reincarnation?

A.: Elizabeth Bacon in New York was giving a reading about the crystal; there were some five hundred people present. She went into her trance, and the people were asking questions about the crystal and the data that came through. She said, "The man who has it used to be called 'Thoth.' "

Q.: Does the crystal vary as to the thought form?

A.: Yes. For instance, I used to display it without a glass bubble around it, and every once in a while someone would touch it. Once, a lady came up who had a very severe pain in the pancreas. She was doubled up. She touched the stone and the pain went away. The lady who touched the stone a few minutes later, got it. It transferred to her through the fingerprint on the stone. Since then I keep it covered.

Q.: What about meditating?

A.: Meditating near this crystal is unbelievable. You must experience it to appreciate it.

Q.: Can you aim the direction of the energy from the crystal?

A.: I think so. You can do it more with thought than you can by aiming the point of the pyramids, though. You can actually look into it and transmit the energy to other points, measurably.

Q.: What happens when you place a compass over the crystal?

A.: The compass needle spins—counterclockwise close to the stone, clockwise two inches above it.

Q.: Do you notice any changes, according to lunar cycles, etc.?

A.: No. We've tried to find a pattern or schedule as to when this stone does its thing and doesn't do its thing, and I haven't been able to find any pattern to it whatsoever.

Q.: Have you tried to duplicate a pyramid with the crystal in place?

A.: Yes, although not on large pyramids. We have placed the crystal inside pyramid structures and measured the energy, and it is phenomenal! When you place a pyramid structure over this and place it near the same position that it was in, in the original structure, the measurable energy is outstanding.

Q.: Why didn't you stay in the area and do further exploration?

A.: After the experience that I had, I really felt very uneasy about staying around that area. After the warning I received, I didn't want to spend any further time at all there. If you heard a voice that shook even your bones, I think you'd listen and you would follow the advice in fear for your life. Apparently, from the experience of the others, they paid the penalty by not listening.

Q.: Do you think the other four divers died because they returned to the area after being told not to?

A.: I assume that that was what happened. All died in the water. One fellow died in Bimini—an experienced, skilled diver. He jumped off the boat and broke his neck—struck the sand. Another one was taken by shark 40 miles north of Bimini. Another was in Haiti; went out in a very small boat and never returned. The last one died in an underwater accident somewhere off Jamaica—I don't know the exact details.

Q.: Could you find the pyramid again if you wished to?

A.: I could bring you to the 15-by-5-mile area. Whether I could land you on top of the pyramid structure to dig and uncover, I don't know if I could do that accurately. Remember, we spent a whole summer digging 40-foot holes, and if we had hit it right we should have hit the pyramid, but we didn't. So at the cost of a million and a half dollars, we didn't find anything. Then we came there on a fluke, on a storm day, and we landed right on top of it! Now, that sand of course filled back over the area and has recovered this underwater city. But there will be times when it is uncovered again. We watch the storm patterns, and when the storms hit that area, I'm curious to see if it's time to go back there and film. But you won't catch me underwater there!

Q.: What is the location of the Sargasso Sea in relation to this site?

A.: Due east, maybe 150 miles.

Q.: Where were the devices that the other divers found located?

A.: Two of them were found in one structure that appeared like some type of library or art gallery—some large building. They were lying on a stone table in a position that, whatever they were, they were held in high esteem. The other device, which was quite differently shaped, was found in what appeared to be a home structure. We don't know what it is. It was a square, larger device. The others were small and very streamlined. The corners were rounded and they were of a dull-colored metal.

Q.: Has anyone ever tried to steal the crystal?
A.: Yes. I brought it to a party given by a friend, U. S. Anderson, in California. One of the guests, who ran a shop where they sell occult items, asked to see it. A few minutes later, he and the crystal were gone. Strangely, the next morning the crystal had returned. It was waiting outside in the hall. However, the man who had taken it was never heard from again. He never returned to his home or his business. He just disappeared.

Q.: Does anyone else have a spherical crystal?
A.: There are people who are cutting spherical crystals.

My crystal has a strange energy, a very powerful form of energy around it and will charge other materials placed near it. The charging energy tends to get stronger as time goes on, and not diminish. I have no explanation for this.

As the crystal is exposed it grows in potential energy. If we take it into daylight it gets very strong. But it tends to do something with the energy of people. Its energy is greater with a large crowd around it.

Q.: Have you had the crystal carbon-dated?
A.: No. The curator of the Smithsonian claims that the equipment needed to cut this stone so perfectly was not available prior to 1900.

Q.: Has the crystal ever been checked for radioactivity?
A.: No. We may submit it for testing at UCLA to determine why this strange ionic wind comes out of it.

Q.: Was it really right that you took this stone from the pyramid?
A.: Apparently I was supposed to. I really feel that I was drawn to it. To tell you the truth, I don't know

what the purpose of my having it is. I'm doing things with it, yes, but I just don't know.

Q.: Do you believe that this crystal comes from Earth?
A.: No. But that is only my opinion.

Q.: What are your further plans for the crystal?
A.: I don't know. We're wide open. It isn't just a healing device, although being in the healing arts, that is my first line to look into.

The underwater city that Dr. Brown explored, with its inundated group of buildings, may very well be the ancient civilization of Atlantis. It cannot be proven at this time that the ruins he discovered are Atlantean, but apparently they are in the right place. Edgar Cayce had predicted: "Poseidia will be among the first portions of Atlantis to rise again—expect it '68 and '69—not so far away." (Reading 958-3; June 28, 1940).

In another reading in August of the following year (1152-11; MS-3), Cayce stated that within several years, lands will appear in the Atlantic as well as the Pacific. Interestingly, nearly ten years earlier he discusses that the entire country will find many physical changes, but the greatest change in America will be the North Atlantic seaboard (311-8; MS-7; April 9, 1932). Then again, in 1934, he predicts there will be new land seen off the Caribbean Sea and dry land will appear (3976-15).

Naturally, the Edgar Cayce readings can be interpreted in many different ways, but this does not necessarily hamper their validity. In one aspect, his readings consistently referred to the reappearance of lands in Atlantic waters, as well as their disappearance.

The existence of Atlantis has been cogitated, conjectured, considered, contemplated, meditated, mulled or brooded over, deliberated, envisioned, philosophized, pondered, propounded, reasoned, speculated, surmised, and weighed; as well as examined, investigated, researched, and scrutinized. One of the most valuable records of antiquity is the history of Atlantis partially preserved for us through the writings of Plato, who lived about four hundred years before Christ's birth.

For thousands of years hence, the story of Atlantis has usually been regarded by both wise man and fool as a fable signifying nothing; nonetheless, it bears witness to the question of Atlantis as an inestimable record of the past. Plato's narrative contains nothing improbable, insofar as it simply describes a great, rich culture of educated people; the tale is unpretentiously independent of marvels and myths. Thus the story is a reasonable history of people ruled by Kings, living and progressing as other nations have done, but who also reached out, touched, and revolutionized the civilizations of the world.

If the pyramid is assumed to be a singular architectural construction, which the Hindu Puranic writings also indicate as existing far anteriorly in time to any that has survived to our day; and assuming that the existence of Atlantis dates back beyond the known birth of history, then it is quite possible to conclude that the original model for all existing pyramids cannot only be identified with Atlantis, but will also be confirmed upon its discovery.

Over the course of centuries, many have tried to discover Atlantis—or some evidence of it—within and without the boundaries of the Atlantic Ocean. Just as the cities of Herculaneum, Pompeii, Troy, and others were resurrected from their sepulchers of myths and legends, so will it be of Atlantis.

Through the intuitive scholarship of Ignatius Donnelly, a wealth of detail and information is amassed in his book *Atlantis: The Antediluvian World,* published in the late 1800s. His patience, and the seemingly infinite work required to assemble facts supportive of the existence of Atlantis, are assimilated into this voluminous writing, which remains unsurpassed for being vitally essential and having extreme validity.

The underwater city with its pyramid, which had been observed some years prior to Dr. Brown's experience of rediscovering it, is slowly—albeit sporadically—

documented with various and even controversial evidence. For ever so many years, there have been profuse reports by pilots, crew members, and passengers sighting a submerged pyramid or other structures while flying over the waters off the Bahamas. The documented reports of these sightings are usually "officially" dismissed by authorities as visual aberrations due to a host of "optical illusions" experienced by the observers.

The inability to confirm these sightings, even though photographic evidence exists, is the result of the inability to again locate the exact position where the inundated structures were seen. This has become an illusive phenomenon that apparently cannot be repeatedly experienced, even though observers retrace their flight path as accurately as possible.

Ocean exploration, using surface craft with sophisticated electronic equipment designed to locate submerged objects, has recently been employed in an attempt to find the city. But even this undertaking has not been as successful as was initially anticipated; the phenomenon is just as elusive from the surface as it is from the air.

Charles Berlitz, in his book *Without A Trace,* presents "strong evidence" documented by sonar tracings that reveals a massive pyramid structure at the purported site explored by Dr. Brown and others. The disturbing fact about this "strong evidence" is that it clearly lacks any sonar-tracing definition of adjoining ruins known to be part of the complex at this site. Therefore, one of several conclusions can be drawn with varying degrees of strength concerning the sonar location of the pyramid without its surrounding buildings.

The most plausible conclusion is that the explorers are confusing their site with that of Dr. Brown's. The least plausible is that the sand uncovered only the pyramid and remained as a blanket, shielding the ruins from sonar detection. However, when Dr. Brown explored the pyramid, a height of only 90 feet was exposed through the sand, and the subsidiary ruins were also visually discernible at that level; whereas the "sonar pyramid" is

297

claimed to be 420 feet high on an "otherwise flat ocean bottom"—with no ruins ostensibly in evidence.

The most probable conclusions are either that the sonar equipment was malfunctioning and the horizontal contour of the ocean floor was misinterpreted as being a vertical structure (which, by the way, is known to occur quite frequently), or, as has been suggested by reputable authorities, that it was "fabricated" to simultaneously keep alive the controversies surrounding the mysteries and enigmas of the Bermuda Triangle, the Lost City of Atlantis, and the pyramid.

The greatest obstacle to accepting the existence of this pyramid (or pyramids) is its elusiveness—its perpetual process of appearing, disappearing, and then reappearing. However, even this phenomenon loses its mystique once it is understood that the sand of the ocean floor can suddenly—within a matter of hours—be redistributed by the frequent storms between Bimini and the Bahamas.

Dr. Brown states that after spending an entire summer searching underwater at huge expense, nothing was found; but then, revisiting the site on a stormy day, there they were—the ruins and the pyramid! He further states that the shifting sands sporadically cover and uncover the underwater city and that the storm patterns in the area must be closely observed in order to be aware of when the complex will once again be uncovered.

Dr. Brown's incredible quartz crystal ball, with its quality of energy and quantity of strength is, as stated earlier, the symbolic key of the pyramid structure.

Many of us have a misconception concerning the words "crystal" and "quartz." The word crystal actually means a formation by chemical solidification of a mass whose atoms are internally arranged with a regularly repeating pattern, or lattice structure, and usually with external geometric facets. Most minerals develop into crystals when they solidify from a liquid or gas state, because crystallization is the condition of least energy and therefore greatest stability.

Crystals begin from a microscopic point. They have the ability of growing like living organisms, except that the process is by accumulation from the outside, where more of the same material is added, rather than expanding from within. Crystal growth is usually slow—at times, so slow it takes thousands of years for crystals to reach sizable dimensions—while some crystal growth is observable on a day-to-day basis. They are also known to grow into giant forms weighing several tons.

Crystallization occurs in many shapes, forms, and groups. Crystals are referred to as "flowers of the mineral kingdom" because of their fine symmetry and delicate colors. The internal lattice structure of the crystal, determining its outward form, is constructed from orderly arranged atoms held together by electrical attraction of opposite-charged ions.

The word crystal was historically applied to clear quartz, which Greek philosophers thought was water frozen into a six-sided mass by the intense cold of the Alps. Therefore, the rock-crystal variety of quartz is considered the original of all crystals. Quartz is the most widespread and commonest mineral found in the world. It is basically made of silicon dioxide, which may be clear or colored, and always occurs in hexagonal form. The larger quartz crystals are only found in cavities or caves, but they also pervade and form within the tiniest spaces of rocks and other mineral formations.

The apparent mystery regarding the presence of gold and quartz as the two prevalent minerals of pyramid civilizations is unveiled by the fact that gold is usually found in quartz veins. Historical records document the astonishment of various conquerors finding gold used as a virtually commonplace decoration. The application of gold was primarily for the symbolic representation of the sun, because of its brilliance and fiery reflection. Copper, bronze, or any other metal did not have this precise reflective quality, and it was logical for the sun-worshiping civilizations to adopt gold as the symbol of their sun god.

It is quite possible that gold was not the primary product sought after, but rather that it later developed as the by-product of quarrying for the more precious and valuable commodity—quartz. In our current value system, the world uses gold as the standard commodity of exchange, and relegates quartz to a far lesser value. There are, however, some members of the quartz family that are considered expensive gems, such as amethyst, rose and smoky quartz, agate, onyx, jasper, bloodstone, etc. From the dawn of mankind, quartz in its various species has represented powers and mysteries of the cosmos. Various types of quartz, along with other gems and stones, were ascribed to individual zodiacal signs.

How the quartz crystal in its spherical shape became a symbol unto itself, and what in fact it represents, is little understood. The "crystal ball" has long been mis-used as a medium for the enhancement of psychic powers when its true force emanates from its shape and symbolism. Its value to the ancients was more priceless than anything else they possessed, for it had a threefold symbol to them. First, it was the pure representation of the cosmos prior to becoming matter; second, it signified the "Universal Egg" in whose transparence exists creation; and finally, it represented the etheric sphere of the world, in whose translucent essence is preserved the perfect image of all terrestrial activity.

Knowing full well about the electrical properties of quartz, scientists of our day have perfected the artificial production of quartz, virtually free of flaws, for commercial purposes. Unblemished quartz cut into wafer-thin slices and suspended under tension at both ends produces a measurable electrical impulse when flexed. This electrical impulse is quite proportional, up to a point, to the degree of flexion. The internal lattice structure of its atoms in an orderly arrangement is responsible for the production of electrical impulses when the crystal is either momentarily stretched or compressed. It is because of this property that the crystal plays a very important part in commercial and industrial applications, as well as consumer-oriented products. Perhaps the ancients also knew full well of its electrical properties, and had developed an application of the crystal that is still unknown to us—but that undoubtedly was a primary and important force.

Many theories abound concerning the use of the crystal and the purpose for which it was applied by the masters. For example, it is thought that when specifically located and perhaps oriented within the pyramid, the crystal will attract or accumulate cosmic forces, which then will cause it to function by radiating its own energy force. It has been postulated that this force was once used as a vehicle for the transmission of thoughts; as a generator to power all things needing energy; or as a functioning cosmic timepiece.

The description recounted by Dr. Brown is of the quartz crystal ball cradled by two metallic, human-sized hands, bronze-colored with gold coloring on the palms. Directly above the hands was a metallic gold-colored rod extending from the ceiling, directed straight to the crystal, and terminating an estimated 4 feet above it. The end of this rod had a sharply pointed, faceted red stone aimed at the crystal.

The rod may very well have been the conductor of cosmic energy forces, while the red stone concentrated and precisely directed the energy force, perhaps at a certain point of the crystal. Thus the crystal would be activated and its multiple functions could be finely tuned by simply redirecting the concentrated beam from the red stone to a different point of the crystal.

Conversely, the quartz crystal ball, as situated in the hands, could have been heated by fire or flame, which would cause it to emit electrical impulses. These electrical impulses may then have been detected and accumulated by the sharply pointed red stone, which transmitted these energy impulses along the rod, possibly leading to the apex of the pyramid. Once at the apex, the energy impulses then radiated like transmission signals, not only to the surrounding area, but into the cosmos as well.

There are countless theories as to the purpose of radiating these energy impulses from the apex of the pyramid.

Perhaps when viewed from the purely metaphysical plane, within which is epitomized the mystery of human evolution, the crystal in reality took on the role of an experimental animal. A metaphysical philosophy contends that the spirit, by ensouling matter, becomes the indwelling power that gradually and sequentially raises the mineral to the status of the plant; the plant to the animal plane; the animal to the level of man's dignity; and finally, man elevated to the realm of the gods.

These masters would attempt to imbue their spirit into this mineral which, if the process were properly executed, would subsequently transform this mineral into a plant. Being true or perfect masters, they could have indeed transmuted the mystery of human evolution into an actual process in their research laboratory; this undoubtedly has been handed down to us under the guise of rituals and ceremonies of the many religions of the world.

Two important stones or gems of great significance to the mystic emerged as he developed spiritually. The metaphysician who possessed the philosopher's stone possessed the greatest of all treasures—truth. He was therefore wealthy beyond the calculation of man. He became immortal simply because he was able to strengthen that noncorporeal element in all man that does not die, and he became healed of the most loathsome of all diseases—ignorance. The philosopher's stone is an ancient symbol of perfect love, which transmutes all that is base and raises all that is dead. It reflects the perfected and regenerated man whose divine nature shines forth.

The metaphysician also strove to attain possession of the Hermetic Stone, symbolic of divine power—a strength that all men seek but that is found only by exchanging it for temporal power, which is then transformed into the service of the divine.

These two significantly important stones for the metaphysician may in fact have been, at one time, one and the same quartz crystal!

⟨[11]⟩

PYRAMYTHOLOGY

Over the past few years, a wealth of interesting data have been collected concerning the original pyramids, the use they were truly intended for, and the people who built them.

Part of this information comes from hypnotic sessions where individuals were regressed back to flourishing pyramid civilizations; some information comes from psychics and sensitives while they were in trance medium states; and still other ideas have been volunteered by individuals who have expressed their thoughts as to why pyramid civilizations are scattered throughout the world.

The following story has been compiled from a combination of all these data; and while it is a nonfactual, fabricated tale, it does contain fascinating points of information that are quite plausible and simply await verfication.

Pyramythology

What is this place? I'm in a huge . . . vast . . . area . . . there are no bounds. A cloudlike mist seems to billow from all around, and silently settles like fog on a warm, damp dusk. Illumination is diffused throughout the off-white haze, just being, not originating from any source. Where can I be? I don't remember how I've come to be here. I have a vague recollection of who and what I am, but the harder I try to remember, the more difficult it is.

I am aware of my body, but I cannot see it. Slowly wandering in a hapless pattern, in and out of huge pockets of the billowing, smokelike clouds, I feel neither warmth nor cold. The mist is neither moist nor dry. I experience no current of air. I can't even feel the surface on which I am walking. . . . Am I walking? I don't know. Yet I have this sensation of unhurried movement propelling me listlessly through the area. Am I dreaming? How else can I explain this? What am I doing here, alone, in an apparent state of limbo?

The Old Couple and the Master Book

Suddenly I perceive two figures seated in front of me. They are just far enough away that I cannot distinguish their faces too clearly; the tumbling smoke clears from around them just enough that I catch a fleeting glimpse.

I get the impression that it is a man and a woman, even though they are dressed alike, in bright white linen-type gowns that cover their feet and have flowing sleeves down to their hands. Both have illuminescent hair down to their shoulders. One of them has a short beard.

Now I can distinguish coloring in their garments. There is blue . . . there is green . . . yellow . . . red . . . and orange. There is purple, or is it lavender? Perhaps it is lilac. Strange . . . the colors appear not to remain in the same place when I glance and search for them. It is not as light where the couple is as it is where I am; however, I can see the sparkle in their eyes.

The two are kindly-looking, and I judge their age to be sixty-five or so; but to my amazement, I feel . . . I sense . . . my intuition suddenly tells me . . . they are hundreds—thousands of years old. Wait. Incredible! They are ageless! Am I imagining this? To what new world have I been transported?

Now I can see that there is a table on each side of the couple. One table holds an open book—a huge book. I've never seen a book so large! It must be 4 feet thick! And it has to be at least 6 feet long, and perhaps 4 feet wide!

On the table next to the male figure is what appears to be an altar setting: several pieces of gemlike stones; a goldlike chalice; a big crystal ball, with a rod appearing from above with a colorless faceted stone on its end, nearly touching the crystal.

Behind the altar-table hangs a symbol, suspended—a symbol that I've seen before . . . and yet haven't seen. It reminds me of an ankh. But instead of having a horizontal bar below the loop, it has two horizontal loops; and instead of having a straight stem, its stem is like an old-fashioned skeleton key, but more complex, with its triple-sidedness and additional ridging.

I try to approach the couple, but find that I cannot get any closer than I am now. Is it in my mind, or are they real? They seem to speak, but I don't see their lips move. Maybe their lips don't move! Maybe I am hearing them within my mind instead of with my ears! For when I think to myself, "Why am I here?" I perceive her answering, "My daughter, you have been chosen to come before us to learn of some of the secrets that the ancients possess."

Now the old man speaks. "Yes, my son, but not so much secrets as history—the history of the earth, and why the anvil of civilization is so shrouded by mystery in the minds of men."

She speaks again. "We will present you with some of the historical background, some of the knowledge, and some of the wisdom. It shall not be in cipher, for it is difficult for people of your time, at your point of development, to understand our codes. Yet, some of the cipher will be understood by you once you learn of our history—and your history."

I slowly realize that they are ancient souls . . . ancient bodies . . . ancient masters. Yet when I hear them, they don't sound old. Their movements are very soft and very specific. Timelessness is before me.

He points to the big book. "This contains the history of what was—and the history of what is—and the history of what is to be. This book shall never be lost, for it is perpetually guarded by certain individuals, within and without your plane of existence. The guardians within your plane of existence are unaware of their specific mission, until it is necessary for them to defend the Master Book.

"Many individuals on your plane have been designated as guardians for different purposes. Some are meant to guard history; some guard knowledge of universal and earthly science; some are guardians of other individuals on your plane; while others guard the flow of things.

"Individuals become guardians when they are entrusted, unbeknownst to them, with a specific category of wisdom. Some who are called upon to apply their guardianship may not necessarily leave your plane of existence. They become whom you know to be geniuses."

Now the old woman continues: "Existences on your plane grow and continue in positive and negative directions, yet in a never-ending way; for as it has been said by your people, 'History repeats itself,' and civilization repeats itself. Events, everything on earth and in the universe repeats itself. There are cycles within cycles— wheels of existence within wheels. You are entrusted with this knowledge, and now you understand that what is written about today—happening today—has happened in the past, and will happen in the future—not once, but many times again.

"Time and history folds into itself many times over.

Some events have a short cycle and they repeat and recur within a matter of minutes, or days, or months, or years. Other things repeat and recur within decades, or centuries, or millennia—but they do recur. It is the basic rule of nature. The law of the Almighty says life comes and goes, but what happens to man happens over and over again."

At this point I am aware of mounting apprehension. The contents of what the old people have said is beginning to have its impact. Can it be that that's all there is to life's existence as man? What exactly will be the outcome of life itself? And what are the worlds like that are yet to come?

Now another, more immediate, thought passes through my mind. She refers to me as her daughter—he refers to me as his son. Why are they seeing me as two different people? *Am* I two different people? I am aware of my existence in front of them, but I cannot fully perceive a body.

The woman smiles—and I feel slightly reassured. She says, "My daughter, I know you are very puzzled. You see, you *are* my daughter, and yet at the same time, you are his son; for man has the qualities of both sexes in a proportional ratio within the same earthly body. Your life's energy form is equally female and male.

"You also have much apprehension, but you must learn not to allow apprehension to grow into fear; for when fear is allowed to get a stronghold, thoughts become very, very darkened and you cannot see or think clearly."

I feel a calmness descending over me. The apprehension disappears, and a peaceful, near emotionless feeling fills my existence. I believe I can comprehend everything that will be entrusted to me.

And she continues, "You are man on earth today—this very moment. We, too, have existed like you in the past. Your existence to us is in the future. We have been allowed to reach the ultimate energy form. We are the chosen few to watch over and guide those who are the guardians of the laws of nature.

"The basic laws of nature must be maintained by life forms, and must also have overseers in the energy form, for this too is a cycle within a cycle. When a life form ceases to exist on earth it may cease for eternity, or it may just be chosen for its energy form as the caretaker, the overseer, or other life forms who are designated keepers of the laws of nature.

"Our energy form is very powerful compared to your lower form of energy, and that is why you cannot come closer to us than you are now."

A hundred questions begin running through my mind. I want to know so much! But she holds up her hand, the long sleeve draping gracefully around her arm.

"It is better that you not ask many questions. Rather, listen with intent, for we have much to give your mind; then there will be no need for questions."

Atlantis and Lemuria

Now the man begins to speak: "Son, as you question your ancestry, and have only scant knowledge of the beginnings of man on your world, so had we questioned our ancestors. Our knowledge, our information, our written records, our documentation, is as scant as yours. All we are allowed to be aware of and to know is that our ancestors—which are yours, too—came from the civilization called Maoth which—yes—still exists in the center of the earth. Whence was their beginning we do not know.

"We were born and schooled on the continent that today you call Atlantis. At that time there was another continent, located in the Pacific Ocean, known to you as Lemuria, whose people were not so rich in knowledge and in technical skill.

"The Lemurians were at the stage of exploration with their limited sciences. They had only developed the technology for travel across water; and they were in this manner setting out to explore and to settle in other parts of earth.

"We Atlanteans, however, not only had the ability to travel on the water, but also the ability to travel within the water; and we had the ability to travel in the air, and we were able to visit other civilizations in the universe and then travel back to Maoth.

"Before there was Atlantis and Lemuria, there were periods of upheavals and destruction that befell the lands both inside and on the surface of the earth. Such events must occur in all cycles."

The old woman nods in agreement, and takes up the story.

"You see, daughter, we had obtained great ability to harness both the energy from within earth and the cosmic energy from the universe, but we did not know that we were gathering too much. Nor did we have the knowledge or capability to store what we had been gathering. To clarify this in your mind, think of what happens with fruits and vegetables, the produce of the earth. As you know, if too much produce is gathered and it is not stored properly, it will simply decay and wither away. When energy is gathered and not totally consumed, it continues to amass, never dissipating but becoming bigger and bigger. The greater the energy becomes, the less controllable it is—and that is what happened.

"We had attracted more energy than we were able to store and consume. As a result, it discharged from our stockpile in a huge spark, traveling between the North Pole and the South Pole. This spark was great enough to cause a catastrophe that we had not foreseen, nor could ever have conceived, even with all our technical abilities and wisdom of the ages.

"Once this spark was generated, a chain reaction occurred that could not be stopped. It had to be allowed to go and reach its full force, at which point the continents of Atlantis and Lemuria met their catastrophic end. Both continents shattered! Lemuria was more vulnerable, and that unfortunate land mass actually disintegrated; whereas Atlantis, being a more stable continent, broke into a half-dozen pieces before being inundated by the waters of the ocean."

The old man now speaks. "Yes, the various pieces of Atlantis sank beneath the surface of the water. And now, after tens of thousands of years it has become totally covered by the ocean debris that slowly sifted upon it. However, as Earth continues to experience quakes and underwater disturbances, more and more of Atlantis shall become uncovered once again. A cyclical earth change shall be heralded when the land masses of Atlantis resurface, when mountains go back to being ocean bottoms.

"Before Atlantis sank, much had been achieved by our fathers and our forefathers. We were taught that the Almighty was present throughout the entire universe. We had learned to chart the cycles of the universe and to equate these cycles with the cycles of time, the cycles of history, and the cycles of humanity. Our energy knowledge was given to us by our ancestors.

"We had been taught to build one structure—one structure to house the sciences; that same structure housed religion; that structure housed the knowledge. That structure stored the energy, and was simultaneously the sender and the giver of this energy. All of us and our machines were powered or energized through this one structure. Our minds as well as our bodies were nurtured by this structure. Our bodies were formed through this structure.

"Yes—that structure is the pyramid! We needed only one, and that structure was a design of ancient knowledge from Maoth, the world within.

"Some of our Maothan ancestors developed and colonized Atlantis on the surface of the earth, as an experiment to see if the development of the Atlanteans on the surface would parallel that of the inner world. They knew of Lemuria's existence, which was progressing through its normal chain of evolution upon the surface. The Maothans knew, also, that the Atlanteans would

310

developmentally surpass the Lemurians within a brief span of time. And this, indeed, came to pass.

"The Atlanteans erected a pyramid structure on their continent, similar to that of the Maothans in the land within the earth. However, they did not realize that the attraction of energy to the Atlantean pyramid was becoming violently imbalanced. This imbalance occurred because the pyramid was exposed directly to the energies of the universe.

"The same structure within the world only had access to the cosmic energy that filtered through the earth's crust. On the surface, however, there was nothing to filter—to regulate—the amount of energy being attracted and absorbed by the Atlantean structure.

"The balance of polarity between the outer and inner surfaces began to change, becoming erratic. As the millennia went by, the difference in electrical potential became more immense and more threatening, until finally the equalization potential, which is a basic law of nature, sought to stabilize this great buildup of energy, and the spark was born."

Preparing for the Holocaust

Now the old woman speaks. "The spark lasted for seven years. In that period of time we managed to take our wise ones, our scholars, our engineers, our religious people, and place them in ships—those that traveled on the sea, those that traveled in the sea, and those that traveled in the air.

"There were fifty-four ships—eighteen in the water, eighteen on the water, and eighteen in the air. From each of these three groups, nine were selected for our outposts of other civilizations from the other continents around the earth. At that time, all around the surface of the earth, we had religious figures, educators, mathematicians, engineers, astronomers—wise men from all disciplines who had volunteered to go into the sparse, wild country to tame its life forms and to teach them some knowledge.

"One of these outposts is recorded in your current history data, and is known as the Ark. The name of our master there has been translated as you know it today to be Noah. He was knowledgeable of all the animals of the world. During the seven years that the spark lasted, he gathered together as many of the animals as he was able to place on the ship you call the Ark, in order to save these species from the destruction that was yet to occur to the entire surface and, yes, to a degree, to the inner surface of the earth. Noah's Ark was able to travel in and on the water, as well as in the air. Before the catastrophic destruction peaked, the master was able to take two thirds of the animal life existing at that time and save it.

"Elsewhere, other ships were being prepared to contain masons, engineers, scientists, religious ones, et cetera. We were in two separate ships," she gestures toward the old man, then goes on, "and our ships were among those surviving the holocaust. Of the original fifty-four ships that were launched, only nine survived." She pauses a moment, then adds, "Forty-five ships, and all who were on them, were lost."

Her eyes begin to sparkle with greater intensity. I cannot tell whether it is due to tears for the past, or to the tears of gladness that the holocaust had finally ended. She straightens in her chair and continues: "Fortunately, as the Almighty One constantly governs the existence and nonexistence of all energy forms, I was on one of the surviving religious ships. The religious ships did not have as much electrical potential within, and did not suffer as many of the equalizing potential shocks as did others."

Reconstruction After the Catastrophe

Now the old man is speaking again. "When the catastrophe ended, the surviving ships gathered together and a meeting was held, at which the Survey Committee gave its report.

"The entire surface of the earth had changed. Waves and waves of water spread around the globe very quickly, inundating everything many times over. New land appeared where oceans once existed; oceans and bodies of water covered old land masses. The poles of the earth repositioned themselves due to the electrical equilibrium and subsequent repolarization process. Ice began to form at the new poles, threatening to seal in the Maoths. The environment had changed drastically, causing severely different climate conditions to develop in various locations on the earth. The positions of the stars appeared to have changed, but it was only due to the rotational shift of the earth. The gravitational pull became stronger, and we found ourselves having more difficulty in levitating. The postdevastation climatic changes, which were mainly rains, floods, and tidal waves, lasted for forty years.

"At our meeting it was decided that we would not begin anew on only one continent. We decided to equally subdivide our knowledgeable masters and place ourselves on different parts of Earth. One of the elder masters suggested that a group be sent to another planet, to accomplish colonization and expansion of our outposts already established on twenty-one different planets. This was agreed upon, and a ship was sent out to establish a central base for the universe in what you know as the Pleiades. Those of us left behind vowed to remain earthbound forever and to rely on those from the central base traveling to us.

"We decided to dispatch another shipload back to the continent of Maoth, in the inner world. This ship contained neophytes who would receive further intensive education; and also included on this ship was original documentation to be stored in Maoth for safekeeping.

"The seven remaining ships were dispersed to geographical locations most suited, both in climate and temperament, for our reconstruction; and which also had

313

beings inhabiting them. These were the prime areas of Atlantean reconstruction.

"Several of these sites are already known to you. Some others will be rediscovered around your year 2000, while the remainder have since been obliterated by history. One of our group settled in what is now known as Egypt; another in South America; a third went to North America; a fourth went to the Himalayas; and the remaining three were dispatched to Antarctica, Australia, and Greenland.

"Each group took a portion of the writings, deciding to preserve them forever in such a manner that neither catastrophe as we had experienced, nor human intervention, could ever destroy them. Seven groups . . . seven divisions of our secret written knowledge."

The woman picks up the narrative. "We began to build anew. We built our pyramid structure civilization at all seven points of our distribution. Each of our pyramids was exactly as the original on Atlantis. It housed the storage of energy. It was the repository of knowledge. It was the center of our religion. All the energy that was needed was once again available from the pyramid; and, yes, we were wiser now. We knew how to attract just enough energy to be collected in this pyramid. The excessive energy potentially built up was mechanically shunted or freed, for we did not want it to be trapped like before.

"The electromagnetic and cosmic energy were collected at the apex by the master crystal control, and stored in the bottom portion of the pyramid. Our wisdom and knowledge were stored in the middle, or center portion; and our religion was housed near the apex.

"The pyramid was redesigned so that the initiates— those who wanted to become religious ones—had to pass through the pyramid in prescribed steps. Those failing to reach mastery from the initiate level were reabsorbed, for once an individual becomes an initiate, even the smaller bits of knowledge are very dangerous if not handled correctly."

The illumination around me is beginning to fade. The visions that were so vivid while the two spoke are disappearing; and suddenly I am in total darkness. I see nothing and hear nothing. A feeling of desolation descends over me. I am in a total void.

I yearn for more knowledge; my desire becomes stronger and stronger. I am being entrusted with a portion of the wisdom of the ages, but it appears to be given painstakingly; slowly; in bits and pieces like a puzzle. Each time a piece is found that fits, the picture gets clearer, and information conveyed by the *Gestalt* of the puzzle becomes more evident.

The darkness engulfs me—and I am beginning to feel apprehensive again. What is happening? Where should I go? What should I do? Suddenly I hear a voice within me—a different voice: "Fear not the darkness, for this darkness is not forever. Light always follows darkness and, yea, darkness always follows the light. This is but one of the many laws of nature—that of the cycle of nature that states, 'One follows the other.' The laws of nature are what man must understand first before he can even begin to comprehend the ancient masters, for the ancients know what you, man, have forgotten."

Now light is beginning to reinfiltrate the darkness; and once again I am in front of the couple. The man speaks:

"Following several millennia of existence and re-development, we learned that dividing into seven different groups was not necessary. We found that the division, the splitting up of the groups, actually weakened the total energy upon which we depended. So we decided to regroup into one community; and upon consulting our inner world, we agreed that we must go back to the beginning. We stripped our structures and went back to the Center. With what we had given the beings on earth, we knew that they would progress slowly; and we also knew that at their rate of development it would take aeons for them to reach the status of the Center."

Now the woman speaks: "Our group in space

315

received much support from the Center, because the Center realized the space stations on the various planets in the universe were able to significantly regulate the cosmic energy radiated to earth. Then the Center dispatched more groups into the universe, for in space we are able to look at and monitor the voltage gradient between the outer and inner surfaces of the earth, along with the voltage potential among earth, the planets, and other stellar bodies. Our extraterrestrial groups are now able to foresee some, but not all, future catastrophes, for another law of nature states that spontaneity is a necessary existence in nature's cycle."

A New Catastrophe

The old man speaks: "One day, from data submitted by every universal station to the Center, we became aware that a large mass was approaching earth. A plan was designed in an attempt to circumvent the encroaching catastrophe.

"The seven surface pyramids had to be reactivated, in order to collect the energy force radiated by this oncoming mass. We planned to beam the energy force back to repel the approaching object, creating a braking force—a counterforce—to prevent this mass from striking and annihilating earth. The plan did succeed in slowing the mass down, and it prevented a collision with earth; yet its proximity caused new catastrophes—earthquakes, floods. By the time the beings on the surface of the earth realized that they had survived the catastrophe, they subsequently beheld a body in orbit with the earth—the moon. It was the largest of three. The other two collided with each other and broke into pieces. Some of those fell upon the earth; others shot into space."

Now she speaks. "When the catastrophe was over, we surveyed the surface and saw that the Almighty

Power had saved a sampling of the lives of the many creatures on the surface of the earth; and it was then that we realized that it wasn't really possible to intervene upon the laws of nature, for as its laws govern itself, its laws are self-protective within each cycle. It becomes more like a weeding-out process where those who are scheduled—who are selected to survive—will; and those who are not, will not.

"The beings surviving regressed and degenerated back to the times before our living on the surface, and our governing committee agreed to bring to these beings a program of education, to re-establish some of the lost knowledge. We intervened. We went to many groups of beings throughout the surface of the earth, to educate them, to give them back basic knowledge of the laws of nature, and to speed up their progress of development.

"It was also decided that we should attempt to shut off the energy in the pyramid that had sunk with Atlantis; and to do the same with some other generating plants that we and the Lemurians had long ago distributed throughout the world. These had acted as relay stations, supplying energies to our various surface outposts that were no longer extant.

"We successfully deactivated all but three—one in the Western Hemisphere, the Atlantean pyramid generator, and the Lemurian Cubic generator in the Pacific Ocean. These three energy-collecting and -regenerating structures had developed a strong energy field around the crystal nucleus, which our science to this day has not been able to penetrate to safely deactivate the units. The energy from these structures will continue to amass and intermittently discharge their stored energy in a burst until such a natural catastrophe occurs to annihilate them. Until that occurs, the intermittent discharge of energy will continue to be disruptive to man, for the collected energy is like the sands of time—it will never run out. Energy is energy. It has existed, it continues to exist, and it will exist forever."

317

The Rites of Initiation

Now the old man speaks. "We decided to conduct an experiment to see if we could lead some of the surface beings back to some of the basic forms of knowledge and wisdom. We revived in the minds of the survivors the significance of the pyramid structure in their area, but we limited them to use it only for religious purposes. They were taught to fear light and to fear darkness. We taught them how to fear themselves and then how to fear the unknown, for we had to teach them how not to fear—how to see through and beyond their fears. They were passed through the rites of initiation in exactly the same manner as our initiation rites exist.

"They were placed into the pyramid in total darkness. It was up to them to find various points from which they could develop and reach the next level of knowledge. The pyramid is so built as to have hidden chambers, doors, and passageways equivalent to various trials, tribulations, and rewards—or death.

"The first fear we developed in the initiates was the fear of darkness. They were plunged into the beginning passageway of the labyrinth. From there the initiate had to find his first chamber. The environs of the pyramid had been so designed as to place the first chamber down below. Once the initiate reached the lowest chamber in total darkness, his fear either engulfed him or enlightened him. The next step was to confront him with the unknown.

"The chamber and passageway were flooded with water. In total darkness, the initiate now had to make his next decision—either to accept the fate confronting him and move with it, or to struggle and fight and ultimately lose. Those who accepted willingly and faithfully the flooding of the chamber and passageway learned as they floated on the water that they floated up into another passageway; and they would continue to float up to the very top. But this top was closed—it had no opening. If the initiate did not give up, he

318

would find that the flooding stopped in plenty of time and the water slowly receded, bringing him back to the lower chamber. Once there, the initiate had to learn again, through his own intuition, that he had to see, but not with his eyes. He had to see with his mind's eye. His intuition must see for him, just as a blind man 'sees' more than a sighted individual. The initiate had to see what he had learned from this experience; for, after all, going down a pitch-black passageway into a blank chamber and then suddenly having water rush in, floating him up in a vertical shaft to an end again should enlighten him. He should see a light in his mind that made him realize that there was some place he had to go—some secret door or some secret passageway that he had yet to find. He learned to see with the eyes of his senses—his mind's eye."

The woman speaks: "The first or lower chamber is so constructed as to have smoothness to its ceiling and the upper part of its walls, so as not to cause undue injury to the initiate's body during the flotation process.

"After the initiate was unsuccessful in locating the shaft through which he had been floated, his next decision would be to retrace his steps. Because the descending passageway is so long, he would sooner or later realize that there might be an opening to another passageway from within the descending passageway. Finally he arrived at the correct decision and began his trek back up the descending passageway. In total darkness, he physically had to grope around with his hands—'seeing' with his sense of touch, his sense of feeling. Somewhere along the wall of the passage, he ultimately found some grooves. In the near vicinity of these grooves there would be a stone that felt different to the touch, having a different texture from the rest of the stones in the passageway. Once found, the initiate should—and most of them did—reason correctly that this was the entrance to another chamber or passageway."

The man speaks: "Now it was up to the initiate to determine how this stone would move—would open to

319

allow him passage. All the initiate would have to do was to properly recite a psalm that was taught to him, with the reason not given, during the preparatory stage. After he recited the psalm correctly with the proper inflection, the elder masters would cause this great massive door to open.

"This door is a very guarded door and many people who wandered in between initiations, or the nomads who found their way in, would not be able to open it. The door is actually in three parts, one behind the other. They are called plugs today, but these are the actual doors by which the entrance to the main ascending passage was closed, prohibiting entry to the uninitiated.

"The doors were opened in such a way that the initiate had to crawl around to find the spot. There was just enough room for him to squeeze through. Once past the first door, he found he had another door to squeeze through, but now he had to rest, and in his period of rest the initiate learned about dedication. He learned that life has many difficult obstacles to surmount. If he rested too long, the doors would begin to close; at this point he would have to hurry and start squeezing through the second door, and then the closings would halt. Once squeezed through the second doorway, he would again find himself in a narrow area, with yet another door. Now the initiate would ask himself how many doors he would have to squeeze past in order to reach his goal. The ones who had gained sufficient intuition would sense that there was only a third door to go, and with this thought in mind they rested less the second time than the first. Those who felt hopeless, resting longer, would find the door again beginning to close. The ones who did not scurry fast enough terminated their initiation, as well as their existence, at this point.

"Once past the third door, the initiate realized that this passageway was very long—a passageway through which he had to again gropingly crawl upward to reach the other end. Upon reaching the end, the passageway opened into a vast, huge chamber. The initiate had to learn once again, to see with a different part of his senses. Like the blind person relying on his sense of hearing, the initiate who learned quickly now learned to 'see' with his ears. No longer having to crawl, he was able to stand up. By reciting the psalm once again, he was able to readily find the end of the chamber by seeing it with his ears—leading him to the next phase of his initiation."

The woman speaks: "Those who did not realize that they could find their way through their sense of hearing groped along from side to side of the chamber. They thought that it was one solid room with very high walls that they were not able to climb to reach the ceiling. Some of them made many complete circuits around the chamber, not sensing and realizing that one side of this huge chamber contained a passage through which they could gain exit, entering into a strange passageway; and still others did not realize that, once crawling to the junction point allowing them to stand, the passageway split in two directions.

"Some initiates took very long in realizing the floor plan of this vast chamber. Those who were unable to locate either end of the chamber actually gave up. They waited for days and days before finally being led out of the pyramid and their initiation, as well as their lives, were terminated.

"The initiate who discovered the junction point the moment he was able to stand erect was confronted with another decision—which way to go. Some continued their trek along the straight horizontal course, while others continued along the ascending floor of the huge chamber —reciting their psalm to reach the other end. Curiously, most of the beings initiated chose the straight course and reached the chamber at the end of this straight, horizontal passageway. Those initiates first choosing to ascend into the chamber rather than following the horizontal passage did not find an entrance open at the other end of the chamber, and their reasoning should have guided them back to the junction point, to then follow along the horizontal passageway."

He speaks: "In this chamber is an altar; and an image of our God, fashioned in the rarest of metals and gems, was encouched in one wall of the chamber. Once the initiate entered this chamber he had to observe a long period of fasting and meditation. He was not allowed to leave this chamber until he experienced a period of inner peace.

"Three masters came to him and taught him how to see and know with the senses. One taught him the mysteries of the sense of touch, the other hearing, and the third with the sense of smell. When the period of initiation in the small chamber was completed, the initiate was allowed to return to the junction point.

"Now he had to continue his ascent through the long chamber. Upon reaching the top, he had to surmount a huge step, at the end of which was a short, small tunnel through which he had to crawl.

"Once again, he was confronted with a doorlike obstacle. These doors, unbeknownst to him, were permanently positioned in place. They were not intended to be moved mechanically any longer. What the initiate had to learn was that he now had to physically exert himself, surmounting the obstacle in his path by climbing over it. The climb itself was very difficult and when he completed it he was confronted with another small, short tunnel.

"His ability to see that he would have to climb over the doorlike obstacle was presented to his sense of smell, by the aroma of herbs whose scent he had to learn to follow.

"Upon crawling through the last low, short tunnel, the initiate finally gained entrance to the temple proper, where five elder masters now attended to him. They taught him the remainder of the senses of his body and mind. Then they taught him to control his senses. He learned the physicalness of his body, and how to control every organ. They trained him to slow his body functions down to the point where he transcended the state of sleep and entered into a suspended state of animation. He had to learn about the functions of his body completely and totally within forty days.

"Once the masters were convinced that he had sufficient control and maintenance of his body's functions, they placed him into a container and sealed it. At this point, the initiate had to slow down the physiological functions of his body to a degree where he could exist in this airtight, sealed container for three consecutive and inclusive twenty-four-hour periods of time. When the container was opened, he was supposed to be able to reawaken his body and continue the initiation. If he failed to have complete control over his body functions, then of course he terminated his own initiation rites in the sealed container.

"Upon reviving his body, the initiate was then taken by the five masters through a secret door in the temple wall and led up a long, twisting, narrow flight of stairs, to a much larger temple containing only a table. He lay upon his back on this table, and the masters connected cables to his ankles and wrists. A large crystal was placed on his forehead. The initiate was instructed to keep his eyes closed and to place his body back into the state of suspended animation. Now the ceiling of the room swung aside, showing that the apex had actually moved, exposing the chamber to the full force of the cosmic energy.

"The energy force, capable of blinding the uninitiated, also caused the initiate in the rite to leave his body and enter the crystal on his forehead, at which time he came in complete communion with the Almighty Power. He was now entrusted with every secret of the universe. A blue glow was seen around his physical body, which transformed his physical body into the body of a master. The top stone of the pyramid swung back into place, once again becoming the ceiling for the chamber of the cosmic energy rite. A few moments later, the blue glow melted into the initiate's body and the four cables and the crystal were removed.

"The initiate-now-neophyte-master was garbed in the traditional white robe. He then left, leading the elders down a second flight of secret steps, which he then intuitively knew, and entered the chamber of universal instruction. This room, along with the rest of the world, would be his university."

Powers of the Neophyte Master

The woman speaks: "Upon becoming the neophyte master, he could come and go from the confines of the pyramid. He then joined the select group of individuals who were to work and earn their way to becoming elder masters, for as one elder master attains the existence of pure energy, a new elder master has to replace him to perpetuate and keep the secrets of our universe.

"The neophyte master now had to learn that as an individual he could do very little. He could do what you would call tricks of magic, but yet the common people would view these accomplishments of his as miracles. The neophyte was taught how to heal, how to take his bodily energy and redirect it, focusing it to cause restructuring of the energy within a sick individual and reversing or halting the progress of the illness. People who were in comas and thought dead could be revived by the neophyte. Blind people could be made to see again because of the tremendous energy control of the neophyte.

"But yet the neophyte could not, on his individual basis alone, control the flow of rivers, the growth of plants, or the clouds in the sky. The neophyte had to learn to do those things collectively. Minds must be brought together into a unified form of energy that has the strength—that has the power—of the Almighty to affect nature. All three ranks of mastership—neophyte master, master, and elder master—had perfected this ability, and with this ability there was no need for the Maoths to have armies for protection or aggression.

"By grouping our mental energies together, a great wall of energy was established that invaders could not penetrate. The masters created spheres of great energy, and when directed at invaders, it startled them and made them return whence they came, not recalling where they had been."

The old man speaks: "It was difficult during the time we were on the planet surface because there were many beings from far-off countries who felt that we had riches that they wanted, needed, or couldn't live without. As in everything, in our ability to ward off these invaders, some of them died. It is true they died as a result of our energy, but we have never directed our energy for the malicious purpose of termination.

"In their fear they would trample their kind. In their fear they would fall and die. In their fear they would fight blindly, killing those of their own around them. Yet these beings never seemed to stop. Oh, they would stop for a while, only to regroup and plan new strategies of attack. Our elder masters would sit together and listen into their camp, or into their cities, far, far away, and hear what was being plotted—what campaigns were being drawn up for a new attack. At times we were forced to have an elder master or two project to their cities and cause a cataclysmic problem, in order to make them attend to that disaster and forget about us.

"Our other groups around the world were experiencing the same problems. We learned that it was difficult for us to control these things because separated, our power was not that great; so we agreed to rejoin and go back to the Center.

"We sealed all the pyramids, removed our statues and altar, removed the lid from the container, dug a vertical shaft from the junction point down to the first chamber after permanently setting the three doorlike plugging stones into position, and abandoned the pyramids."

The woman speaks: "We were sad, yet even with our sadness there was much, much joy; for we realized that the surface beings were beginning to develop in a way we had developed. It is taking man much longer, and he has lost much of the knowledge and ability we had given him. Periodically the Maothans intervene by coming and directly guiding man, and watching over him so that he does not destroy himself through war."

He speaks: "When the pyramids were sealed they were left in a condition appearing to have never been completed. The design of the pyramid is such that the apex, the top portion of the structure containing the energy collection and converting capability, is easily removable. We had no need for it any longer, because we were going back to the Center, so we buried it in the ground in the vicinity of each pyramid. Once the apex is removed from the pyramid, it no longer has the energy collection, conversion, generation, regeneration, transmission, and amplification capabilities.

"The committee of elders decided that if the moment should come where a spontaneous disaster terminates Maoth, some evidence and knowledge must be passed on to surface man developing; so the knowledge of where the apex is buried, and certain formulae allowing the user to activate the pyramid once again, have been placed in a secret chamber inside the pyramid. It was decided that the Great Pyramid in Egypt contain this information, while the other pyramids around the world contain specific information governing the laws of science, history, and the universe. The secret chamber containing this knowledge is within one of the granite plugs in the ascending passageway of the Great Pyramid in Egypt.

"Another large pyramid in Egypt, labeled the Bent Pyramid, contains the reasons for the interaction of several smaller pyramids in Egypt and how to interconnect the functions of all pyramids around the world. The energy generating-converting device will also be found in the Bent Pyramid. Yes, it is a crystal. The ones formed into a ball are not the primary sources, but

326

are secondary sources that actually are the translators—
the communications devices—that enable them to communicate with Maothans throughout the world and the
universe. One such ball of crystal has already been found
and taken from one of the secondary pyramids of
Atlantis."

She speaks: "The crystal ball itself is useless. It
must be used the way it was found, but it will be quite
a while before the doors of that pyramid will again be
opened, giving access to it."

Returning to the Present

The clouds, the billowing mist, are getting thicker
and thicker, obscuring my view of the old couple. I seem
to be moving away from them. The illumination is fading.
I want to remain with the old couple, but I can barely
see them now. Darkness is descending over me. I know
I have been entrusted with some knowledge because I
have been chosen to be a guardian—a keeper of the
knowledge. Now the last light fades, and the couple disappears; but I can feel—I sense—that although I am
going away, they will always be with me. I enter darkness,
and from the darkness a flash of light. I feel pressure on
my right shoulder; and I hear a deep, gruff voice. I
open my eyes.

The bus driver is leaning over me—shaking my
shoulder. He looks a little annoyed.

"Hey, buddy! Wake up. This is the end of the
line."

I squint sleepily at him—glance around at the empty
bus—and yawn as I stretch. I feel great! Boy, that was
a good nap! I wonder if I dreamed anything?

But what's the difference? I never remember my
dreams anyway.

{12}

CONCLUSION

What I have endeavored to do in the preceding chapters was not so much to present a work that would answer the age-old questions and mysteries surrounding the Great Pyramid; but rather, I have tried to combine into one volume all the information and the questions that have perplexed scholars and metaphysicians alike for centuries. My purpose has been to instill in the readers the ability to arrive at their own conclusive answers—if they can ever find that possible. My conclusion at this point is that I have not been able to reach a definite answer myself.

There are many vexing questions, and I am basically back at square 1: Was the Great Pyramid used as a tomb? Was the Great Pyramid a temple for religious and ritual ceremonies? I just don't know!

Any Egyptologist who bombastically asserts that the Great Pyramid was nothing more than a tomb is citable for the same narrow-mindedness in his thinking as those pyramidologists and metaphysicians he accuses for believing that it was only a temple of initiation. The possibility is great that the Pyramid was used for both purposes—as a temple of initiation originally, and subsequently as a tomb, which then became the example of tomb construction for future dynasties. It is as difficult to prove that the Pyramid was a temple as it is to prove that it is a tomb.

Egyptologists, in their attempt to date pyramids, unwittingly have divided all pyramid structures into two categories: pre-Fifth Dynasty and post-Fourth Dynasty. This classification is not based on an exact or even approximate knowledge of the dates of individual pyramids. Rather, pre-Fifth Dynasty pyramids are grouped together due to similarities in architectural design, and post-Fourth Dynasty pyramids, due to lack of similarity and the assumption that they are copies of earlier designs. Given this division, we can then do a little bit of investigative research, and look at some of the features of all the pyramids classified in the Fourth Dynasty and prior to it.

The Great Pyramid has been singled out as a significant structure based upon three fundamental reasons. First, it is the largest physically extant pyramid in all of Egypt. Second, its linear dimensions correlate to nearly every cosmic aspect of our universe, as well as to the religious foundation of the Bible. Finally, the third reason for its prominence is its unique interior design of passageways and chambers, which no other pyramid seems to come close to.

However, if we take a look at some other pyramids, as I have outlined in the following chart according to their height, length of base, and slope angle of their faces, some additional interesting features and possibilities begin to take shape. The Pyramid of Chephren, which stands virtually next to Cheops' Pyramid, is the second-largest pyramid in Egypt; while the Pyramid of Mycerinus —the third in the Giza group—is really the sixth-largest pyramid in Egypt.

The third-largest pyramid is the Bent Pyramid of

73. A View of the Giza Complex

Chart VII

Pyramid	Height	Base Length	Face Angle	Alignment Deviation	Number of Entrances
Cheops	481 ft.	755 ft.	50°51′	1′57″ S of W	One
Kafra Chephren	471 ft.	708 ft.	52°20′	5′26″ W of N	Two
Bent/Dahshur Southern Pyramid Snofru	336 ft.	620 ft.	54°31′/42°21′	9′12″ W of N	Two
Northern/Dahshur Snofru	300 ft.	675 ft.	43°40′	None available	One
Meidum Snofru	276 ft.	450 ft.	51°53′	24′25″ W of N	One
Mycerinus	218 ft.	356 ft.	51°	14′3″ E of N	One existing One closed
Zoser at Saqqara	200 ft.	410 ft. x 360 ft.	75°(?)	None available	One

Note: All values are either original, current, or averaged.

74.

331

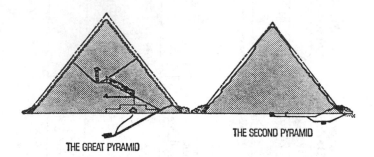

THE GREAT PYRAMID

THE SECOND PYRAMID

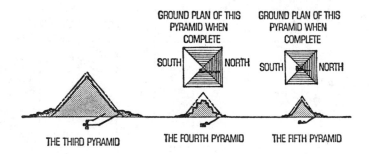

GROUND PLAN OF THIS
PYRAMID WHEN
COMPLETE

SOUTH   NORTH

GROUND PLAN OF THIS
PYRAMID WHEN
COMPLETE

SOUTH   NORTH

THE THIRD PYRAMID

THE FOURTH PYRAMID

THE FIFTH PYRAMID

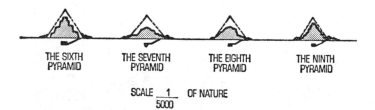

THE SIXTH
PYRAMID

THE SEVENTH
PYRAMID

THE EIGHTH
PYRAMID

THE NINTH
PYRAMID

SCALE $\frac{1}{5000}$ OF NATURE

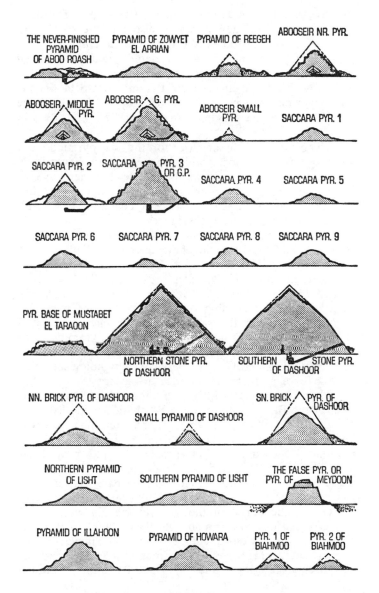

75. Chart of significant Egyptian pyramids

Snofru, also known as the Southern Pyramid at Dahshur.

The fourth-largest pyramid, also credited to Snofru, is simply known as the Northern Pyramid at Dahshur.

Finally, the fifth-largest pyramid, again considered belonging to Snofru, is known as the Pyramid of Meidum.

The heights from Cheops' Pyramid down to Mycerinus' Pyramid range from 481 feet to 218 feet, and the lengths of the base sides range from 755 feet to 356 feet.

The slope angle of three of the six pyramids has been in the 51° range, while the Northern Pyramid is in the 43° range; and the Bent Pyramid actually incorporates both these angles. I find it significant that all six pyramids appear to have a correlation to each other in the slope angle of their faces.

In addition, the Pyramid of Chephren, Snofru's Bent Pyramid, and the Pyramid of Mycerinus all have or had two entrances. This leads me to believe that the Pyramid at Meidum, Snofru's Northern Pyramid, and Cheops' Pyramid indeed must also have a second entrance. My path of logical reasoning is simply that these pyramids seem to be within the same genre of construction, and it is because of this that I believe all six pyramids were built with two entrances.

Moreover, using the classical Egyptologist's reasoning for a moment, if we were to accept the fact that the Pharaohs had a tomb and a cenotaph constructed— one for the Ba and one for the Ka—there would also have to be one for the Khat, which is the Pharaoh's physical body as a whole. It is my firm conviction that the pyramid—if used as a burial place—would have been used for the ritual burial of the abstract Ba and Ka together, and the Khat would be physically buried elsewhere, as in the Valley of the Kings near Karnak and Thebes. If the burial of the Ba and the Ka were to be properly performed through the prescribed ritual practices, they each would require their own entrances and passageways, and, therefore, chambers. The Pyramids of Chephren, Mycerinus, and the Bent Pyramid of Snofru strongly indicate this with their two entrances, and it would seem that along with the other pyramids, Cheops' Pyramid would have to have another entrance.

John Phillips, in his small Arizona-published pamphlet entitled *The Great Pyramid and Its Design,* locates the probable second entrance to the Great Pyramid through simple geometric construction techniques, as slightly more than halfway up from the ground level on the North face. It is an interesting theory and coincides with the higher entrance of the Bent Pyramid, but while the two entrances to the Bent Pyramid are on different faces, it is quite possible that the other entrance of the Great Pyramid has also been put on a different face.

In observing the illustrations of these six pyramids, the internal architecture does make the Great Pyramid unique among the others, because of its chambers and passageways situated high within the superstructure of the pyramid itself; only the Northern and Southern pyramids of Snofru show complexly built chambers within the superstructure of the pyramid, but at ground level. However, if the stone concealing the Ascending Passageway had not fallen, to this very day the only impression we would have of the internal architecture of the Great Pyramid would be its Descending Passageway to the Subterranean Chamber, making it basically equal with all the other pyramids in Egypt.

This particular point leads me to consider the possibility that there are ascending passageways in Chephren's Pyramid, in Mycerinus' Pyramid, and in all three Pyramids of Snofru. The reason why these have not been discovered is because contemporary investigators have not had the good fortune of Al Mamoun's men who, hearing the stone hiding the Ascending Passageway fall out of place, realized that the passageway existed. All investigators—Egyptologists, pyramidologists, archaeologists—have touted in agreement the unique ability and craftsmanship of the architects and masons involved in constructing the pyramids; and the fact that other chambers and passageways have not been found is history's greatest testimonial to the master Egyptians' ability. These passageways and chambers are there, but how do we find them without causing undue damage to the internal architecture?

Dr. Louis Alvarez, in 1968, failed to detect secret chambers or passageways in Chephren's Pyramid using a scientific method of cosmic-ray-bombardment measurements; and no scientific individual will act upon the statements of a dowser. So what is left? Do we need another act of divine intervention to bring to light that which modern man has failed to accomplish with his scientific prowess? Apparently so, because investigators in all branches seem quite content to make cursory visits to the pyramids, performing the modicum of investigative attempts, all the while spending a great deal of time on speculations.

Two very interesting facts prove to me that there is at least one other chamber in the Great Pyramid, and a passageway leading to it.

First, the story related by Herodotus stating that Cheops was buried on an island surrounded by water in the pyramid may in fact be true. This chamber may have been tightly sealed so as to have been filled with water, and the sarcophagus of Cheops may have floated in this chamber. I derive this from the statements of several investigators in the late 1800s and the early 1900s, who wrote detailed accounts of the chambers and passageways of the Great Pyramid. To wit, in a letter dated Saturday, July 17, 1909, is the one reported by John and Morton Edgar and published in their book *Great Pyramid Passages*:

> . . . but beyond this, on to the Queen's Chamber, the very thick and hard incrustation of salt which entirely covers the walls of this passage, made it impossible for us to locate the joints with any certainty. This salt incrustation is peculiar to the Horizontal Passage and Queen's Chamber, although a little of it may also be seen on the walls of the First Ascending Passage.

336

This statement and other similar ones indicate to me that a chamber does exist either above or alongside the Queen's Chamber. This yet-to-be-discovered chamber could very well have been filled with water and ingeniously sealed; or perhaps the passageway leading to this "secret" chamber was filled with water. In either case, over the centuries or the millennia, this water had to have seeped out, causing the incrustations on the Queen's Chamber walls and the Horizontal Passageway. For very interestingly, this incrustation exists nowhere else in the pyramid—not even in the Subterranean Chamber, where it would be expected to have seepage.

There could have been several purposes for the water. It could be directly related to a ritual of burying the Pharaoh back onto the primeval mound of earth surrounded by the primordial waters, as stated in the mythohistory of the origin of the Egyptians. Or the water could have been simply the ultimate deterrent against tomb robbers, whereby if the despoilers did stumble upon *the* passageway and chamber they would be drowned by the release of thousands of gallons of water.

The filling of the secret chamber and passageway could very easily have been accomplished if we consider Mr. Nelson's theory of damming the River Nile, explained in Chapter 4. As the Giza Plateau was being flooded to higher levels to raise the next course of stone into position, when the "secret" burial chamber was at the point of completion it would have been a simple process to allow it to fill with water before the final ceiling blocks were positioned—simply and efficaciously accomplishing everything in one process. The pyramid then would have been complete in its construction and the damming would be removed. As the water receded, it would automatically empty out of the King's Chamber and Queen's Chamber down along the Ascending Passageway, and the remaining water in the Descending Passageway and Subterranean Chamber could be efficiently pumped out through a hydraulic pump system.

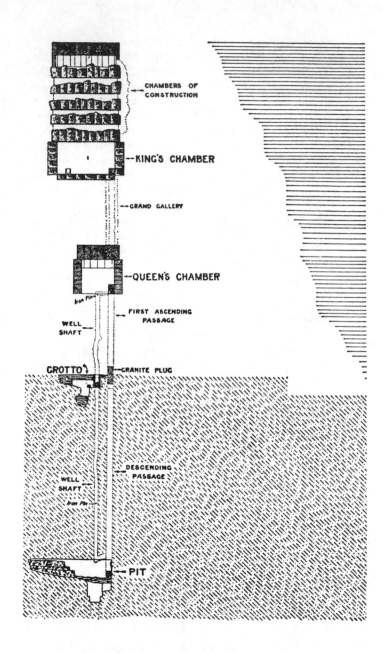

CHAMBERS OF
CONSTRUCTION

KING'S CHAMBER

GRAND GALLERY

QUEEN'S CHAMBER

Iron Pin

FIRST ASCENDING
PASSAGE

WELL
SHAFT

GROTTO

GRANITE PLUG

DESCENDING
PASSAGE

WELL
SHAFT

Iron Pin

PIT

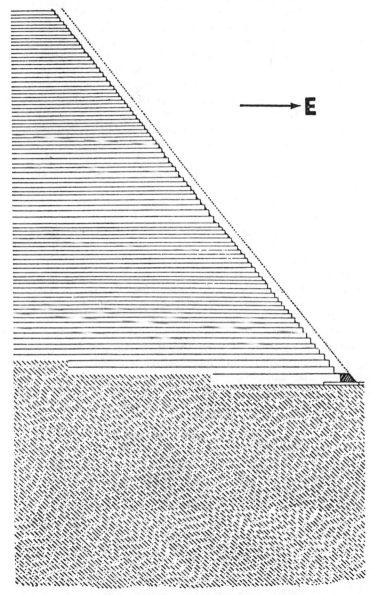

76. South section of the Great Pyramid

The second fact that leads me to believe that there is a passageway leading to a secret chamber in the Great Pyramid is the evidence of a huge block of stone, designed to be slid into place covering the entrance to a passageway in another pyramid, namely Snofru's Bent Pyramid. This sliding stone block in the Southern Pyramid at Dahshur (Snofru's) was so designed as to permanently seal access to the entrance of the chambers. If we follow the concept of architectural similarity in the pyramids, this method of obstructing entranceways should also be used in the other pyramids.

To date, there is only one pyramid having blocks of stones that might hint at their being blocking stones rather than plugging stones. These are what are known as the three Granite Plugs in the Ascending Passageway in the Great Pyramid. Rather than plugging stones, I believe these are designed to block at least one entrance passageway, if not two.

In addition, I agree with Mr. L. Dow Covington, an American who had worked at the Great Pyramid between 1901 and 1910, who theorized that one of the Granite Plugs in the First Ascending Passageway conceals the lower end of a small vertical shaft.

Mr. Covington frequently expressed his opinion to John and Morton Edgar, the brothers who made significant contributions of passage and chamber measurements in the field. Mr. Covington based his theory on the fact that a small, vertical, well-like shaft in the Trial Passages joins at the junction of two inclined passages, and he therefore argued that a similar shaft should be found at the junction of the Descending Passage with the First Ascending Passage within the Great Pyramid. To test the truth of his theory, he had wanted to have the plugs removed, but the Edgar brothers apparently dissuaded him from doing so.

The Trial Passages are thought to be architectural guides for the workmen constructing the actual passage system for the pyramid, and have been cut into the rock about 300 yards east of the actual pyramid site. Accord-

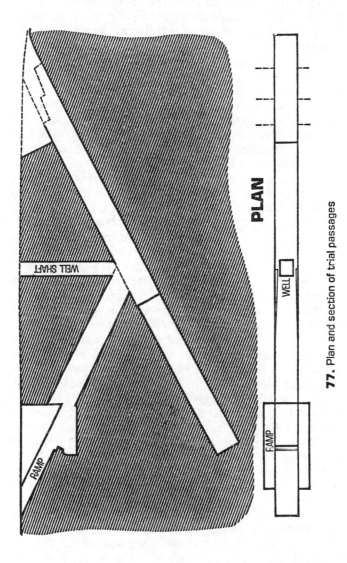

PLAN

WELL SHAFT

RAMP

FAMP

WELL

77. Plan and section of trial passages

ing to Petrie, the Trial Passages appear to be a model for the Great Pyramid passages, having the same width and height, but being much shorter in length. It is also thought that the vertical shaft shown at the junction of the Descending and Ascending Passages had its position altered when the pyramid passageways were constructed, and it is now called the Well Shaft.

I believe that if these three Granite Blocks were to be pulled up into the Ascending Passageway, at least one hidden entrance leading to a new passageway would be revealed, shedding more information on the customary use of the pyramid in ancient dynastic Egypt.

Psychics and seers, both contemporary and ancient, have stated that there is another chamber and passageway yet to be found, but none has been able to scientifically assess the location of the chamber and its passage.

The Granite Plugs may also contain niches within them that may be repositories of ancient records, and these too may be discovered once the three Granite Plugs are slid up for closer and total investigation. This procedure would cause minimal damage to the internal structure and would, I am quite certain, reveal a greater find than that of Tutankhamen's tomb.

I have always been curious as to whether or not this secret passageway and chamber had already been found by the investigators of the 1800s. Waynman Dixon discovered air channels in the Queen's Chamber; Capt. G . B. Caviglia unplugged the Well; Colonel Richard Howard-Vyse discovered the Chambers of Construction above the King's Chamber; and so forth (see Chapter 7). These investigators and others were very adept at these discoveries, especially the one made by Mr. Dixon —in which the air channels to the Queen's Chamber were so well concealed that I am surprised they were found at all!

According to Professor Piazzi Smyth in his book *Our Inheritance in the Great Pyramid,* Mr. Waynman Dixon perceived a crack in the south wall of the Queen's Chamber. He decided to push in a wire to see how deep the crack was. The wire had gone in for an "unconscionable length," at which point Mr. Dixon proceeded to chisel into this crack, revealing the first air channel. The result of his excavation showed that the air channel had a neatly squared inner end. Mr. Dixon theorized that there would be a second air channel on the opposite wall, and his excavation proved him to be correct. That find had raised a question in the minds of the nineteenth-century pyramidologists as to what purpose the ancient architects could have had in mind to expend so much time and trouble in constructing two long air channels in such a way that they would be useless as conductors of air, for the portion of the uncut stone leading to the wall of the Queen's Chamber was 5 inches thick.

It is well known that these investigators were following their instinct as well as ancient writings and tales, which is what led Colonel Vyse to dig a pit in the Subterranean Chamber, to dig into the niche in the Queen's Chamber, and to dig into the ceiling of the King's Chamber. Is it possible that one or more of these investigators did, in fact, find the hidden passage and secret chamber—sealing it up again, never to disclose that they had found it, nor what its contents were? I doubt if this will ever be known, but it does stand to reason that more has been found than was actually recorded, or importantly noted; for just as the piece of iron found by Vyse and the basket found in the Queen's Chamber were not greatly advertised, other finds could also very possibly not have been mentioned at all.

The ritualistic symbolism of a pyramid complex is more pronounced than one is led to believe. Because of the religious ritualistic overtones of the earlier pyramid complex, Egyptologists have rightly concluded that the largest pyramid structure in the complex would therefore be the burial tomb of the Pharaoh, while smaller subsidiary pyramids in the complex would be the tombs of nobles connected with the Pharaoh and his dynasty.

The early dynastic Pharaohs, such as Zoser of the Third Dynasty, are recorded to have celebrated a jubilee

343

ceremony called the Heb-Sed. Egyptologists conclude that courts with surrounding buildings in the pyramid complex were built for the prime purpose of providing the Pharaoh with the necessary setting for repeating the Heb-Sed ceremony in his afterlife. According to records, it seems that every Pharaoh was subject to celebrating this jubilee ceremony after a certain period of time on the throne.

Egyptologists believe that the Heb-Sed ritual was essential for the welfare of the kingdom, whereby the physical vigor of the King would be shown to be unimpaired. This equates to the barbarian ritual of "the stronger being the ruler" theory. Accordingly, as Egypt became more civilized under unification, it was not necessary to physically kill or dispose of the ruler—as it apparently was prior to unification—but his strength could be perpetuated through this jubilee or festival ceremony.

The origin of this festival is as obscure as all other knowledge of ancient Egypt, but seems to date back to the remote past when Kings ruled for a definite limited period of time before being ceremonially put to death. This might be the ceremony that metaphysicians claim was the initiation rite, making it seem like the initiate was dead, after which resurrection occurred.

Apparently, one of the most important elements in the Heb-Sed was the coronation re-enactment, involving two thrones—one each for the Red and the White crowns. Another ceremony thought to be part of the Heb-Sed depicts the Pharaoh with a flail, running a fixed course around the court. He was accompanied by the priest who was the guardian of the "Souls of Nekhen": the spirits of the prehistoric Kings of Upper Egypt. According to the Egyptologists, this running may have been derived from a primitive belief that the fertility of the fields depended in some way upon the physical agility of the Pharaoh. The Pharaoh's dress is depicted as a short, close-fitting garment, and in his hands he carries the emblems of the god Osiris.

In the later dynasties after the Tenth Dynasty, it is thought that the cenotaph became the mock burial chamber for the Pharaoh, who ceremoniously celebrated the Heb-Sed in his thirty-ninth year of reign.

Another ritual that seems to be connected with a fertility rite is one that depicts the Pharaoh standing near a high pole that is supported by four wooden stays. Two men are represented in the act of climbing these stays, one above the other; while others, acting perhaps in the capacity of attendants, hold ropes attached to both the stays and the poles. This scene looks very much like the medieval Maypole dance.

It can only be mere conjecture on the part of the Egyptologists—or anyone else, for that matter—that the subsidiary courts and buildings of the pyramid complex were used for the afterlife of the Pharaoh.

I contend that the pyramid complex containing the various courts and subsidiary buildings were constructed in the reign of the Pharaoh for the Pharaoh's specific ritualistic use as dictated by the then current standards of religious observance. I look at it as his "stadium" in which he developed and maintained the spiritual and physical training needed to be the sovereign of the two lands, and its spiritual leader. The high priests were his judges and referees and his trainers, who would insure the Pharaoh's ability and who maintained a level of perfection befitting a Pharaoh. This, then, in a sense, was the Pharaoh's religious training ground, which insured for him his rightful place among the gods when he died.

The Great Pyramid itself could very specifically have played an important role in the continuation of the initiation of the Pharaoh into his ultimate role of "one who walks with the gods." Upon his death, the Pharaoh would then be symbolically buried in the Pyramid, as represented by the ceremonies involving his Ba and Ka, and the entire pyramid complex would then be considered a religious site that would be maintained by the high priests who served the Pharaoh during life and who con-

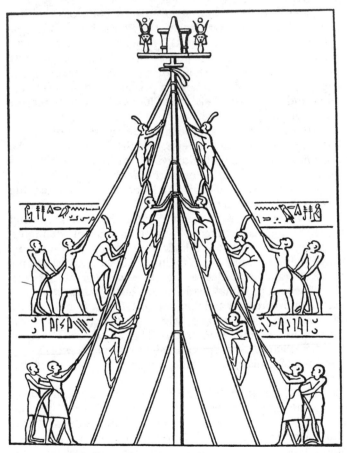

78. Illustration of Egyptian fertility ritual

tinued to serve his spirit in death. Because of the highly religious significance that the pyramid complex served, the nobles in the court of the Pharaoh would then be interred within the confines of the complex.

Following this reasoning, because the Pharaoh would be considered a god at the time of his death, his body became very sacred and required hiding in such a way and manner as to never be found by anyone; and it is logical that his body would not be concealed in the pyramid complex because that would be too obvious a place.

The nobles in the Pharaoh's court, however, had the religious right to be buried in the complex, allowing their mortal body to rest as near to the symbol of the Pharaoh's immortal essence as possible. This theory explains the complex of tombs around the Great Pyramid, and especially why the Pharaoh's mummy has not been found in any of the early dynastic pyramids, much less the record of where they were buried.

As one Pharaoh succeeded another, and depending on how much he identified with his ancestors, that Pharaoh attempted to restore and rehabilitate the statues and structures of his ancestors. It is a well-documented fact that during the Saite Period, in the Twenty-sixth Dynasty, much restoration was done on the ancient structures. Apparently the Pharaohs in this dynasty had a strong affinity to their ancestors, and attempted to bring about a renaissance of ancient history.

This act might be responsible for causing so many problems to the Egyptologists in specifically dating the pyramids and ascribing them to a certain dynasty. As stated earlier, dating of the pyramids solely depended upon what evidence Egyptologists deemed relative to the structure. This evidence is in the form of stellae, carvings, or paint marks on passageways and chambers, and the writings of succeeding dynasties giving credit to a particular Pharaoh. Egyptologists accept some evidence as legitimate, and other evidence is discounted by them. Nonetheless, it is the restoration attempts and the chronicling of successive dynasties that has definitely misled Egyptologists in correctly locating Pharaohs and structures to specific older dynasty periods.

Religious power appears to have reached its highest peak in the Third Dynasty, when Snofru's Bent Pyramid and his other two pyramids—the Northern Pyramid at Dahshur and the Pyramid at Meidum—were built. Not even the attempted renaissance in the Eighteenth Dynasty came close to matching the power and energy expended by the late Third Dynasty and early Fourth Dynasty Pharaohs. The priests of Ra of the Third and Fourth Dynasties attained a level of power that they magnificently transferred into the pyramid structures of that period.

I am certain that the Bent Pyramid has many secrets and much information to reveal once its upper chambers are located, through the discovery of the hidden ascending passageways.

In retrospect, the Great Pyramid remains an enigma. It has been, and it could very possibly always be, to the end of time. It presents mind-boggling problems to scientists who cannot arrive at sufficient answers to explain all of its features, and to mystics who search for the Pyramid's code in its symbolism.

The ancient Egyptians expended tremendous energy in exhibiting their knowledge of the sciences both in the Pyramid's measures and its construction. This energy was imparted to the very stones themselves. It is on this thought that I conducted an experiment, many times over, with psychometrists. These are individuals who, through a process called psychometry, are able to tune in, or become sensitive to, the energy of a particular object, and can envision its past, present, and future by the vibrations sensed in the object.

I had acquired several pieces of limestone rock from the Great Pyramid at Giza. These were then mounted for me into a small, solid, clear-plastic replica pyramid.

I decided to take two of these Giza Rock plastic pyramids and seal them in an unidentifiable box, which I then gave to several individuals who acted as my researchers. My instructions to them were very simple: "Please give this box to individuals you know who have proven themselves to be very adept at psychometry, and ask them to psychometrize the contents of the box, recording exactly what they say."

Of the eight responses, I have selected one that exemplifies all of the psychometrists' impressions. Anna M. is a Long Island, New York, psychic in her thirties. The box rested between her hands on the table before her, and upon entering a light trance she relayed the following psychically perceived impressions:

> I see a pyramid, but at the same time I see a mountainous shape. I see an eye; just one eye. I get a feeling of happiness. I feel a warm climate. The sky is a beautiful blue with some puffy white clouds. I feel there should be water nearby, but I don't see it. I can't tell where it should be coming from. The terrain is very sandy. There's some rock of deep red color. There's a tunnel of some kind. I can't tell whether it's large or small. Now I see nighttime. I'm drawn to one very bright star in the sky. I'm getting the Star of Bethlehem. Although it's nighttime, it's very bright. I see a cross in the distance and a temple.

The impressions of Anna M. typify the response of all of the individuals tested. They all perceived at least the pyramid, sandy terrain, and water. While each individual's psychically perceived impression varied in detail and length, the one striking phenomenon that manifested itself was that the piece of rock from the Great Pyramid is imbued with the energies of time past —which still can be tapped into after all these millennia, affording us one more avenue into its secrets.

In the warm, peaceful, and powerful faces that are so common to Egyptian monuments and art, there lies an understanding and unity of consciousness that was the spirit upon which the Great Pyramid was built. The tremendous effort and technical knowledge needed to build such an impractical and nonutilitarian wonder as the Great Pyramid must have been based and in essence

349

represent the Egyptian cultural unity and spiritual power. It is my belief that when humanity rediscovers and realigns itself with this spiritual power and thus finds unity both within itself and the world at large, the secret chambers and mysterious passageways of the Great Pyramid will burst open and herald a new Golden Age.

BIBLIOGRAPHY

Adams, Walter Marshal. *The Book of the Master.* Putnam, New York, 1898.

Adler. *Mathematics for Science and Engineering.* McGraw-Hill.

Aldersmith, Herbert. *The Great Pyramid; Its Divine Message.* London, 1932.

Amkraut, Joel. "Pyramid Power," *Spaceview* Magazine, Jan.–Feb. 1973.

Anderson, U. S. *The Secret Power of the Pyramids.* California, 1977.

Andrews, E. Wyllys. "Chronology and Astronomy in the Maya Area" in *The Maya and Their Neighbors,* pp. 150–161. New York, 1940.

Anonymous. *The Bible and the Forgotten Books of Eden.* New York, 1926.

Anonymous. *Season of Changes, Ways of Response.* Virginia, 1974.

Archibald, R. C. *Notes on Logarithmic Spiral of the Golden Section.* New Haven, 1920.

———. "The Pyramids and Cosmic Energy." Aleph Enterprises, Palo Alto, Calif., 1972.

Austin, Marshall. *Solved Secrets of the Pyramid of Cheops.* California, 1976.

Aziz, Philippe. *The Mysteries of the Great Pyramid.* Geneva, 1977.

Bache, Richard M. *The Latest Phase of the Great Pyramid Discussion.* Philadelphia, 1885.

Badaway, A. *A History of Egyptian Architecture,* Vols. I–III. Cairo, Berkeley and Los Angeles, 1954–68.

Baikie, J. "The Sphinx" in J. H. Hastings, *Encyclopedia of Religion and Ethics,* Vol. XI, pp. 767–68. Edinburgh, 1920.

————. *A History of Egypt,* Vols. I and II. London, 1929.

Ballard, Robert T. *The Solution of the Pyramid Problem.* New York, 1882.

Balsiger, D., and Sellier, C. E., Jr. *In Search of Noah's Ark.* U.S.A., 1976.

Bandelier, Adolf Francis. "The Ruins at Tiahuanaco," American Antiquarian Society Proceedings, XXI, pp. 218–65, 1911.

Barton, George A. *The Religion of Ancient Israel.* New York, 1961.

Bell, Edward. *The Architecture of Ancient Egypt.* London, 1915.

Benavides, Rudolfo. *Dramatic Prophecies of the Great Pyramids.* Mexico, 1961.

Bennett, Wendell C. "Chavin Stone Carving," Yale Anthropological Studies, New Haven, Conn., 1942.

————. Excavations at Tiahuanaco," *Anthropological Papers,* American Museum of Natural History, Vol. 34, pp. 359–494. New York, 1934.

Bennett, Wendell C. (ed.), "A Reappraisal of Peruvian Arts," *Archaeology Memoir* 4, Society for American Archaeology, Menasha, 1948.

Berlitz, Charles. *Mysteries from Forgotten Worlds.* New York, 1972.

————. *Without A Trace.* New York, 1977.

Bernard, Raymond. *The Hollow Earth.* New Jersey, 1969.

Blavatsky, Helene P. *Isis Unveiled.* Los Angeles, 1931.

————. *The Secret Doctrine,* 2 vols. London, 1888.

Blumrich, Josef F. *The Spaceships of Ezekiel.* New York, 1974.

Bonwick, James. *Pyramid Facts and Fancies.* London, 1877.

Bothwell, A. *The Magic of the Pyramid.* Goose, 1915.

Boyce, Shirley. "The Pyramid Pioneers Fire Safety," *Buildings,* Vol 66, No. 6, June 1972.

Breasted, James H. *A History of Egypt from the Earliest Times to the Persian Conquest.* New York, 1909.

————. *The Development of Religion and Thought in Ancient Egypt.* New York, 1912.

Bristowe, E. S. G. *The Man Who Built the Great Pyramid.* London, 1932.

Bromage, Bernard. *The Occult Arts of Ancient Egypt.* London, 1953.

Brooke, M. W. H. L. *The Great Pyramid of Gizeh.* London, 1908.

Brown, Les. *The Pyramid—How to Build It, How to Use It.* Canada, 1976.

Brunhouse, Robert L. *In Search of the Maya.* New York, 1973.

Brunton, Paul. *A Search in Secret Egypt.* London, 1936.

Budge, E. A. Wallis. *Egyptian Language.* New York, 1977.

————. *The Egyptian Heaven and Hell.* U.S.A., 1905.

————. *The Egyptian Book of the Dead* (Egyptian text and translation). New York, 1967.

————. *The Gods of the Egyptians,* Vols. I and II. New York, 1969.

————. *The Mummy.* New York, reissued 1972.

————. *Egyptian Magic.* New York, reissued 1971.

Burgoyne, Thomas H. *The Light of Egypt.* Denver, Colo., 1963.

————. *The Holy Bible.* New York, 1901.

Caffery, Jefferson and Boyer, David S. "Fresh Treasures from Egypt's Ancient Sands," Vol. CVIII, No. 5, Nov. 1955.

Capt, E. Raymond. *The Great Pyramid Decoded.* California, 1976.

Carey, George W. *God-Man: The Word Made Flesh.* Los Angeles, Calif., 1920.

Carter, Howard. *The Tomb of Tutankhamen.* Great Britain, 1972.

Carter, Mary Ellen. *Edgar Cayce on Prophecy.* U.S.A., 1968.

Case, Paul Foster. *The Great Seal of the United States: Its History, Symbolism, and Message for the New Age.* New York, 1935.

Cayce, Edgar Evans. *Edgar Cayce on Atlantis.* U.S.A., 1968.

353

Cerny, J. *Ancient Egyptian Religion*. London, 1952.

Cerve, W. S. *Lemuria: The Lost Continent of the Pacific*. California, 1931.

Chapman, Arthur Wood. *The Prophecy of the Pyramid*. London, 1933.

Chapman, Francis W. *The Great Pyramid of Gizeh from the Aspect of Symbolism*. London, 1931.

Charroux, Robert. *One Hundred Years of Man's Unknown History*. New York, 1970.

Cheetham, Erika. *Prophecies of Nostradamus*. Great Britain, 1973.

Churchward, James. *The Sacred Symbols of Mu*. New York, 1933.

———. *The Cosmic Forces of Mu*. New York, 1934.

———. *The Second Book of the Cosmic Forces of Mu*. New York, 1935.

———. *The Children of Mu*. New York, 1931.

———. *Understanding Mu*. New York, 1970.

Clarke, Somers and Engelbach, Reginald. *Ancient Egyptian Masonry: The Burning Craft*. London, 1930.

———. *Ancient Egyptian Masonry*. Oxford, 1930.

Clement, Alan B. *Earth Changes—Past, Present, Future*. Virginia, 1959.

Cole, J. H. *Determination of the Exact Size and Orientation of the Great Pyramid of Giza*. Cairo, 1925.

Collier, Robert. *The Secret of the Ages*. South Carolina, 1948.

Corbin, Bruce. *The Great Pyramid, God's Witness in Stone*. Guthrie, Okla., 1935.

Cormack, Maribell. *Imhotep, Builder in Stone*. New York, 1965.

Cottrell, Leonard. *Lost Worlds*. New York, 1962.

———. *The Anvil of Civilization*. New York, 1957.

———. *The Mountains of Pharaoh*. London, 1956.

Crowley, Aleister. *The Book of Thoth by the Master Therion*. New York.

Cummings, Jennie. "Pyramid Church," *Houston Review*, Vol. 1, No. 4, Dec. 1973.

———. *The Pyramid Guide*, Nos. 1, 2, 4, 5. Elsinore, Calif., 1973.

Cummings, Violet M. *Noah's Ark: Fable or Fact?* California, 1973.

Dane, Christopher. *The American Indian and the Occult*. New York, 1973.

Darter, Frances M. *Our Bible in Stone*. Salt Lake City, 1931.

Davidson, David and Aldersmith, H. *The Great Pyramid: Its Divine Message*. London, 1924.

Davies, A. Powell. *The Meaning of the Dead Sea Scrolls*. New York, 1956.

De Campe, L. Sprague. "How the Pyramids Were Built," *Fate*, Vol. 15, No. 12, Dec. 1962.

———. *The Ancient Engineers*. New York, 1960.

De Lubicz, Isha Schwaller. *Herbak, Egyptian Initiate*. New York, 1978.

———.*Herbak, the Living Face of Ancient Egypt* and *Herbak: Egyptian Initiate*. Inner Traditions International, 1978.

Donnelly, Ignatius. *Atlantis: The Antediluvian World*. New York, 1971.

Dunham, D. "Building an Egyptian Pyramid," *Archaeology*, 9 (1956), No. 3, pp. 159–65.

Earll, Tony. *Mu Revealed*. New York, 1970.

Ebon, Martin (ed.). *Mysterious Pyramid Power*. New York, 1976.

Edgar, John and Morton. *The Great Pyramid Passages and Chambers*. Glasgow, 1910.

Edgar, Morton. *The Great Pyramid: Its Scientific Features*. Glasgow, 1924.

———. *The Great Pyramid: Its Spiritual Symbolism*. Glasgow, 1924.

———. *The Great Pyramid: Its Time Features*. Glasgow, 1924.

Edwards, I. E. S. *The Pyramids of Egypt*. New York, 1972.

———. *The Early Dynastic Period in Egypt*. Cambridge, 1964.

Emery, Walter B. *Archaic Egypt*. Baltimore, 1961.

———. *Archaic Egypt*. Harmondsworth, 1962.

Erman, A. *A Handbook of Egyptian Religion* (English translation by A. S. Griffith). London, 1907.

———. *The Literature of the Ancient Egyptians*. New York, reissued 1971.

Evans, Albert. "Metaphysical Mysteries of the Great Pyramids," *The Osteopathic Physician*, May 1972.

Fish, Everett W. *Egyptian Pyramids: An Analysis of a Great Mystery.* Chicago, 1880.

Flanigan, G. Patrick. "The Pyramid and Its Relationship to Biocosmic Energy," 1972.

Forlong, J. G. R. *Rivers of Life,* Vols. 1 and 2. London, 1883.

————. *Science of Comparative Religions.* London, 1897.

Gardiner, Sir Alan. *Egypt of the Pharaohs.* New York, reprinted 1969.

Gardner, Martin. *Fads and Fallacies.* New York, 1957.

Garnier, Col. J. *The Great Pyramid: Its Builder and Its Phophecy.* London, 1912.

Gaster, T. *The Dead Sea Scriptures* (English translation). New York, 1956.

Goneim, M. Z. *The Lost Pyramid.* New York, 1956.

————. *The Buried Pyramid.* London, 1956.

Goose, A. B. *The Magic of the Pyramids.* London, 1915.

Gordon, Cyrus H. *Before Columbus.* New York, 1971.

Gray, Julian Thorbirn. *The Authorship and Message of the Great Pyramid.* Cincinnati, 1953.

Grinsell, Leslie V. *Egyptian Pyramids.* Gloucester, 1947.

Haberman, Fredrick. *The Great Pyramid's Message to America.* St. Petersburg, Fla., 1932.

Hall, Manly P. *The Secret Teachings of All Ages.* Los Angeles, Calif., 1969.

————. *The Judgment of the Soul: The Mystery of Coming Forth by Day.* California, 1935.

Hayes, W. C. *The Scepter of Egypt,* 2 vols. New York, and Cambridge, Mass., 1935.

Hick, John. *The Myth of God Incarnate.* London, 1977.

Higgins, Godfrey. *Anacalypsis,* Vols. 1 and 2. New York, 1965.

Holt, Etelka. *The Sphinx and the Great Pyramid.* Los Angeles, 1968.

Hunt, Avery. "Harnessing Pyramid Power, Pyramid Power?" *Newsday,* Sept. 24, 1973.

Hunter, C. Bruce. *A Guide to Ancient Maya Ruins.* Oklahoma, 1974.

Hurry, J. B. *Imhotep.* Oxford, 1926.

Ibek, Ferrand. *La Pyramide de Cheops, a-t-elle livre son secret?* Malines Celt, 1951.

Ions, Veronica. *Egyptian Mythology.* England, 1965.

Ivimy, John. *The Sphynx and the Megaliths.* U.S.A., 1975.

James, T. G. H. *Myth and Legends of Ancient Egypt*. New York, 1972.

Jeffers, James A. *The Great Sphinx Speaks to God's People*. Los Angeles, Calif., 1942.

Jeffery, Edmond C. *The Pyramids and the Patriarchs*. New York, 1952.

Johnson, Fredrick (ed.). "Radio Carbon Dating." *Memoirs of the Society of American Archaeology*, Salt Lake City, 1951.

Keller, Werner. *The Bible As History*. New York, 1956.

Kellison, Cathrine. "If Pyramids Could Talk . . . !!!" *Playgirl*, Nov. 1973.

King, Francis. *Wisdom from Afar*. New York, 1976.

Kingsland, William. *The Great Pyramid in Fact and in Theory*. London, 1932.

Klein, H. Arthur. *Great Structures of the World*. New York, 1968.

Knight, Charles S. *The Mystery and Prophecy of the Great Pyramid*. San Jose, Calif., 1933.

Kolosimo, Peter. *Not of This World*. New York, 1973.

Kozyrev, Nikolai. "Possibility of Experimental Study of the Properties of Time," Joint Publications Research Service, NTIS. Springfield, Va. 1968.

Kueshana, Eklal. *The Ultimate Frontier*. Chicago, 1963.

Kuhn, Alvin Boyd. *The Lost Light*. New York: Columbia University, 1940.

Landone, Brown. *Prophecies of Melchi-Zedek in the Great Pyramid*. New York, 1940.

Larson, Kenneth L. *The Topstone*. California, 1970.

———. *Great Pyramid Designs, UFO's and Planet Earth*. California, 1973.

Lehner, Mark. *The Egyptian Heritage*. Virginia, 1974.

Lemesurier, Peter. *The Stones Cry Out*. Great Britain, 1976.

Lewis, David H. *Mysteries of the Pyramids*. Florida, 1978.

Lewis, Havre Spencer. *The Symbolic Prophecy of the Great Pyramid*. San Jose, Calif., 1936.

———. *The Mystical Life of Jesus*. California, 1929.

———. *The Secret Doctrines of Jesus*. California, 1937.

Lichtheim, Miriam. *Ancient Egyptian Literature*. California, 1973.

Lucas, A. *Ancient Egyptian Materials and Industries*, 4th edition revised by J. R. Harris. London, 1962.

MacQuitty, W. *Tutankhamen: The Last Journey.* New York, 1977.

Manning, Al G. "Can Pyramid Power Work for You?" *Occult,* Vol. 4, No. 3, October 1973.

————. "How to Use the Mystic Pyramid," Los Angeles, Calif., 1970.

Marriott, Alice and Rachlin, Carol K. *American Indian Mythology.* New York, 1968.

Martin, Russ. "Building the Great Pyramid A.D. 1973," *TWA Ambassador,* Vol. 6, No. 7, July 1973.

Mason, J. Alden. *The Ancient Civilizations of Peru.* New York, 1957.

Massey, Gerald. *The Egyptian Book of the Dead and the Mysteries of Amenta,* an exact reprint of Book IV of *Ancient Egypt: The Light of the World.* London, 1907.

————. *The Natural Genesis,* Vols. 1 and 2. London, 1883.

————. *Ancient Egypt,* Vols. 1 and 2. London, 1907.

McCollum, Rocky. *The Prime Mover.* Michigan, 1971.

————. *The Giza Necropolis Decoded.* Michigan, 1975.

Mendelsohn, Kurt. *The Riddle of the Pyramids.* New York, 1974.

Mercer, S. A. B. *The Pyramid Texts in Translation and Commentary,* 4 vols. New York, 1952.

Mertz, Barbara. *Temples, Tombs, and Hieroglyphs.* New York, 1964.

Michell, John. *The View over Atlantis.* New York, 1969.

————. *City of Revelation.* New York, 1972.

Montet, Pierre. *Eternal Egypt.* New York, 1964.

————. *Isis or the Search for Egypt's Buried Past.* France, 1956.

Naud, Yves. *The Curse of the Pharaohs,* Vols. 1 and 2. Geneva, 1977.

Neugebauer, O. *The Exact Sciences of Antiquity.* Princeton, 1951.

Norton, Roy. "Monuments to UFO Space Pioneers," *Saga,* Vol. 44, No. 3, June 1972.

Nuttall, Zelia. *The Codex Nuttall.* New York, 1975.

Ostrander, Sheila and Schroeder, Lynn. *Psychic Discoveries Behind the Iron Curtain.* New York, 1970.

Owen, A. R. G. "The Shapes of Egyptian Pyramids," *New Horizons,* Toronto, Ont., 1973.

Pace, Mildred M. *Wrapped for Eternity: The Story of the Egyptian Mummy.* New York, 1974.

Palmer, Ernest G. *The Secret of Ancient Egypt.* London, 1924.

Parker, Richard A. *The Calendars of Ancient Egypt.* Chicago, 1950.

Patrick, Richard. *Egyptian Mythology.* Hong Kong, 1972.

Pauwels, Louis and Bergier, Jacques. *The Morning of the Magicians.* New York, 1960.

———. *Impossible Possibilities.* New York, 1968.

———. *The Eternal Man.* New York, 1972.

Pawley, G. S. "Do the Pyramids Show Continental Drift?" *Science,* Vol. 179, March 1973.

Pearl, Richard M. *Rocks and Minerals.* New York, 1956.

Petrie, W. M. F. *The Royal Tombs of the First Dynasty,* Part I. London, 1900.

———. *The Royal Tombs of the Earliest Dynasties,* Part II. London, 1901.

———. *The Pyramids and Temples of Gizeh.* London, 1883.

Phillips, John. *The Great Pyramid and Its Design.* Arizona, 1977.

Pickthall, M. M. *The Glorious Koran* (explanatory translation). New York, 1953.

Platt, Paul T. *Secret: The Pyramid and the Lisa.* New York, 1954.

———. *The Secret of Secrets.* New York, 1955.

———. *Psychic Observer.* Entire Issue, Vol. XXXIII, No. 7, Nov. 1972.

———. *Pyramid News,* No. 7, Sept. 26, 1973 (edited by Transamerica Corporation).

Pochan, A. *The Mysteries of the Great Pyramids.* New York, 1978.

Prabhavananda, Swami and Isherwood, C. *The Song of God: Bhagavad-Gita.* New York, 1972.

Racey, Robert R. *The Gizeh Sphinx and Middle Egyptian Pyramids.* Winnipeg, Man., 1937.

Rand, Howard B. *The Challenge of the Great Pyramid.* Haverhill, Mass., 1943.

Rawlinson, G. *History of Herodotus* (Every Man's Library), edited by E. H. Blakney. London, 1912.

Reich, Wilhelm. "Cosmic Superimposition," The Wilhelm Reich Foundation, Orgonon. Rangeley, Me., 1951.

————. *The Murder of Christ.* New York, 1976.

Reisner, G. A. *Mycerinus: The Temples of the Third Pyramid at Giza.* Cambridge, Mass., 1931.

————. *The Development of the Egyptian Tomb Down to the Accession of Cheops.* Cambridge, Mass., 1935.

Riffert, George R. *Great Pyramid Proof of God.* England, 1932.

Robb, Stewart. *Phophecies on World Events by Nostradamus* (English translation). New York, 1961.

Roberts, Jane. *The Seth Material.* New Jersey, 1970.

Robinson, Lytle. *The Great Pyramid and Its Builders.* Virginia, 1966.

Roche, Richard. *Egyptian Myths and the Ra Ta Story.* Virginia, 1975.

Russell, Walter. "The Secret of Light," University of Science and Philosophy. Waynesboro, Va.

Rutherford, Adam. *Pyramidology,* Books I, II, III, IV. Dunstable, Bedfordshire, 1961.

————. *Outline of Pyramidology.* London, 1957.

Schure, Eduard. *The Mysteries of Ancient Egypt, Hermes/ Moses.* New York, 1971.

Sédir, Paul. *Initiations.* England, 1967.

Seiss, Joseph A., D.D. *The Great Pyramid: A Miracle in Stone.* New York, reissued 1973.

Sendy, Jean. *Those Gods Who Made Heaven and Earth.* New York, 1972.

Shealy, Julian B. *The Key to Our God-given Heritage.* South Carolina, 1967.

Shirota, Jon. *Legacy of the Unknown,* Vols. 1 and 2, March 1973.

Silverberg, Robert. *Mound Builders of Ancient America.* New York, 1968.

Sinnett, Alfred P. *The Pyramids and Stonehenge.* London, 1958.

Skinner, J. Ralston. *The Source of Measures.* Minnesota, reissued 1972.

Smith, E. Baldwin. *Egyptian Architecture as a Cultural Expression.* New York, 1938.

Smith, G. E. and Dawson, W. R. *Egyptian Mummies.* London, 1924.

Smith, Joseph Jun. *The Book of Mormon* (translation). Utah, reissued 1961.

Smith, Robert W. *Mysteries of the Ages*. Utah, 1936.

Smith, Warren. "Mysterious Pyramids Around the World," *Saga*, Vol. 47, No. 1, October 1973.

———. *Ancient Mysteries of the Mexican and Mayan Pyramids*. New York, 1977.

Smith, W. S. *Art and Architecture of Ancient Egypt*. Middlesex, 1958.

———. *A History of Egyptian Sculpture and Painting in the Old Kingdom*. Oxford, 1946.

———. *The Art and Architecture of Ancient Egypt* (The Pelican History of Art). London, 1958.

Smith, Worth. *The House of Glory*. New York, 1939.

———. *Miracle of the Ages: The Great Pyramid of Gizah*. New York, 1937.

Smyth, Piazzi. *Our Inheritance in the Great Pyramid*. New York, reissued 1977.

Stewart, Basil. *The Mystery of the Great Pyramid*. London, 1929.

———. *The True Purpose of the Great Pyramid*. Exeter, 1935.

———. *The Witness of the Great Pyramid*. London, 1928.

———. *Times of the Gentiles*. England, 1928.

Straub, W. L. *Anglo-Israel: Mysteries Unmasked*. Nebraska, 1937.

Talbott, Stephen. *Velikovsky Reconsidered*. U.S.A., 1966.

Tellefsen, Olaf. "A New Theory of Pyramid Building," *Natural History*, Vol. LXXIX, No. 9, Nov., 1970.

Temple, Ronald. *The Message from the King's Coffer*, California, 1920.

Thompson, J. Eric. *The Rise and Fall of Maya Civilization*. Oklahoma, 1954.

Tompkins, Peter. *Secrets of the Great Pyramid*. New York, 1971.

———. *Mysteries of the Mexican Pyramids*. New York, 1976.

Toth, Max. "The Mysterious Pyramids," *Beyond Reality*, Vol. 1, No. 2, Dec., 1972.

Toth, Max and Nielsen, G. *Pyramid Power*. New York, 1974.

Touny, A. D. *Sport in Ancient Egypt*. Leipzig, 1969.

Trench, Brinsky L. *Secret of the Ages*. New York, 1974.

Tucker, William J. *Ptolemaic Astrology*. Sidcup, Ky., 1962.

Tunstall, John. "Pharaoh's Curse," Toronto *Globe and Mail*, July 30, 1969.

Vaillant, George C. *The Aztecs of Mexico*. New York, 1962.
Vandenberg, Philippe. *The Curse of the Pharaohs*. New York, 1975.
Velikovsky, Immanuel. *Oedipus and Akhnaton*. New York, 1960.
———. *Earth in Upheaval*. New York, 1955.
———. *Ages in Chaos*. New York, 1952.
Von Daniken, Erich. *Chariots of the Gods?* New York, 1970.
———. *Gods from Outer Space*. New York, 1968.
———. *The Gold of the Gods*. New York, 1973.
———. *Miracles of the Gods*. New York, 1974.
———. *In Search of Ancient Gods*. New York, 1974.
Von Hagen, Victor W. *World of the Maya*. New York, 1960.
———. *Realm of the Incas*. New York, 1957.
———. *The Aztec Man and Tribe*. New York, 1958.
Vyse, H. and Perring, J. S. *Operations Carried Out on the Pyramids of Gizeh,* 3 vols. London, 1840–42.
Waddell, L. A. *Egyptian Civilization: Its Sumerian Origin and Real Chronology*. London, 1930.
Weeks, John. *The Pyramids*. London, 1971.
Weeks, Kent and Edwards, I. E. S. "The Great Pyramid Debate," *Natural History,* Vol. LXXIX, No. 10, Dec., 1970.
Weigall, Arthur. *A History of the Pharaohs,* Vol. I. New York, 1925. Vol. II, New York, 1927.
Wheeler, N. F. "Pyramids and Their Purpose," Antiquity, IX (1935), pp. 172–85.
Williamson, George H. *Secret Places of the Lion*. New York, 1977.
Winlock, H. E. *The Rise and Fall of the Middle Kingdom in Thebes*. New York, 1947.
———. "Pyramid Meditation," *National Enquirer,* Jan. 13, 1974.
Wynne, Barry. *Behind the Mask of Tutankhamen*. New York, 1972.
Zim, Herbert S. and Shaffer, Paul R. *Rocks and Minerals*. New York, 1957.

INDEX

364

Other titles of interest from
Destiny Books...

SECRET PLACES OF THE LION

By George Hunt Williamson
ISBN 0-89281-039-4
$14.95, paperback

Early traditions speak of the arrival of "radiant beings from heaven," self-sacrificing guardians of the human race who have reincarnated as pivotal figures in the panorama of history to assist in human evolution. These great ones have helped mankind for thousands of years, hiding their secrets in tombs, caverns, temple ruins, and catacombs. *Secret Places of the Lion* brings these records to light.

PENDULUM POWER

A Mystery You Can See, A Power You Can Feel

By Greg Nielsen and Joseph Polansky
ISBN 0-89281-157-9
$8.95, paperback

Dowsers have used pendulums for centuries to locate buried treasure, find lost objects, discover hidden sources of water, and divine the future. In this guide, the authors show you how to make your own pendulums and how to put them to immediate use for success in every area of life—including career and personal relationships, healing, development of intuition, and increased mind power.

PYRAMID POWER

Max Toth and Greg Nielsen
ISBN 0-89281-106-4
$9.95, paperback

The #1 bestseller on pyramid energies offers fascinating information on pyramids around the world, revealing the powers harnessed by the ancients. The authors give instructions for building your own pyramid and show how you can put the power of the pyramid to work for you.

MANITOU
The Sacred Landscape of New England's Native Civilization

By James W. Mavor and Byron E. Dix
ISBN 0-89281-078-5
$18.95, paperback

This remarkably detailed book can be your guide to the discovery and exploration of stone structures found throughout New England that are believed to be ancient native ritual and calendar sites. Hundreds of these ancient sites are scattered throughout the region—some may be in your backyard.

> *". . . among the few innovative advances in the field of New England archaeology in recent years."*
> **Massachusetts Archaeological Society**

THE WAY OF THE ESSENES
Christ's Hidden Life Remembered

By Anne and Daniel Meurois-Givaudan
ISBN 0-89281-322-9
$16.95, paperback

Enter into the daily life of the Essenes, a mystical society that originated in Palestine 2,000 years ago, believed to have influenced Christ's life and teachings. Through direct revelation, the authors received detailed knowledge of the community, their beliefs, and way of life. This is the first English language edition of the European bestseller.

THE SECRET BOOKS
OF THE EGYPTIAN GNOSTICS

By Jean Doresse
ISBN 0-89281-107-2
$18.95, paperback

Believed by many to surpass the Dead Sea Scrolls in importance, the Gnostic texts included here bring a new perspective to the vanished world of early Christianity. This prodigious collection of sacred writings, concealed for sixteen centuries, came to light in the late 1940s, when the documents were unearthed in Chenoboskion, a remote village in Upper Egypt. Included is *The Gospel According to Thomas*.

SECRET OF THE RUNES

By Guido von List
Translated and edited by Stephen Flowers
ISBN 0-89281-207-9
$9.95, paperback

Guido von List, renowned for his studies in Indo-European Germanic linguistics and mythology, is also a major figure in the Western mystical and occult tradition. Here, for the first time in English, is his original 1908 work on the ancient Germanic-Runic alphabet, that reveals the cosmology and occult understanding of the primeval Teutonic peoples.

AMERICA'S SECRET DESTINY
Spiritual Vision and the Founding of a Nation

By Robert Hieronimus
ISBN 0-89281-255-9
$14.95, paperback

A wealth of little-known facts, critical to our understanding of this nation's development, are revealed in this fascinating book. Tracing the Native American influence as well as that of esoteric orders— among them the Masons and Rosicrucians—upon key figures such as Washington, Jefferson, and Franklin, the author shows how a spiritual vision of America's future was established in those early days, and encoded in our most important national documents and symbols.

SECRETS OF THE STONES
New Revelations of Astro-Archaeology
and the Mystical Sciences of Antiquity

By John Michell
ISBN 0-89281-337-7
$10.95, paperback

Since the beginning of the twentieth century, when Sir J. Norman Lockyer discovered astronomical orientations in Egyptian temples and the stone circles of Britain, the subject of astroarchaeology has expanded worldwide. In Secrets of the Stones, John Michell traces the development of this science, detailing principle sites and the people involved.

THE DIVINING MIND
A Guide to Dowsing and Self-Awareness

By T. Edward Ross 2nd and Richard D. Wright
ISBN 0-89281-263-X
$10.95, paperback

Using a step-by-step approach, dowsers Terry Ross and Richard Wright explain how to use various dowsing devices, including the L-rod, Y-rod, and pendulum to sharpen your intuition and to access hidden knowledge of every kind—from the location of missing persons, gold, buried artifacts, and ancient ritual sites to predicting future conditions and events.

> *"This must be one of the best books for the beginner to appear for*
> *a long time. It tackles dowsing from square one, but unlike many*
> *others, really tries to build into the dowser's mind an awareness*
> *of the deeper philosophical and mystical aspects*
> *of the process, so that you understand the why as well as the*
> *how as you progress on the path."*
> **Journal of the British Society of Dowsers**

THE SIRIUS MYSTERY

By Robert Temple
ISBN 0-89281-163-3
$16.95, paperback

Author Robert Temple traces the traditions of four African tribes back 5,000 years to the ancient Mediterranean cultures of Sumer and Egypt, showing that these cultures possessed great knowledge, much of which they claimed was given to them by visitors from a planet in the Sirius star system. Many authors have speculated on the subject of extraterrestrial contact, but never before has such a detailed theory been formulated.

"Temple's massive research into the ancient mythologies
of numerous civilizations and cultures
one can only regard with awe."
The London Sunday Times

" . . . a cautious, honest, and scientific attempt."
Columbus Dispatch

THE BODY OF MYTH

Mythology, Shamanic Trance,
and the Sacred Geography of the Body

J. Nigro Sansonese
ISBN 0-89281-409-8
$24.95, paperback

"Illustrates convincingly the interconnections between myth and
body, with real flashes of creative and intuitive brilliance that
make even the unfamiliar exciting. What Sansonese has discovered
and documented is the symbolic presence of the human organism
in those least 'physical' of all events, myth and dream. Even the
very attentive and sophisticated reader will marvel at the detail
and subtlety Sansonese has brought to his investigation."
Steve Larsen, Ph.D.,
author of The Shaman's Doorway and
Fire in the Mind: The Life of Joseph Campbell

EARTHMIND

Communicating with the Living World of Gaia

Paul Devereux, John Steele, and David Kubrin
ISBN 0-89281-367-9
$12.95, paperback

Is the Earth alive? This idea, now known as the Gaia hypothesis, was self-evident until a few hundred years ago, but in modern times we have lost touch with this ancestral wisdom. *Earthmind* looks back at traditional societies and their relationship with the earth, examining the history of electromagnetic phenomena at sacred sites. Then, exploring the sensitivity of human and other life forms to the subtle electromagnetic frequencies of the earth, the authors seek ways in which we might interface and communicate with the terrestrial environment for the purpose of planetary healing.

THE STONES OF TIME

Calendars, Sundials, and
Stone Chambers of Ancient Ireland

By Martin Brennan
ISBN 0-89281-509-4
$19.95, paperback

In this absorbing work, Martin Brennan describes the exciting discovery and deciphering of glyphs in the 5,000-year-old stone chambers and standing stones of pre-Celtic Ireland. Through a combination of careful observation during solar and lunar cycles, analysis of the astronomical alignment of the sites, and personal insight into the meanings of megalithic symbols and carvings, Brennan demonstrates that the passage mounds and chambers are actually sophisticated calendar devices.

"A pioneering work . . . we may have been given a revelation of the cosmological beliefs of our distant forefathers."
The Times Literary Supplement

"The most complete record of Irish megalithic art ever published . . . calculated to overturn some fundamental doctrines of prehistoric archaeology and initiate an entirely new mode of enquiry."

John Michell,
author of Secrets of the Stones

BETWEEN THE LINES
Understanding Yourself and Others
Through Handwriting Analysis

By Reed Hayes
ISBN 0-89281-371-1
$14.95, paperback

A Certified Master Graphologist who specializes in jury selection explains the fascinating science of handwriting analysis, showing what individual styles reveal about personality. He uses handwriting samples from famous people as illustrations.

THE OCCULT CONSPIRACY
Secret Societies—Their Influence and Power
in World History

By Michael Howard
ISBN 0-89281-251-6
$12.95, paperback

From the time of ancient Egypt to the present, secret societies and occult groups have exercised a strong and often crucial influence on the destiny of nations. In *The Occult Conspiracy*, the author reveals how secret societies, including Freemasons, Knights Templar, and Rosicrucians have influenced politics and statecraft throughout history. He details their influence in the lives of many well-known figures, including Frederick the Great, John Dee, Francis Bacon, Benjamin Franklin, Comte Cagliostro, Helen Blavatsky, Rasputin, and Woodrow Wilson. We are left with little doubt that the secret societies—largely ignored by orthodox historians—have survived and continue to operate powerfully in world affairs today.

> " . . . *sheer comprehensiveness and sense of continuity from*
> *age to age . . . demonstrates a well-documented and sane*
> *approach to conspiracy theory, while offering those*
> *wonderful 'Aha!' experiences."*
>
> **Gnosis**